TAKING BACK
PHILOSOPHY

TAKING BACK PHILOSOPHY

A MULTICULTURAL MANIFESTO

BRYAN W. VAN NORDEN

Columbia University Press *New York*

Columbia University Press
Publishers Since 1893
New York   Chichester, West Sussex
cup.columbia.edu

Library of Congress Cataloging-in-Publication Data
Names: Van Norden, Bryan W. (Bryan William), author.
Title: Taking back philosophy: a multicultural manifesto /
Bryan W. Van Norden.
Description: New York: Columbia University Press, [2017] |
Includes bibliographical references and index.
Identifiers: LCCN 2017031091 | ISBN 9780231184366
(cloth: acid-free paper) | ISBN 9780231184373 (pbk.: acid-free paper) |
ISBN 9780231545457 (e-book)
Subjects: LCSH: Philosophy.
Classification: LCC B53.V28 2017 | DDC 101—dc23
LC record available at https://lccn.loc.gov/2017031091

Columbia University Press books are printed on permanent and
durable acid-free paper.
Printed in the United States of America
Cover design: Lisa Hamm
Cover photo: Herve BRUHAT/Gamma-Repho via Getty Images

To the Memory of
Rev. Charles E. Van Norden, DD (1843–1913)
our family's first philosopher
and
Warner Montaigne Van Norden (1873–1959)
our family's first Sinologist

I am a citizen of the world.

—Diogenes

*Only those who are petty regard themselves as separate from
others solely because of the space between their bodies.*

—Wang Yangming

CONTENTS

Foreword *xi*
JAY L. GARFIELD

Preface *xxiii*

1 A Manifesto for Multicultural Philosophy 1
Why Multicultural Philosophy? 3
A Second-Best Approach 8
The Quality Argument 12
Essentialist Ethnocentrism 16
The History of Philosophical Ethnocentrism 19
Avoiding Intellectual Imperialism 29
Where Do We Go from Here? 31

2 Traditions in Dialogue 38
Metaphysics 40
Political Philosophy 52
Ethics 62
Weakness of Will 72
Other Voices 82

3 Trump's Philosophers 85
Building Racial Walls in American Politics 86

Building Walls to Protect Chinese Civilization   88

Building Walls to Protect Western Civilization   98

Jericho   107

4 Welders and Philosophers   110

Philosophy and Occupational Training   112

Philosophy and Democratic Citizenship   115

Philosophy's Value to Civilization   130

5 The Way of Confucius and Socrates   138

Philosophy's Special Role Among the Humanities   138

So What Is Philosophy?   142

Recovering the Way of Confucius and Socrates   151

Notes   161

Index   203

FOREWORD

JAY L. GARFIELD

This book has its origins in what Bryan Van Norden and I had thought was an innocuous opinion piece in *The Stone* column of the *New York Times*, one we thought likely to be completely ignored, but which instead, to our astonishment, ignited a firestorm of controversy across the philosophy blogosphere. That column had its origin in a rather wonderful conference on minorities in philosophy, hosted by the University of Pennsylvania philosophy department, and organized by its graduate students. The graduate students and the many others who attended that conference were delightful.

Bryan and I were struck, however, by the fact that, despite including the keynote address in the regular department colloquium series, and even though the conference was held at the philosophy department, the Penn faculty almost entirely boycotted the proceedings. Most members of that department were simply not interested in hearing about non-Western philosophy, even if their own graduate students organized a conference on the topic in their own department.

We found that surprising. And out of that surprise came our short editorial, which is reproduced in chapter 1 of the present volume. From our previous experiences, we expected that most of our colleagues would roll their eyes and ignore it as one more lunatic fringe call for change in a field notoriously resistant to change. We hoped that a few would take us seriously and either bite the bullet and agree that their departments should be renamed or think about expanding their curriculum and hiring (and indeed a very few have taken the latter course).

We thought that a few more would offer the same tired arguments against change: It is too hard to cover the "core," so how can we possibly devote scarce resources to the non-Western fringe? There just aren't any good graduate programs training people in these areas, so how can we hire? We don't read the languages, so how can we seriously address these texts and traditions? We lack the expertise to determine what is good and what is bad in non-Western philosophy, so how can we hire or assess our colleagues' work? What would we cut to make room for this?

We know how to respond to those rejoinders, and we find ourselves doing so all the time. Indeed, the present volume addresses these arguments carefully and in detail. But while there were a few of those in the eight hundred replies we received the first day on the *Times* website (a record for *The Stone*) and in the thousands of others that quickly populated other philosophy sites, we were not prepared for the level of vitriol, personal attacks, and frank racism that characterized most of the replies, including many from within our own profession. Nor were we prepared for some of the spectacularly ill-informed essays that appeared subsequent to our editorial in response to it. On the one hand, we regretted having provided an occasion for some of this rhetoric; on the other hand, we are glad that it is out in the open, as it demonstrates clearly what is at stake as we consider the future of our profession. This book is a careful, if polemical, consideration of that future in response to this wave of hostility.

One philosopher wrote that Native Americans have not been literate long enough to produce philosophy; many connected Kongzi to fortune cookies; others tarred us with the brush of "political correctness." (We think that it is in fact correct from a political point of view not to be explicitly racist, or even to perpetuate structural racism; we also think, perhaps charitably, that our opponents agree; one must then wonder how bad one's own position is if the best way to defend it is to concede that the opposition is correct, if only on matters of politics.) Many argued, either without citing any textual support or by providing a single snippet of some non-Western text out of context as evidence, that there simply is nothing valuable in any non-Western tradition. If this kind of argument were emblematic of the greatness of Western philosophy, then, quite frankly, we would think it is better off abandoned. Our colleagues in Asian traditions can't afford to offer such patently racist or lame arguments, and they don't.

Two responses stick in my mind. One scholar, who chose to remain anonymous, wrote that while Kongzi might have had some good philosophical ideas, China never produced a tradition of argument and commentary following his work, and so there was no real philosophical tradition in China. This is what White Privilege looks like. This author obviously knows absolutely *nothing* about the history of Chinese philosophy (which has a very rich and ongoing "tradition of argument and commentary"); she or he also presumably also *knows* that she or he knows nothing about that vast tradition; nonetheless, she or he feels perfectly comfortable pontificating about it in public. Imagine a Chinese scholar conceding that the West had produced Heraclitus, and that he is worth studying, but asserting that the West has no tradition of debate and argument after him.

And indeed this invocation of White Privilege is common not only among our recent critics, but among so many with whom I have discussed this issue over the years. It combines the assumption that being European, or being educated in the European tradition, authorizes one to pronounce on all things intellectual with the casual assumption that the ocean of texts with which one is unfamiliar contain nothing worthwhile, nothing worth studying, nothing worth teaching, and could not possibly measure up to Western philosophy in profundity or rigor, and even that they could not possibly be doing the same thing. One is reminded of Thomas Babington Macaulay's infamous remarks:

> I have no knowledge of either Sanscrit or Arabic.—But I have done what I could to form a correct estimate of their value. I have read translations of the most celebrated Arabic and Sanscrit works. I have conversed both here and at home with men distinguished by their proficiency in the Eastern tongues. I am quite ready to take the Oriental learning at the valuation of the Orientalists themselves. I have never found one among them who could deny that a single shelf of a good European library was worth the whole native literature of India and Arabia. The intrinsic superiority of the Western literature is, indeed, fully admitted by those members of the Committee who support the Oriental plan of education.[1]

Nicholas Tampio wrote a sustained reply to our editorial, titled "Not All Things Wise and Good Are Philosophy."[2] While his article is well intentioned, it illustrates the central fallacies and prejudices that serve to maintain the Eurocentrism of our discipline. Tampio takes as his initial premise the claim, "Philosophy originates in Plato's *Republic*." Let us leave aside the point that this ignores all of Plato's earlier dialogues as well as the pre-Socratic tradition in Greece, and let us charitably read *The Republic* as a metonym for *Greece*. Even so, in an argument for the claim that all philosophy is Western, the initial premise is that philosophy starts in Greece. You just couldn't beg the question more obviously. Tampio asserts just before this that while "it might seem broadminded to call for philosophy professors to teach ancient Asian scholars such as Confucius and Candrakīrti in addition to dead white men such as David Hume and Immanuel Kant, . . . this approach undermines what is distinct about philosophy as an intellectual tradition, and pays other traditions the dubious compliment of saying that they are just like ours." This sets out his two lines of argument. First, neither Confucius (Kongzi) nor Candrakīrti is really a philosopher (and therefore presumably—given the conclusion of the essay—no alleged non-Western philosophers are real philosophers), and, second, it is more respectful to classify them as "sages" rather than philosophers.

Tampio describes both Kongzi and Candrakīrti as "sages . . . on mountaintops" in contrast to those engaged in *real philosophy*, which takes place "among ordinary human beings in cities." This characterization is important not only because of its historical inaccuracy, but because of what it shows about the prejudices that keep our field so narrow. Kongzi taught in a series of cities in China, and Candrakīrti taught at what was the largest university in the world at the time (Nālandā). Neither, so far as anyone knows, came anywhere near a mountaintop, and each was part of an urban intellectual elite. The important point is that even though this information is easily available, Tampio doesn't bother to get it right; European scholars don't have that burden to bear. The presupposition that non-European intellectuals spend their time on mountaintops and in caves is not an irrelevant factual error, but a form of condescending romanticism. It suggests a quaint detachment from the need to test one's arguments against other philosophers. The reality that both the Indian and the Chinese traditions are richly dialectical is of course important, as it ought to persuade those who close the door to these traditions on these grounds to open them. But it also important to confront the underlying prejudice that leads those who tout the "unique" commitment to reason of the Western tradition to fail to meet those standards themselves.

In addition to the curious claim that some thinkers cannot be philosophers because of the physical environments in which they wrote, Tampio argues that Kongzi is not a philosopher because of the content and form of his writing. This at least is *relevant* (although, even were this argument sound, the most it could show is that *Kongzi* was not a philosopher, not that there was no philosophy in China, which is the intended conclusion). The evidence that Tampio offers that Kongzi is not a philosopher is a single remark about *xiào* (filial duty) from the *Analects*, taken out of all context—a remark that, in context, is actually an important part of a larger argument that this disposition is a standing character trait continuous with respect for the law and authority instead of a momentary attribute. Tampio does nothing to search for this context or even to explore how other scholars read these passages. Imagine quoting Plato in the *Symposium* on the original humans—"Then also people were shaped like complete spheres. Their backs and sides made a circle. They had four hands, with the same number of legs and two faces—completely the same—on top of a circular neck. . . . and whenever they got running fast, it was just like acrobats revolving in a circle—legs straight out and somersaulting!"—and concluding not only that *Plato* was not a philosopher, but also that there are no philosophers in the West.[3] In subsequent correspondence, Tampio acknowledged that he hasn't actually read Kongzi or Candrakīrti, let alone any of the thinkers who are in dialogue with them. (In this respect, he is less qualified to have an opinion than even Macaulay was regarding Indian philosophy.) Nonetheless, he is comfortable dismissing their work. Here is one reason to extend the canon: perhaps if philosophical education were sufficiently broad, philosophers would neither think nor write like this.

Finally, Tampio suggests that exalting non-Western intellectual activity (no matter what its form) as "the possession of wisdom" (rather than philosophy, the *love* of wisdom) is more respectful than the colonialist impulse to assimilate it to what *we* do. We should not, that is, take our own practices to be honorific standards against which to hold others. Fair enough. But what do we mean by apparently innocuous phrases like "wisdom traditions"? There are two things to say about this: First, this is not a way of honoring, but of condescendingly disparaging a tradition. We have departments of philosophy because we value philosophy as an activity. Those departments are resolutely Eurocentric because we take European philosophy as the default, or paradigm, case of philosophy, conceived, as Tampio himself puts it, as reflective rational investigation of an argument about the fundamental nature of reality, or, as Sellars so perfectly put it, the attempt "to understand how things in the broadest possible sense of the term hang together in the broadest possible sense of the term."[4] We don't have departments of "wisdom traditions," because we don't value what we take them to be—nonrational exercises in mythopoetic thinking, or something like that. To praise Kongzi and Candrakīrti by putting them in that category is to justify ignoring them as sources of reflection, consigning them to the status of the objects of anthropological research.

Moreover, to draw this distinction, and to draw it on the basis of cultural location, as not only Tampio but the vast majority of philosophers do (either explicitly as so many of our critics have, or implicitly in curricular and staffing decisions that replicate that distinction), is to regard, usually with no evidence whatsoever, the intellectual efforts of those in East Asia, Africa, and India, and of the indigenous communities around the world, as of a fundamentally different character from our own. And that almost always amounts to presuming it to be irrational, or at least incompetently rational, as does Tampio. Imagine, for instance, defining "food" as that which the Italians and the French prepare, and then defining the cuisines of Asia as "fodder," politely saying that we don't want to condescend to it by suggesting in a colonialist voice that they are doing the same thing that we do when they cook and eat!

I belabor Tampio's essay and the remarks of our anonymous critic because they are typical of the arguments that we so often hear, and Tampio's has the virtue of being articulated with great clarity in an extended essay. Let me repeat the central point: Most professional philosophers have neither studied nor taught, nor considered creating positions for those who do study or teach, nor considered giving centrality in the philosophy curriculum to *any* philosophy pursued in *any* non-Western culture. Nonetheless, everyone in our profession who *has* studied or taught this material seriously *agrees* that there is a massive body of philosophically sophisticated, well-argued, and important work in non-Western philosophical traditions. Moreover, scholars who have studied this literature agree that it is of the same *kind* as philosophy pursued in the West, and that it addresses similar issues, albeit with distinct perspectives, and that it offers distinctive arguments and positions.

It follows that ignoring this work is both epistemically and morally reprehensible. It is epistemically reprehensible since it requires us to ignore arguments, positions, and perspectives on issues we care about that we have good reason to believe are valuable. And its requires us to do so simply on the grounds that the material we ignore is written by people inhabiting cultures different from our own. The only arguments for doing so are clearly bankrupt. If you don't believe this now, you will believe it by the time you finish reading this book. But there is a moral issue as well: ignoring non-Western philosophy in our research, curriculum, and hiring decisions is deeply racist, and is a practice we cannot endorse in good faith once we recognize this.

In leveling the charge of racism—a charge I recognize to be serious and not to be leveled lightly—I do not mean to suggest that our colleagues in philosophy individually harbor or act upon racist views. That would be irresponsible, and, I believe, false. But there is a distinction to be drawn between individual and structural racism. A social structure can be racist without any individual who participates in it being racist when it serves to establish or to perpetuate a set of practices that systematically denigrate—implicitly or explicitly—people of particular races.

Philosophy as it is practiced professionally in much of the world, and in the United States in particular, is racist in precisely this sense. To omit all of the philosophy of Asia, Africa, India, and the Indigenous Americas from the curriculum and to ignore it in our research is to convey the impression—whether intentionally or not—that it is of less value than the philosophy produced in European culture, or worse, to convey the impression—willingly or not—that no other culture was capable of philosophical thought. These are racist views.

When we academic philosophers have a position open— perhaps because our Kant specialist retired, or our metaphysician who works exclusively on possible-worlds modal realism took a job elsewhere—and we decide that we now have a big "hole" in Kant or modal metaphysics, and take that hole to be *bigger, more in need of filling* than one that comprises all of East Asia, India, Africa, and Indigenous America, we have endorsed a racist view of the relative importance of these areas. We have to decide whether we can reflectively endorse these views, and whether we can reflectively endorse the practices that express and entrench them.

It is worth reflecting for a moment, as we consider this question, on the fact that, in the contemporary humanities, philosophy stands magnificently *alone* in this respect. You can't run an art history program that attends only to Anglo-European art anymore; you can't run a literature program that reads only works written in English and European languages; and you can't run a history department in which only European and American history are studied. You could once upon a time, but if you tried now, you would be ridiculed, and properly so. So, ask yourself, is it different in philosophy because we just have higher standards, or is it different because we are simply institutionally less reflective, more retrograde? An honest answer is deeply troubling.

It is clear, as Bryan Van Norden argues in this book, that this situation requires remediation, and fortunately, it is not hard to see how to remediate it. But that will require a collective will and a collective effort. We must begin to see our current departments and journals, and our own philosophical educations, as inadequate because of serious lacunae. We must see filling those lacunae as an internal intellectual need and as a moral imperative. And we must come to realize that doing so will make us each better philosophers, will make our departments better departments, will allow us to educate our students better, will make philosophy a more valuable social asset, and will not be a cost we must bear, but an enjoyable and exciting intellectual adventure. That is, we must now act in good faith, enacting the values we all endorse. This book shows us why we must do that, how we can do that, and that it really is in each of our interests to do so. I urge you to read on.

PREFACE

Jay Garfield and I did not anticipate the storm of controversy that would result when we published "If Philosophy Won't Diversify, Let's Call It What It Really Is" in *The Stone* column of the *New York Times* blog (May 11, 2016). Perhaps we should have: after all, we were calling upon ethnocentric philosophy departments to rename themselves "departments of Anglo-European philosophy" to reflect their intentional disregard of everything outside the mainstream philosophical canon. However, it immediately became obvious that our challenge to the chauvinism of US philosophy departments had struck a nerve. This book is an effort to develop in detail the case for a multicultural approach to philosophy.

Like the original editorial, this book is polemical and intentionally provocative in the hope that it will incite discussion and raise awareness. This work is also intended to be interesting and accessible to general readers. Since the point is to get nonspecialists excited about the issues so they will want to read more and gain a deeper understanding, my argumentation is less guarded and less detailed than I would produce in a work intended solely for my fellow scholars. In addition, my editor specifically asked for a work that is "cheeky," so I tried to deliver that tone, and have not shied away from being openly partisan in my presentation, and sometimes sardonic in a manner I would eschew in the classroom or in a scholarly publication.

To assist those who want to learn more about philosophy outside the Anglo-European canon, I maintain a bibliography, "Readings on the Less Commonly Taught Philosophies," at http://bryanvannorden.com. I am grateful to James Maffie and Sean Robin for suggestions of some titles to include related to Native American thought, and to Travis W. Holloway for advice about readings in Continental thought.

I owe thanks to Jay Garfield for many things: for providing an inspiring example of how to engage in multicultural philosophy, for the initial suggestion about renaming ethnocentric philosophy departments, and for writing the generous foreword to this book. (Unfortunately, his numerous other commitments made it impossible for him to be a coauthor.) I am indebted to Wendy Lochner, my editor at Columbia University Press, for suggesting a book developing in more detail themes from the editorial Jay and I wrote. Wendy has also provided much helpful feedback on earlier drafts of this book, as did Erin Cline, Benjamin Huff, Jeffrey Seidman, Victor Mair, David E. Mungello, Matthew Walker, and two anonymous referees. My copyeditor, Robert Demke, did a thorough job of correcting a number of careless mistakes in my original manuscript. I am also thankful to Lewis Gordon, Charles Goodman, and Kyle Whyte for advice about doctoral programs in Africana, Indian, and Indigenous philosophy, respectively. William Levitan helped me to avoid a mistaken attribution to the learned abbess Héloïse. I offer prospective thanks to Professor Wu Wanwei of the Wuhan University of Science and Technology, who is already at work on the Chinese translation of this book. Of course, I owe an especially great debt to Barbara, Charles, and Melissa Van Norden, both for feedback on the manuscript and for putting up with my busy schedule of naps, watching zombie movies, playing zombie video games, and more naps.

The editorial that inspired this book was intended to have a list of cosignatories from the "Minorities and Philosophy" conference at the University of Pennsylvania in 2016. Their names could not be included because of the editorial policy of the *New York Times*, but Jay and I are very grateful for the support of Nalini Bhushan, department of philosophy, Smith College; Aditi Chaturvedi, department of philosophy, Ashoka University; Alan Fox, department of philosophy, University of Delaware; Alexander Guerrero, department of philosophy, University of Pennsylvania; Nabeel Hamid, doctoral student in philosophy, University of Pennsylvania; Jennie Innes, philosophy major, Brooklyn College; Julie R. Klein, department of philosophy, Villanova University; James Maffie, department of philosophy, University of Maryland; Deven Patel, South Asian studies, University of Pennsylvania; Jessica Taylor (Treijs), philosophy major, Brooklyn College; Christina Weinbaum, philosophy major, Brooklyn College; and Kathleen Wright, department of philosophy, Haverford College. (None of them should be blamed for anything I say in this book, nor should Jay.)

Parts of this book appeared previously in Skye Cleary, "Chinese Philosophy in the English-Speaking World: Interview with Bryan Van Norden," *Blog of the APA*, May 17, 2016, http://blog.apaonline.org/2016/05/17/chinese-philosophy-in-the-english-speaking-world-interview-with-bryan-van-norden/; Jay Garfield and Bryan W. Van Norden, "If Philosophy Won't Diversify, Let's Call It What It Really Is," *The Stone*, blog, *New York Times*, May 11, 2016, www.nytimes.com/2016/05/11/opinion/if-philosophy-wont-diversify-lets-call-it-what-it-really-is.html; and my articles "Chinese Philosophy Is Missing from

U.S. Philosophy Departments: Should We Care?" *Conversation,* May 18, 2016, https://theconversation.com/chinese-philosophy-is-missing-from-u-s-philosophy-departments-should-we-care-56550; "Confucius on Gay Marriage," *Diplomat,* July 13, 2015, http://thediplomat.com/2015/07/confucius-on-gay-marriage/; "Problems and Prospects for the Study of Chinese Philosophy in the English-Speaking World," *APA Newsletter on the Status of Asian and Asian-American Philosophers and Philosophies* 15, no. 2 (Spring 2016): http://c.ymcdn.com/sites/www.apaonline.org/resource/collection/2EAF6689–4B0D-4CCB-9DC6-FB926 D8FF530/AsianV15n2.pdf; "Three Questions About the Crisis in Chinese Philosophy," *APA Newsletter on the Status of Asian and Asian-American Philosophers and Philosophies* 8, no. 1 (Fall 2008): 3–6, https://c.ymcdn.com/sites/www.apaonline.org/resource/collection/2EAF6689-4B0D-4CCB-9DC6-FB926D8FF530/vo8n1Asian.pdf; "What Happened to the Party of Lincoln?" *Hippo Reads,* http://read.hipporeads.com/what-happened-to-the-party-of-lincoln/. The penultimate paragraph of this book includes a paraphrase of a line from the poem "Dion" by William Wordsworth: "And what pure homage then did wait / On Dion's virtues, while the lunar beam / Of Plato's genius, from its lofty sphere, / Fell round him in the grove of Academe."

TAKING BACK
PHILOSOPHY

1

A MANIFESTO FOR MULTICULTURAL PHILOSOPHY

Philosophy is not to be found in the whole Orient.
—Immanuel Kant

We're going to let our children know that the only philosophers that lived were not Plato and Aristotle, but W. E. B. Du Bois and Alain Locke came through the universe.
—Martin Luther King, Jr.

P hilosophy has been a favorite whipping boy in the culture wars since 399 BCE, when an Athenian jury sentenced Socrates to death. However, philosophers nowadays are seldom accused of "corrupting the youth." Instead, a surprisingly wide range of pundits—from celebrity scientist Neil deGrasse Tyson (majoring in philosophy "can really mess you up") to Senator Marco Rubio ("Welders make more money than philosophers. We need more welders and less philosophers")—assert that philosophy is pointless or impractical.[1] Tyson's comment is ironic, since he is a PhD, a doctor of *philosophy*, reflecting the historical fact that natural science developed out of the field he denigrates. Moreover, truly great scientists recognize the continuing importance of philosophy. Einstein even remarked that the "independence created by philosophical insight is—in my opinion—the mark of distinction between a mere artisan or specialist and a real seeker after truth." Rubio's claim is simply inaccurate. Not only do philosophy majors earn more than welders, but they also earn more on average than political science majors like Rubio. In addition, those who study philosophy score at or near the top in admission tests for law school, medical school, and even business school. One businessperson who majored in philosophy was even on the stage when Rubio made his dismissive comment: former Hewlett-Packard CEO and Republican presidential candidate Carly Fiorina majored in philosophy.[2]

Although the critics of academic philosophy are mistaken about where the problem is, departments *are* failing their students in a crucial way: they are not teaching the profound, fascinating, and increasingly relevant philosophy that is outside the traditional Anglo-European canon.

Among the top fifty philosophy departments in the United States that grant a PhD,[3] only six have a member of their regular faculty who teaches Chinese philosophy.[4] There are only three additional doctoral programs in the United States outside the top fifty that have strong faculty in Chinese philosophy.[5] I am focusing here (and in the remainder of this book) on Chinese philosophy, because it is my own area of expertise. However, Chinese philosophy is only one of a substantial number of less commonly taught philosophies (LCTP) that fall outside the Anglo-European mainstream. For example, only six doctoral programs in philosophy in the United States have specialists on Indian philosophy, and only two of those departments are ranked among the top fifty.[6] Only two US doctoral programs in philosophy regularly teach the philosophies of the

Indigenous peoples of the Americas.[7] Most US philosophy departments have no regular faculty who teach courses on African philosophy.[8] Even some major forms of philosophy deeply influenced by the Greco-Roman philosophical traditions are largely ignored by US philosophy departments, including African American, Christian, Continental, feminist, Islamic, Jewish, Latin American, and LGBTQ philosophy.

What are these departments teaching instead? Every one of the top fifty schools has at least one (and often more than one) faculty member who can lecture competently on the ancient Greek Parmenides. There is only one surviving work by Parmenides. It is a philosophical poem, and includes gems like "It is right both to say and to think that what-is is: for it can be, / but nothing is not: these things I bid you ponder."[9] If we turn to contemporary philosophy, we find that almost every leading US philosophy department has a specialist in the philosophy of language, someone prepared to heatedly debate whether the sentence "The present king of France is bald" is false (as the Bertrand Russell camp claims) or neither true nor false (as the Peter Strawson wing asserts).[10] It appears that contemporary philosophers are more likely to be accused of boring the youth to death with their sentences than they are of being sentenced to death for corrupting the youth!

WHY MULTICULTURAL PHILOSOPHY?

In order to appreciate why the narrowness of philosophy departments is so problematic, let's consider one example of a less commonly taught philosophy (LCTP). Chinese philosophy deserves greater coverage by US universities for at least three reasons. First, China is an increasingly important world power,

both economically and geopolitically—and traditional philosophy is of continuing relevance. Chinese businessmen pay for
lessons from Buddhist monks, Daoism appeals both to peasants
(for whom it is part of tradition) and to many intellectuals (who
look to it for a less authoritarian approach to government), and
China's current President, Xi Jinping, has repeatedly praised
Confucius.[11]

What should we make of the Chinese government's support
of Confucius? At the beginning of the twentieth century, Chinese modernizers of the May Fourth Movement claimed that
Confucianism was authoritarian and dogmatic at its core, so
that China must "overturn the shop of Confucius" in order to
become a strong, democratic nation. Many contemporary Chinese intellectuals agree. (One Chinese professor told me that
the US NBA is more relevant to the lives of contemporary Chinese than Confucianism.) In response to this critique, "New
Confucians" claim that Confucianism can and should be made
compatible with Western democracy, but can also contribute to
Western philosophy insights about communitarian modes of
political organization and the cultivation of individual virtues.
Other commentators suggest that Confucian meritocracy is actually superior to the mob rule of Western democracy. (After
watching the last US election, it is tempting to agree with
them.) Still others would argue that President Xi's invocation
of Confucius is simply a tool in the service of a chauvinistic
nationalism.[12]

Having an informed opinion about issues like the preceding
is important for understanding China's present and future.
How will the next generation of diplomats, senators, represen-
tatives, and presidents (not to mention informed citizens) learn
about Confucius and his role in Chinese thought if philosophers refuse to teach him? Some of my philosophical colleagues

would reply that students can learn about Confucianism from religious studies or area studies departments. I would remind them how vociferously they would complain if their dean told them they don't need to hire a Kant specialist, because the German department can teach him, and they don't need to hire a political philosopher, because the political science department has someone who covers "that sort of thing." Philosophers ask certain questions of texts and use certain methods for discussing them that are not necessarily practiced in other humanities or social science disciplines. Other disciplines have equally valuable methodologies, but there is no substitute for reading a text philosophically.[13]

A second reason that Chinese philosophy should be studied in US philosophy departments is that it simply has much to offer as philosophy. Consider the revelations in just a few of the seminal works about Chinese philosophy in the English-speaking world. Lee H. Yearley started a minor revolution in comparative philosophy with his book *Mencius and Aquinas: Theories of Virtue and Conceptions of Courage*, which shows how the concepts of Western virtue ethics can be applied to the study of Confucianism.[14] Yearley argues that the two traditions are similar enough for comparisons to be legitimate, but different enough for both traditions to learn from each other. For example, both the Thomistic tradition and the Confucian tradition have lists of "cardinal virtues" (the major virtues that encompass all the lesser ones); however, the lists overlap only partially. The Confucian cardinal virtues are benevolence, righteousness, propriety, and wisdom, while the Thomistic list of natural virtues is wisdom, justice, courage, and moderation. Thinking about different conceptions of the cardinal virtues gives us a broader range of possible answers to the question: What is it to live well?[15]

Many philosophers are doing fascinating work on other aspects of Confucian philosophy: comparing Confucian and Western conceptions of justice,[16] discussing how Confucian views of filial piety and childhood education can inform specific public policy recommendations,[17] bringing seminal Western philosophers like Hobbes and Rousseau into productive dialogue with Mengzi and Xunzi,[18] examining the similarities and differences between Christian and Confucian views of ethical cultivation,[19] and combining insights from Chinese philosophy with contemporary psychology and metaethics to formulate powerful alternatives to conventional Western ethics.[20] Some leading mainstream philosophers have also been open-minded enough to engage in dialogue with Confucian thought, including Alasdair MacIntyre and Martha Nussbaum.[21]

Asian philosophy can also make important contributions to the philosophy of language and logic. For example, most Western philosophers (going back to Aristotle) have argued that no contradiction can be true. However, there are a surprisingly large number of statements that seem to be both true and false. Some are sentences in ordinary language (like the Liar Paradox, "This sentence is false," which is false if it is true, and true if it is false), while others are generated by formal logico-mathematical systems (like Russell's Paradox, "There is a set that has as a member every set that is not a member of itself," which both does and does not have itself as a member). Asian philosophers have been more willing to entertain the possibility that some statements might be both true and false. Consequently, some contemporary philosophers are attempting to synthesize Buddhist and Daoist insights about paradoxes with "paraconsistent logic" to defend dialetheism, the claim that some contradictions are true.[22] This is not the only technical topic on which Asian philosophy anticipates Western philosophy by millennia: the ancient Mohist philosophers recognized that "opaque contexts" block the substitutivity of coreferential terms, something not fully appreciated in the West until the twentieth century.[23]

The third reason that it is important to add Chinese philosophy to the curriculum has to do with the fact that philosophy faces a serious diversity problem. As researchers Myisha Cherry and Eric Schwitzgebel pointed out recently,

> Women still receive only about 28% of philosophy PhDs in the United States, and are still only about 20% of full professors of philosophy—numbers that have hardly budged since the 1990s. And among U.S. citizens and permanent residents receiving philosophy PhDs in this country, 86% are non-Hispanic white. The only comparably-sized disciplines that are more white are the ones that explicitly focus on the European tradition, such as English literature. Black people are especially difficult to find in academic philosophy. Black people or African Americans constitute 13% of the U.S. population, 7% of PhD recipients across all fields, 2% of PhD recipients in philosophy, and less than 0.5% of authors in the most prominent philosophy journals.[24]

[handwritten margin note: Good Data]

Least well represented among PhDs in philosophy are Native Americans, of whom there are estimated to be twenty *individuals*, in total, working in higher education.[25] Both my own experience and that of many of my colleagues suggest that part of the reason for homogeneity among philosophers is that students of color are confronted with a curriculum that is almost monolithically white. As Cherry and Schwitzgebel note, white male students "see faces like their own in front of the classroom and hear voices like their own coming from professors' mouths. In the philosophy classroom, they see almost exclusively white

Double consciousness
W.E.B. PPL

men as examples of great philosophers. They think 'that's me' and they step into it." Students of philosophy are ill served by a narrow, ethnocentric education. Fixing the problem of philosophy's homogeneity is a matter of justice, but it is also about the very survival of philosophy as an academic discipline. Women and students of color are an increasing percentage of college students, and by 2045 whites will be a minority in the United States. Philosophy must diversify or die.

For all the geopolitical, philosophical, and demographic reasons I have given, philosophy departments in the United States need to increase offerings in not just Chinese philosophy, but other LCTP. So how is philosophy doing in the process of diversifying the curriculum? A decade ago, among the top fifty doctoral programs in philosophy in the United States, four offered courses in Chinese philosophy.[26] We are now up to eight, if we include departments that cross-list courses by faculty in other departments. It would be a mistake to infer from this that we will continue to see slow but regular growth in coverage of Chinese philosophy. Some departments that previously had faculty specializing in Chinese philosophy lost them. In addition, some departments that currently have faculty in this area are *not* committed to replacing them when they retire. Can't we do better than this?

A SECOND-BEST APPROACH

At the "Minorities and Philosophy" conference on non-Western philosophical traditions at the University of Pennsylvania in 2016, my colleague Jay Garfield (an analytically trained philosopher who has become a leading expert on Buddhism) suggested, half-jokingly, that any philosophy department that does not teach any Africana, Arab, Chinese, or Indian philosophy should be forced to change its name to "department of Anglo-European philosophy." I was taken with the idea, and suggested that we cowrite an editorial on this topic. It appeared in *The Stone*, the philosophy blog of the *New York Times*:

We ask those who sincerely believe that it does make sense to organize our discipline entirely around European and American figures and texts to pursue this agenda with honesty and openness. We therefore suggest that any department that regularly offers courses only on Western philosophy should rename itself, "Department of European and American Philosophy." This simple change would make the domain and mission of these departments clear, and would signal their true intellectual commitments to students and colleagues. We see no justification for resisting this minor rebranding, . . . particularly for those who endorse, implicitly or explicitly, this Eurocentric orientation.

Some of our colleagues defend this orientation on the grounds that non-European philosophy belongs only in "area studies" departments, like Asian Studies, African Studies, or Latin American Studies. We ask that those who hold this view be consistent, and locate their own departments in "area studies" as well, in this case, Anglo-European Philosophical Studies.

Others might argue against renaming on the grounds that it is unfair to single out philosophy: we do not have departments of Euro-American Mathematics or Physics. This is nothing but shabby sophistry. Non-European philosophical traditions offer distinctive solutions to problems discussed within European and American philosophy, raise or frame problems not addressed in the American and European tradition, or emphasize and discuss more deeply philosophical problems that are marginalized in Anglo-European philosophy. There are no comparable differences in how mathematics or physics are practiced in other contemporary cultures.

Of course, we believe that renaming departments would not be nearly as valuable as actually broadening the philosophical curriculum and retaining the name "philosophy." . . . We hope that American philosophy departments will someday teach Confucius as routinely as they now teach Kant, that philosophy students will eventually have as many opportunities to study the *Bhagavad Gita* as they do *The Republic*, that the Flying Man thought experiment of the Persian philosopher Avicenna (980–1037) will be as well-known as the Brain-in-a-Vat thought experiment of Hilary Putnam (1926–2016), that the ancient Indian scholar Candrakirti's critical examination of the concept of the self will be as well-studied as David Hume's, that Frantz Fanon (1925–1961), Kwazi Wiredu (1931–), Lame Deer (1903–1976) and Maria Lugones will be as familiar to our students as their equally profound colleagues in the contemporary philosophical canon. But, until then, let's be honest, face reality and call departments of European-American Philosophy what they really are.[27]

The editorial produced a storm of controversy. The previous five essays in *The Stone* averaged 277 comments per article. Our piece received 797 comments before replies were closed twelve hours later, and over thirty websites commented or hosted discussions. (My own college-age children were most impressed by the fact that we earned a thread on Reddit.)[28] The replies were inordinately passionate for what is essentially a discussion of academic curriculum. Some regarded the movement toward multiculturalism in philosophy as an obvious step.

Patricia McGuire, president of Trinity Washington University, remarked:

> The venerable canon of the liberal arts is largely built upon the hegemony of western, European, and British writing, art, culture and perspectives. Many faculties, including ours at Trinity in Washington, have done great work over the years transforming courses and curricula to include many more voices and contributions from a remarkably broad range of cultures and traditions. These changes have strengthened and enriched the entire liberal arts curriculum, making it more open and accessible to a significantly more diverse generation of students. Let's face facts: there's a Muslim Mayor in London, signifying the fact that even those who revere All Things British need to catch up with the now-settled reality of great diversity in contemporary life. The canon of learning should reflect that, including Philosophy.[29]

However, many responses were quite negative:

> Sure, name the departments in a way that accurately reflects the content and teach global thought traditions but, for better or worse, there is a particular school of thought that caught fire, broke cultural boundaries, and laid the foundation of modern science (Does anyone want to fly in a plane built with non-western math?) and our least oppressive governmental systems. This makes one particular school of thought an appropriate foundation for the study of other schools.[30]

(Personally, I will *only* fly in a plane built with non-Western math. After all, the numeral zero is an Indian innovation, our word "algebra" comes from Arabic, and the ancient Egyptians invented quadratic equations.)[31] Another reader of our editorial was even more dismissive: "Please preserve us from your political correctness. There is much that is of historical interest and value in non-European philosophy, but come on, there's a reason that Europe leaped ahead of the rest of the world. I do not believe that we should sacrifice that merely because of an ooshy gooshy need to pretend that all cultures are equally advanced."[32]

THE QUALITY ARGUMENT

These critical comments suggest that non-European thought somehow isn't as good as European philosophy. Most contemporary Western intellectuals gingerly dance around this issue. The late Justice Antonin Scalia was an exception, saying in print what many people actually think, or whisper to like-minded colleagues over drinks at the club. In the majority decision in *Obergefell v. Hodges*, the Supreme Court decision that legalized gay marriage across the United States, Chief Justice Anthony Kennedy quoted both Confucius and the Roman philosopher Cicero (106–43 BCE) on the "centrality of marriage to the human condition."[33] In his dissenting opinion, Scalia chided Kennedy for daring to invoke the Chinese sage: "The Supreme Court of the United States has descended from the disciplined legal reasoning of John Marshall and Joseph Story to the mystical aphorisms of the fortune cookie."[34] He echoes this sentiment in the conclusion of his dissent: "The world does not expect logic and precision in poetry or inspirational pop-philosophy; it demands them in the law. The stuff contained in today's opinion has to diminish this Court's reputation for clear thinking and sober analysis."[35] Notice that Scalia said nothing that might be interpreted as an aspersion upon Cicero;

only Confucius earned his contempt. Ironically, Confucius is featured on the East Pediment of the Supreme Court Building, along with Moses and Solon, as representing three of the great legal and moral traditions of the world.[36]

It is not only right-wing jurists who impugn non-European philosophy. Many philosophers, including ones who might describe themselves as politically progressive, are also dismissive of it. Massimo Pigliucci, an analytic philosopher of science, wrote an essay, "On the Pseudo-Profundity of Some Eastern Philosophy."[37] (He says "some," but there is no indication in the body of his essay that he sees any limitations to his claims.) Pigliucci concludes that "there is no such thing as Eastern philosophy" based on his exhaustive research—which he admits consisted of reading some kōans and one Wikipedia article on the topic. Philosophy, Pigliucci explains, is inquiry "conducted by the use of logical reasoning, where possible informed by empirical science." (A philosophy graduate student who casually threw around terms such as "logical reasoning" and "empirical" as if they were unambiguous and uncontroversial would be given a remedial reading list including the works of Pierre Duhem, Gaston Bachelard, Thomas Kuhn, Jean-François Lyotard, Paul Feyerabend, Michel Foucault, W. V. O. Quine, Wilfred Sellars, Donald Davidson, and Richard Rorty, for starters.) Pigliucci continues that "Buddhism, Taoism, Confucianism *and so forth*" are not "philosophical in nature because they do not attempt to argue for a position by using logic and evidence." (Italics mine: "and so forth" is, of course, a well-known logical operator, used to make precise generalizations based on empirical evidence.) Finally, Pigliucci explains that, in addition to its logical and empirical basis, actual (that is, Western) philosophy "won't require decades of meditation staring at a wall."

I would ask Pigliucci (or the ghost of Scalia) why he thinks that the Mohist state-of-nature argument to justify government authority is not philosophy.[38] What does he make of Mengzi's reductio ad absurdum against the claim that human nature is reducible to desires for food and sex?[39] Why does he dismiss Zhuangzi's version of the infinite regress argument for skepticism?[40] What is his opinion of Hanfeizi's argument that political institutions must be designed so that they do not depend upon the virtue of political agents?[41] What does he think of Zongmi's argument that reality must fundamentally be mental, because it is inexplicable how consciousness could arise from matter that was nonconscious?[42] Why does he regard the Platonic dialogues as philosophical, yet dismiss Fazang's dialogue in which he argues for and responds to objections against the claim that individuals are defined by their relationships to others?[43] What is his opinion of Wang Yangming's arguments for the claim that it is impossible to know what is good yet fail to do what is good?[44] Does he find convincing Dai Zhen's effort to produce a naturalistic foundation for ethics in the universalizability of our natural motivations?[45] What does he make of Mou Zongsan's critique of Kant,[46] or Liu Shaoqi's argument that Marxism is incoherent unless supplemented with a theory of individual ethical transformation?[47] Does he prefer the formulation of the argument for the equality of women given in the *Vimalakirti Sutra*, or the one given by the Neo-Confucian Li Zhi, or the one given by the Marxist Li Dazhao?[48]

Of course, the answer to each question is that those who suggest that Chinese philosophy is irrational have never heard of any of these arguments because they do not bother to read Chinese philosophy and simply dismiss it in ignorance. Frankly, such comments remind me of the sort of undergraduate who doesn't complete the assigned readings, but thinks he has some "really cool ideas" about the topic anyway, and that the whole class would benefit greatly from hearing them. My grade would be "D-. See me!"

If you are offended when someone says you are wrong, you have no business claiming to be any kind of intellectual. But there is a great difference between a sincerely reasoned argument and an unargued dismissal. As English clergyman William Paley (1743–1805) lamented, "Who can refute a sneer?" After all, "such attacks do their execution without inquiry." Much more of philosophy than we like to admit is simply *argumentum per supercilia*, "argument by raised eyebrows." The great economist John Maynard Keynes gave a wonderful description of how this technique was practiced by one of the founders of analytic philosophy, G. E. Moore (1873–1958):

> Moore was a great master of this method—greeting one's remarks with a gasp of incredulity—Do you really think that, an expression of face as if to hear such a thing said reduced him to a state of wonder verging on imbecility, with his mouth wide open and wagging his head in the negative so violently that his hair shook. "Oh!" he would say, goggling at you as if either you or he must be mad; and no reply was possible.[49]

It should come as no surprise that Moore treated non-Western philosophy with nothing but contempt. After Indian philosopher Surama Dasgupta read a paper on the epistemology of Vedanta to a session of the Aristotelian Society in London, Moore's only comment was, "I have nothing to offer myself. But I am sure that whatever Dasgupta says is absolutely false." The audience of British philosophers in attendance roared with laughter at the devastating "argument" Moore had leveled against Vedanta.[50] This is the level of pseudo-argumentation that is typically used to dismiss philosophy that is outside the Anglo-European canon. When people assert that non-Western philosophy is not *really* philosophy or at least is not good philosophy, it is *never* because they have carefully studied it and have an informed and coherent opinion. I know this because anyone who bothers to learn about it with an open mind *does* recognize it as both philosophical and important.

ESSENTIALIST ETHNOCENTRISM

Another argument against multicultural philosophy appeared in the conservative journal *The Weekly Standard*, in a response to Garfield's and my editorial. D. Kyle Peone argued that, because "philosophy" is a word of Greek origin, it refers only to the tradition that grows out of the ancient Greek thinkers.[51] A similar line of argument was given in *Aeon* magazine by Nicholas Tampio, who pronounced that "Philosophy originates in Plato's *Republic*."[52] (Bad news for those who teach pre-Socratic philosophers like Parmenides!) In other words, the essence of philosophy is to be a part of one specific Western intellectual lineage. This kind of essentialist argument against the existence of non-Western philosophy fails for two major reasons: one conceptual and one historical.

First, the conceptual problem with essentialism: Whether people are engaging in the same kind of inquiry—for example, whether it is philosophical or scientific—cannot depend merely on accidents of history. Consider a parallel case. The Pythagorean Theorem states that for any right triangle, the square of the length of the hypotenuse (the side opposite the right angle) is equal to the sum of the squares of the lengths of the other two sides. Although the discovery of the theorem is conventionally attributed to Pythagoras, it is Euclid who gives the first surviving Western proof of this theorem in his *Elements*. As it turns out, the Pythagorean Theorem was also known in China. The earliest occurrence of it is in the ancient *Zhoubi Suanjing*.[53] The *Zhoubi Suanjing* gives a proof of the theorem that meets the most rigorous mathematical standards, and is arguably more elegant than the proof in the *Elements*. Are we to say that the *Zhoubi Suanjing* is not about "mathematics" because it is not part of the mathematical tradition that grows out of the Pythagoreans and Euclid? This seems patently absurd. If the Pythagorean Theorem were unknown in the West, the proof of it from the *Zhoubi Suanjing* could be translated into English and pass the standards of any top academic journal of mathematics in the United States.

There are also clear historical examples of intellectual traditions accepting and being broadened by alien systems of thought. When Buddhism was brought to China by missionaries from India in the first century CE, there already existed a robust and diverse native spiritual tradition, including Confucianism and Daoism (each of which had a variety of competing interpretations). Buddhism was a completely alien system of thought that challenged many of the fundamental ethical and metaphysical assumptions of the classic Chinese thinkers. However, Chinese philosophers studied Buddhist works, translated them into their own language, learned a new technical vocabulary, and engaged with Buddhist arguments. As a result, the Chinese intellectual tradition was permanently deepened. Even if one refuses to bestow the label of "philosophy" upon any of these systems of thought, the fact that Confucianism and Daoism were able to adapt to and incorporate Buddhist ideas dispels the illusion that intellectual traditions have an unchanging essence that makes them hermetically sealed.

A very similar transformation actually occurred in Western philosophy not too long ago. When a major European university began to teach the ideas of a particular noncanonical thinker, mainstream philosophers on the faculty objected that the new philosophy was not part of "our tradition," and that it was watering down the curriculum in the name of a misguided fad. Because the new philosophy was inconsistent with many widely held positions, some philosophers resorted to a flaccid relativism, arguing that there were "two truths" on these matters. This sort of approach only convinced the mainstream philosophers that the new philosophy was nonsense. However, a brilliant philosopher argued that the best way to discover the truth is through a pluralistic dialogue with all the major world philosophies. This philosophical genius was Thomas Aquinas. In the thirteenth century at the University of Paris, Aquinas, Albertus Magnus, and others encouraged students and colleagues (who had previously only learned a form of Platonized Christianity) to expand the canon and learn not just from the philosophy of the pagan Aristotle (only recently rediscovered in Western Europe), but also from Jewish and Muslim thinkers. The result was to reinvigorate and deepen the Western philosophical tradition. (Siger of Brabant, the infamous "Latin Averroist," was the one who advocated the "two truths" doctrine. Interestingly, there are competing accounts of how Siger died,[54] but I suppose each of them is true, in its own way.) The case of Aquinas and the rediscovery of Aristotle is just one of many examples that illustrate that the Western philosophical canon is not, and never was, a closed system. Philosophy only becomes richer and approximates the truth more closely as it becomes increasingly diverse and pluralistic.

THE HISTORY OF PHILOSOPHICAL ETHNOCENTRISM

The second reason that essentialist arguments against multiculturalism fail is that the definition of philosophy as a self-contained dialogue that begins with the Greeks is a recent, historically contingent, and controversial view. As Peter K. J. Park notes in his book *Africa, Asia, and the History of Philosophy*, the view that "philosophy's origins are Greek was, in the eighteenth century, the opinion of an extreme minority of historians."[55] The only options taken seriously by most scholars during this era were that philosophy began in India, that philosophy began in Africa, or that both India and Africa gave philosophy to Greece.[56]

To Read

Furthermore, when European philosophers first learned about Chinese thought in the seventeenth century, they immediately recognized it as philosophy. The first major translation into a European language of the *Analects*, the saying of Confucius (551–479 BCE), was done by Jesuits with extensive training in Western philosophy. They titled their translation *Confucius Sinarum Philosophus* (Confucius the Chinese Philosopher, 1687). One of the major Western philosophers who read with fascination Jesuit accounts of Chinese philosophy was Gottfried Wilhelm Leibniz (1646–1716). He was stunned by the apparent correspondence between binary arithmetic (which he invented and which became the mathematical basis for all computers) and the *Changes*, the Chinese classic that symbolically represents the structure of the universe via sets of broken and unbroken lines, essentially *0*s and *1*s.[57] Leibniz also famously said that, while the West has the advantage of having received Christian revelation, and is superior to China in the natural sciences, "certainly they surpass us (though it is almost shameful to confess this) in practical philosophy, that is, in the precepts of ethics and politics adapted to the present life and the use of mortals."[58]

In 1721, the influential philosopher Christian Wolff echoed Leibniz in the title of his public lecture *Oratio de Sinarum Philosophia Practica* (Discourse on the Practical Philosophy of the Chinese). Wolff argued that Confucius showed that it was possible to have a system of morality without basing it on either divine revelation or natural religion. Because it proposed that ethics can be completely separated from belief in God, the lecture caused a scandal among conservative Christians, who had Wolff relieved of his duties and exiled from Prussia. However, his lecture made him a hero of the German Enlightenment, and he immediately obtained a prestigious position elsewhere. In 1730, he delivered a second public lecture, *De Rege Philosophante et Philosopho Regnante* (On the Philosopher King and the Ruling Philosopher), which praised the Chinese for consulting "philosophers" like Confucius and his later follower Mengzi (fourth century BCE) about important matters of state.[59]

Chinese philosophy was also taken very seriously in France. One of the leading reformers at the court of Louis XV was François Quesnay (1694–1774). He praised Chinese governmental institutions and philosophy so lavishly in his work *Despotisme de la China* (1767) that he became known as "the Confucius of Europe."[60] Quesnay was one of the originators of the concept of laissez-faire economics, and he saw a model for this in the sage-king Shun, who was known for governing by *wúwéi* (noninterference in natural processes).[61] The connection between the ideology of laissez-faire economics and *wúwéi* continues to the present day. In his State of the Union Address in 1988, Ronald Reagan quoted a line describing *wúwéi* from the *Daodejing*, which he interpreted as a warning against government regulation of business.[62] (Well, I didn't say that every Chinese philosophical idea was a *good* idea.)

So through most of the eighteenth century, it was *not* taken for granted in Europe that philosophy began in Greece, and it *was* taken for granted that Chinese philosophy was philosophy. What changed? As Park convincingly argues, Africa and Asia were excluded from the philosophical canon by the confluence of two interrelated factors. On the one hand, defenders of Immanuel Kant's philosophy consciously rewrote the history of philosophy to make it appear that his Critical Idealism was the culmination toward which all earlier philosophy was groping, more or less successfully. On the other hand, European intellectuals increasingly accepted and systematized views of white racial superiority that entailed that no non-Caucasian group could develop philosophy.[63] (As Edward Said points out, the Orientalist aspect of this racism was correlated with the rise of European imperialism, including the adventures of the East India Company in South Asia and Napoleon's invasion of Egypt.)[64] So the exclusion of non-European philosophy from the canon was a *decision,* not something that people have always believed, and it was a decision based not on a reasoned argument, but rather on polemical considerations involving the pro-Kantian faction in European philosophy, as well as views about race that are both unscientific and morally heinous.

Immanuel Kant (1724–1804) himself was notoriously racist. In his lectures on anthropology, Kant treats race as a scientific category (which it is not), and grades the races hierarchically, with whites at the apex:

1. "The race of the whites contains all talents and motives in itself."[65]

[handwritten margin note: Above hnt of respect for POC a major hist events to exclusion of POC]

2. "The Hindus . . . have a strong degree of calm, and all look like philosophers. That notwithstanding, they are much inclined to anger and love. They thus are educable in the highest degree, but only to the arts and not to the sciences. They will never achieve abstract concepts."

3. "The race of Negroes . . . [is] full of affect and passion, very lively, chatty and vain. It can be educated, but only to the education of servants, i.e., they can be trained." (In another context, Kant dismissed a comment someone makes on the grounds that "this scoundrel was completely black from head to foot, a distinct proof that what he said was stupid.")[66]

4. "The [Indigenous] American people are uneducable; for they lack affect and passion. They are not amorous, and so are not fertile. They speak hardly at all, . . . care for nothing and are lazy."

Kant ranks the Chinese with East Indians, and claims that they are "static . . . for their history books show that they do not know more now than they have long known."[67] So Kant, who is one of the most influential philosophers in the Western tradition, asserted that Chinese, Indians, Africans, and the Indigenous peoples of the Americas are congenitally incapable of philosophy. And contemporary philosophers take it for granted that there is no Chinese, Indian, African, or Native American philosophy. If this is a coincidence, it is a stunning one.

Because of Kant's racism, it is difficult to believe that his judgments on Confucianism in his lectures on *Physical Geography* are based on a rational assessment of the evidence: "Philosophy is not to be found in the whole Orient. . . . Their teacher Confucius teaches in his writings nothing outside a moral doctrine designed for the princes . . . and offers examples of former Chinese princes. . . . But a concept of virtue and morality never entered the heads of the Chinese."[68] Kant also breezily comments: "In China everybody has the freedom to throw away children who become a burden, through hanging or drowning."[69] However, as historian David E. Mungello notes, "the horror felt by Europeans" about the Chinese practice of infanticide "was fed by a chauvinistic hypocrisy that blinded them to the massive infant abandonments that were even then occurring across Europe."[70] Many classic European myths reflect this reality: Rome was supposedly founded by Romulus and Remus, who were suckled by a wolf after being abandoned as infants; the story of Hansel and Gretel is about children being left to starve in the woods. Abandonment of infants became so common in the United Kingdom that in 1872 Parliament had to pass the Infant Life Protection Act, which required registration of all infants.[71] In China, infanticide was hardly treated as a casual matter: Buddhists and Confucians both condemned the practice when it did occur, and funded foundling homes for abandoned children.[72] I am not denying that infanticide is horrific: it is. Nor am I denying that there is something especially abhorrent about the Chinese preference for female infanticide (and the contemporary trend of selective abortion of female fetuses): there is. What I object to is the rhetorical use of infanticide to portray the West as morally superior to China.

G. W. F. Hegel (1770–1831) was one of Kant's most insightful critics, but he shared Kant's casual dismissal of Chinese thought:

We have conversations between Confucius and his followers in which there is nothing definite further than a commonplace moral put in the form of good, sound doctrine, which may be found as well expressed and better, in every place and amongst every people. Cicero gives us *De Officiis*, a book of moral teaching more comprehensive and better than all the books of Confucius. He is hence only a man who has a certain amount of practical and worldly wisdom—one with whom there is no speculative philosophy. We may conclude from his original works that for their reputation it would have been better had they never been translated.[73]

Elsewhere, Hegel opines: "In the principal work of Confucius . . . are found correct moral sayings; but there is a circumlocution, a reflex character, and circuitousness in the thought, which prevents it from rising above mediocrity."[74] Ironically, many people dismiss Hegel's own philosophical writings for the same stylistic flaws of "circumlocution" and "circuitousness."

Note that Hegel is like Scalia in giving Cicero privileged treatment compared to Confucius. Speaking as someone who has actually read both of them, I find Confucius considerably more interesting than Cicero. Cicero reminds me of the uncle who buttonholes you at Thanksgiving to lecture you interminably about fly-fishing. Many others share my opinion. No less an authority than classicist and Nobel Laureate Theodor Mommsen said that "the dreadful barrenness of thought in the Ciceronian orations must revolt every reader of feeling and judgment."[75] In a similar vein, Alston Hurd Chase, a beloved teacher of Greek and Roman literature at Phillips Academy Andover, admitted that "the windy, egotistic orations of Cicero" caused generations of students to abandon the study of Latin.[76] In contrast, Herbert Fingarette, who was originally trained as a mainstream analytic philosopher, said that, when he actually read Confucius carefully, he found him to be "a thinker with profound insight and with an imaginative vision of man equal in its grandeur to any I know."[77]

Essentialist arguments against multiculturalism have continued into the twentieth century. Martin Heidegger claimed that "The often heard expression 'Western-European philosophy' is, in truth, a tautology. Why? Because philosophy is Greek in its nature; . . . the nature of philosophy is of such a kind that it first appropriated the Greek world, and only it, in order to unfold."[78] Similarly, on a visit to China in 2001, Jacques Derrida stunned his hosts (who teach in Chinese philosophy departments) by announcing that "China does not have any philosophy, only thought." In response to the obvious shock of his audience, Derrida insisted that "Philosophy is related to some sort of particular history, some languages, and some ancient Greek invention. . . . It is something of European form."[79] The statements of Derrida and Heidegger might have the appearance of complimenting non-Western philosophy for avoiding the entanglements of Western metaphysics. In actuality, their comments are as condescending as talk of "noble savages," who are untainted by the corrupting influences of the West, but are for that very reason barred from participation in higher culture. Postcolonial feminist Gayatri Spivak, who translated Derrida's *Of Grammatology* into English, acknowledges that "almost by a reverse ethnocentrism, Derrida insists that logocentrism is a property of the *West*. . . . Although something of the Chinese prejudice of the West is discussed in Part I, the *East* is never seriously studied or deconstructed in the Derridean text. Why then must it remain, recalling Hegel and Nietzsche in their most cartological humors, as the name of the limits of the text's knowledge?"[80]

Sometimes the narrow-mindedness characteristic of contemporary philosophers is amusingly baffling. I vividly remember many of my early experiences being interviewed for a job as an assistant professor. The writing sample I submitted as part of my application packet discussed Daoist critiques of Confucian ethics. Part of the Daoist argument is that those who self-consciously advocate virtue (like the Confucians) are the first to "role up their sleeves and resort to force" (as *Daodejing* 38 puts it) when things don't go their way. It is not an implausible argument that a conscious effort to be virtuous is self-defeating because one can easily slide into hypocritical self-righteousness. Confucians typically reply that emphasizing deference and humility as virtues will make self-righteousness less likely. I was looking forward to discussing this debate between Daoists and Confucians with other philosophers. However, in one interview, a leading analytic epistemologist had only one question for me: "You mention that thing about rolling up their sleeves. In all the pictures I've seen of Chinese philosophers, they're wearing robes. Did those guys even *have* sleeves?" He seemed fascinated to discover that they did.

During another interview, a philosopher asked me a long, rambling question that I barely understood at the time and most of which I could not reproduce to save my life. However, I will always remember his conclusion: "So, I guess what I'm saying is, it seems like Chinese philosophers are playing the intellectual equivalent of minor league baseball, whereas Western philosophers are playing major league baseball. Wouldn't you agree?" I did not, nor did I get that job.

The ethnocentrism of professional philosophers is sometimes too offensive to laugh at. Former philosophy doctoral student Eugene Park speaks movingly about his failed efforts to encourage a more diverse approach to philosophy:

> I found myself repeatedly confounded by ignorance and, at times, thinly veiled racism. To various faculty, I suggested the possibility of hiring someone who, say, specializes in Chinese

philosophy or feminist philosophy or the philosophy of race. I complained about the Eurocentric nature of undergraduate and graduate curricula. Without exception, my comments and suggestions were met with the same rationalizations for why philosophy is the way it is and why it should remain that way. To paraphrase one member of my department, "This is the intellectual tradition we work in. Take it or leave it."

The pressure to accept and conform to a narrow conception of philosophy was pervasive. When I tried to introduce non-Western and other noncanonical philosophy into my dissertation, a professor in my department suggested that I transfer to the Religious Studies Department or some other department where "ethnic studies" would be more welcome.[81]

Park eventually dropped out of his doctoral program. How many other students—particularly students who might have brought greater diversity to philosophy—have been turned off from the beginning or have dropped out along the way because philosophy seems like nothing but a temple to the achievement of white males?

The sad reality is that comments like those by Kant, Hegel, Heidegger, Derrida, Scalia, Pigliucci, and the professors Park encountered are manifestations of what Edward Said labeled "Orientalism": the view that everything from Egypt to Japan is essentially the same, and is the polar opposite of the West: "The Oriental is irrational, depraved (fallen), childlike, 'different'; thus the European is rational, virtuous, mature, 'normal.'"[82] Those under the influence of Orientalism do not need to really read Chinese (or other non-European) texts or take their arguments seriously, because they come preinterpreted: "'Orientals' for all practical purposes were a Platonic essence, which any Orientalist (or ruler of Orientals) might examine, understand,

and expose."[83] And this essence guarantees that what Chinese, Indian, Middle Eastern, or other non-European thinkers have to say is at best quaint, at worst fatuous.

While racism is undeniably part of the problem, it is also true that most US philosophers simply don't know anything about Chinese philosophy. As philosopher Eric Schwitzgebel laments: "Ignorance thus apparently justifies ignorance: Because we don't know their work, they have little impact on our philosophy; because they have little impact on our philosophy, we are justified in remaining ignorant about their work."[84] If US philosophers *do* have any familiarity with Chinese thought (perhaps through a nonphilosophical Asian literature survey course they took as an undergraduate), it is probably from the *Analects* of Confucius, the *Daodejing*, or the *Changes*. In my opinion, of all the ancient classics, these three works are the least accessible to contemporary philosophers. As Joel Kupperman explained,

> If educated Chinese, Koreans, and Japanese (along with a small number of Western scholars) think that they understand *The Analects of Confucius*, it is because they have read it all, probably more than once. The pithy sayings take on meaning in the larger context. For the Western reader who is not a specialist *The Analects of Confucius* initially will seem like one of those amorphous blots used in Rorschach tests.[85]

The same could be said about the *Daodejing* and the *Changes*: without a great deal of effort and assistance in understanding their background and influence, it would be easy to walk away from these works thinking that Chinese philosophy is nothing but shallow platitudes or simply word salad. Ironically, beginning the study of Chinese philosophy with the *Analects*, *Daode-*

jing, or *Changes* is a bit like starting to learn about Western philosophy with the pre-Socratics. The fragments of Heraclitus and Parmenides, like the heterogeneous sayings recorded in the *Analects* and *Daodejing*, are crucial background to understanding what comes later, and they do present interesting philosophical and textual issues for those equipped to handle them. However, the beginner needs a lot of help in understanding what is philosophically important about them, and you will get a misleading impression if all you know about their respective traditions is these works.[86]

However, as Schwitzgebel argues, "even by the strictest criteria," the ancient consequentialist Mozi and the Confucian virtue ethicist Xunzi "are plainly philosophers."[87] Schwitzgebel, a highly respected analytic philosopher of mind, goes on to note that the moral realist Mengzi and his antirealist nemesis Zhuangzi are comparable in style to Nietzsche and Wittgenstein, in that they offer strong prima facie arguments even though they do not write in the essay format favored by contemporary philosophers. I would add the Legalists Hanfeizi and Shen Dao to the list of ancient Chinese thinkers who are plainly philosophers.[88] There are also many interesting and powerful philosophers in the later Chinese tradition, particularly in the Buddhist, Neo-Confucian, and New Confucian traditions.[89]

AVOIDING INTELLECTUAL IMPERIALISM

So far, I have replied to those who would deny the title of "philosophy" to non-Western thinkers on the grounds that they don't engage in anything recognizable as competent philosophy (an assertion that can be falsified by simply reading the thinkers in question), and I've challenged the essentialist ethnocentrism that defines philosophy as grounded in a particular historical tradition (a view that is both conceptually confused and historically dubious). However, some argue that characterizing non-Western thought as "philosophy" is itself a kind of intellectual imperialism, since it takes for granted the Western category. I certainly agree that we have to be careful to understand how doctrines and practices of argumentation are situated in their particular cultures. These doctrines and practices will normally not overlap perfectly with our own. However, it is equally important to avoid the misconception that philosophy in the West is monolithic. As Justin E. H. Smith elegantly illustrates in his recent work, "philosophy has in fact been many things in the 2,500 years or so since the term was first used,"[90] and "philosophy's motion throughout history from one self-conception to the next has been at best a sort of random stumbling."[91] In general, I suggest that we should agree to stop using the word "the" in intellectual history. "*The* Western conception of philosophy," "*the* Chinese view of the sage," "*the* Indian view of liberation": these and similar definite descriptions are all non-referring, because "the" suggests uniqueness. Plato, Kant, and Russell do not share one understanding of what philosophy is. Buddhists, Daoists, and Confucians do not agree about what makes someone a sage, nor do they even agree about who is a sage. Indian philosophers do not hold the same doctrines about what you need to be liberated from, or how you get liberated from it, or what you are liberated into. Consequently, the danger is not that we might mistakenly impose *the* unique Western conception of the philosopher onto (for example) *the* unique Chinese conception of the sage. Rather, the temptation to avoid is the assumption that what one Western philosopher does is definitive of all philosophy, and must be what philosophers in other cultures are doing (if they are doing philosophy at all). For example, if we compare the ancient Confucian Mengzi (fourth century BCE) with René Descartes (1596–1650), the founder of modern Western philosophy, they seem to be engaged in activities that are completely unrelated. However, Mengzi *does* seem to be exploring the same fundamental question as the ancient Stoic Epictetus (fl. 200 BCE)—what is the best way to live— even though they offer answers that are different in interesting and informative ways. A more appropriate Asian philosopher to bring into dialogue with Descartes would be the Buddhist thinker Dharmakīrti (fl. 600 CE), who provides alternative conclusions and arguments regarding the same kinds of issues in epistemology and metaphysics that vex Cartesians. In chapter 5, I discuss in more depth the issue of what philosophy is, why we should use a broad characterization of philosophy, and why some kinds of non-Western thought are clearly philosophy. However, I hope the preceding considerations will encourage those who are worried about the danger of intellectual imperialism to keep reading until then.

WHERE DO WE GO FROM HERE?

As the Confucian philosopher Zhu Xi notes, ethical knowledge comes first in time, but appropriate action is what is most important. Consequently, I offer the following concrete recommendations. To my fellow academic colleagues: the next time you are authorized to hire a new philosopher, consider whether it is really best for the long-term health of your department, for the education of your students, and even for the survival of philosophy as an academic discipline to hire yet another person who specializes solely in mainstream Anglo-European philosophy.

One bad argument I sometimes hear against diversifying the curriculum is "What would you have us cut? We can barely cover Western philosophy as it is!" You're right. You can't cover all of Anglo-European philosophy. But guess what? You were never close to covering all of Western philosophy and you never will be! There are more than a dozen distinct "topical" subjects in Western philosophy (including aesthetics, applied ethics, epistemology, logic, metaethics, metaphysics, normative ethics, philosophy of language, philosophy of mathematics, philosophy of mind, philosophy of science, and political philosophy, among others) and at least eight distinct historical subjects in Western philosophy (ancient Western philosophy, Hellenistic philosophy, medieval Western philosophy, early modern Western philosophy, nineteenth-century Continental philosophy, twentieth-century Continental philosophy, history of analytic philosophy, and history of pragmatism). So, if you want to have comprehensive coverage of Western philosophy, you will need a minimum of twenty philosophers in your department. In reality, even large departments in the United States do not try to have comprehensive coverage, but instead have philosophers with overlapping areas of competence. One top philosophy department has nineteen faculty members, seven of whom list philosophy of mind as an area of expertise. (To its credit, this department also has one specialist in Chinese philosophy and one on Africana philosophy.) So, yes, if you are going to add non-Western philosophy or some other LCTP to your curriculum, you will have less coverage in some area. But you are already making compromises about coverage all the time. Furthermore, scholars who teach some kind of LCTP almost invariably also teach and do research in some "mainstream" area. Chinese philosophy pairs well with ethics; Indian philosophy easily meshes with analytic metaphysics, epistemology, and philosophy of language; many other LCTP are directly relevant to political philosophy.

I once approached a leading philosopher for advice about how to increase diversity in the curriculum of US philosophy departments. I deeply admire her and her work, which includes extensive activism as a progressive public intellectual, so I was hopeful that she would be supportive. She replied that, given how few scholars know classical Chinese or Sanskrit well enough to supervise doctoral students, and how few students come into graduate school with any background in these languages, we can't change things without "cutting corners." I concede that part of the reason for the glacial rate of change in philosophy is a pipeline problem. In a vicious circle, few institutions teach philosophy outside the Anglo-European mainstream, so there are few recent PhDs in these areas for institutions to hire, so the number of institutions that teach these kinds of philosophy does not increase.

definition

Although the pipeline problem is real, it is not an excuse for failure to diversity the curriculum. First, the Society for Asian and Comparative Philosophy, which is probably the largest professional organization devoted to the study of non-Western philosophy, has over six hundred members.[92] Consequently, there are enough strong scholars currently doing research that we could double the number of top institutions teaching Asian philosophy overnight if there were the will to do so. Second, many understudied areas in philosophy do not require expertise in what the US Foreign Service Institute describes as "Category III" languages (the most difficult ones for English-speakers to learn). Rev. Martin Luther King, Jr., and Mahatma Gandhi wrote in English; Simone de Beauvoir, the seminal feminist existentialist, wrote in French; Enrique Dussel, a foundational figure in Latin American philosophy of liberation, writes in

seek help for LP.

Spanish. Third, philosophers have both "areas of specialization" (the subjects they publish on and supervise dissertations about) and "areas of competence" (topics they can teach an undergraduate survey course on). Even if you cannot find someone qualified to do research in one of the LCTP, you can at least hire someone who can teach the topic to undergraduates.

What you should absolutely *not* do is go to someone already in your department who teaches Anglo-European philosophy but happens to be of non-European descent and say, "We're getting pressure about teaching Asian/African/Islamic philosophy. Why don't you work up a course on it?" Yes, this really does happen. This is deeply racist. (It's as bad as telling me that I'm of Polish descent, so I must love Kielbasa and Pierogis. I mean, I am and I do, but that's beside the point.) Furthermore, untenured faculty will often have to swallow their pride and accept your request out of fear of losing their job by being "uncollegial."

Finally, some advice to students: Both as individuals and when organized, you have considerable power to encourage the faculty and administration of colleges and universities to teach philosophy outside the Anglo-European mainstream. As a start, form a local chapter of Minorities in Philosophy (MAP) and connect with chapters at other schools.[93] MAP is a student organization devoted to increasing diversity in the field of philosophy in all ways: among students at the undergraduate and graduate levels, among faculty, and in courses offered. Local MAP chapters sometimes organize reading groups or invite speakers to campus to discuss understudied philosophers. Another simple method to effect change is to vote with your add form. When courses on Chinese, Indian, or other LCTP are offered, sign up for them. If no courses are offered in these areas, you can request to do independent studies on them. If no one seems receptive, it is time to request changes by talking to professors, chairs, deans, and your college or university president. If requests don't work, turn to petitions. If petitions, don't work, it's time to organize protests.

If getting your philosophy department to change its curriculum encounters too much resistance at first, follow Garfield's suggestion and fight for the second-best result: demand that philosophy departments change their names to "departments of Anglo-European philosophy" to reflect their actual curriculum. There is really no legitimate way they can reject a demand to admit what they teach. This might seem like giving up. However, I believe that, if this change were enforced, it would be at most a decade before philosophy departments become multicultural. Currently, departments can hide behind the name "philosophy," which represents a topic with cosmopolitan significance, to disguise the fact that their approach is indefensibly parochial. If their shame were exposed to their colleagues and students, the pressure for change would become insurmountable.

I have been warned that linking the call to study non-Western philosophy to issues of diversity and identity politics will politicize it in ways that may lead to outcomes I would not prefer.[94] I agree. As a professor, I jealously guard my right to conduct my own research and teach my own classes as I see fit. This is not arrogance or stubbornness. I have spent years developing expertise in my areas of specialization, and figuring out how best to communicate to my students what I have learned and most importantly my love for philosophy. I am always interested in feedback, positive or negative, and I take it into account in making long-term adjustments. However, in terms of the fundamentals, no one with at most four years of undergraduate education knows better than I do after thirty years of experience in teaching and research. Consequently, in an ideal world, philosophy departments should make their own decisions about their curricula internally.

Sadly, we are not in an ideal world. I and many others have been fighting with rational arguments for decades to try to get greater acceptance of non-Western philosophy into the curriculum. I have appealed to my colleagues in philosophy to make moderate changes on their own terms in response to the realities of a changing world. However, I increasingly think that the only way to effect change in philosophy is by appealing to students to mobilize and demand changes. If and when curricular change is forced upon philosophy departments, it will not be moderate, and it will not be guided by a deep understanding of what philosophy is about or what its intellectual standards are. This is why Garfield and I ended our editorial with this warning:

> We offer one last piece of advice to philosophy departments that have not already embraced curricular diversity. For demographic, political and historical reasons, the change to a more multicultural conception of philosophy in the United States seems inevitable. Heed the Stoic adage: "The Fates lead those who come willingly, and drag those who do not."[95]

It is one thing to suggest that greater pluralism can make philosophy richer and better approximate the truth. It is another thing to show it. Consequently, in chapter 2, "Traditions in Dialogue," I will provide several examples to illustrate how Western and Asian philosophy can be brought into a constructive conversation. Not all beliefs are held for reasons that are conscious or rational, though, so in chapter 3, "Trump's Philosophers," I will argue that the heated opposition we see to multiculturalism in philosophy is motivated, in large part, by the same chauvinistic instincts that inflame nationalism, racism, and other kinds of ethnocentrism. Some people don't see the value of any kind of philosophy. In chapter 4, "Welders and Philosophers," I explain the vocational benefits of a philosophical education, the contributions of philosophy to Western civilization, and the value of philosophy in producing citizens committed to rational, civil discourse. Finally, in chapter 5, "The Way of Confucius and Socrates," I will argue that contemporary philosophers are partially responsible for their own marginalization in society and discuss how they can change that by returning to the exalted aspirations that have always motivated great philosophical work, regardless of its civilization of origin.

2

TRADITIONS IN DIALOGUE

I am a human, and nothing human is alien to me.
—Terence

Within the Four Seas, all are brothers.
—Zigong

n the previous chapter I called for greater inclusivity and
openness to philosophy outside the mainstream Anglo-
European canon. I dropped the names of a few texts,
thinkers, and issues that could contribute substantially to a
broader dialogue. However, it is fair to ask for more detailed
examples. Consequently, in this chapter I provide a few specific
illustrations of how different intellectual traditions can be
brought into dialogue. Some readers will be disappointed to
discover that my comparisons are only between a handful of
Asian and European philosophers. However, I can only re-
sponsibly discuss the areas in which I claim competence. To
advocate that we teach the less commonly taught philosophies
(LCTP) is not to suggest the unrealistic goal that we should all
be equally adept at lecturing on all of them. Moreover, I do not

go into nearly as much depth in this chapter as would be appropriate in a purely academic work. Nonetheless, even the selective, cursory discussions in this chapter demonstrate conclusively just how much room there is for productive dialogue between traditions.

Philosophers—who, as a group, are known for not agreeing about *anything*—agree that modern Western philosophy begins with René Descartes (1596–1650). There is almost as much of a consensus that modern Western political philosophy begins with Thomas Hobbes (1588–1679).[1] The two disagreed about a great deal.[2] Hobbes asserted that "the *universe*, that is, the whole mass of all things that are is corporeal—that is to say, body."[3] Descartes, in contrast, believed that, in addition to physical objects, the universe includes souls that are incorporeal and immortal. However, Descartes and Hobbes agreed on a fundamental claim: the universe is composed of *distinct individual entities*. Although there have been occasional philosophers who have dissented from this view (most notably Parmenides, Spinoza, and Hegel), individualistic metaphysics is something like the orthodoxy in Western philosophy.[4] This belief has been developed in various ways, but it is so fundamental to Anglo-European philosophy that it generally has not been seen as requiring demonstration. The issue has not been *whether* we are distinct individuals, but *how* we are fundamentally distinct and what the implications of this are. However, if we assume that individuals are distinct, it creates a number of problems in metaphysics (our account of the most fundamental kinds of things that exist and how they are related), political philosophy (our conception of how and why human communities should be organized), and ethics (our view of the best way for a person to live). We shall see that Buddhist, Confucian, and Neo-Confucian philosophies offer alternatives on these topics that are undeniably worth taking seriously.

METAPHYSICS

In his major philosophical works, *Discourse on Method* and *Meditations on First Philosophy*, Descartes argues that there are two distinct kinds of *substances* in the universe: things that think (souls) and things that occupy space (material objects).[5] His use of the word "substance" is potentially misleading for us. When we talk about a "substance," we are typically talking about something that lacks individual identity (especially if it is disgusting): "Ew, what is this substance stuck to the bottom of my shoe?" For Descartes, "substance" is a technical philosophical term, which he inherited from Aristotle (384–22 BCE). Aristotle defined a substance as a thing that has qualities but is not itself a quality of anything else.[6] For example, the color red is not a substance, because it is a quality of something else, like a fire hydrant. But a fire hydrant is not a quality of anything else, so it is a substance. The thesis that the universe is divided into qualities of various kinds and the things that they are qualities of sounds simple and accurate. However, as Aristotle himself came to recognize, this seemingly straightforward account generates problems as soon as we think more carefully about what it means.[7] Let's return to Descartes to see how.

In trying to explain what a material object (a substance that occupies space) is, Descartes invites us to consider a piece of wax, fresh from the beehive, and its sensory qualities. It has the taste of honey, a floral scent, is hard and cold to the touch. However, if you melt the same piece of wax, it loses its taste and odor, changes its shape, and feels hot and soft. Descartes then asks his readers, "does the same wax remain? One must confess that it does: no one denies it; no one thinks otherwise. What was there then in the wax that was so distinctly comprehended? Certainly none of the things that I reached by means of the senses. For whatever came under taste or smell or sight or touch or hearing by now has changed, yet the wax remains."[8]

The material thing that remains the same through the various changes is the *substance*. But what is this substance? You cannot identify the substance with any properties, like being hot or cold, hard or malleable. The substance is the thing that has these qualities, and remains the same as the properties change. This led Aristotle to suggest at one point that there must be what he called "prime matter," a quality-less substratum that is the bearer of properties.[9] Something seems incoherent, though, about the notion of a thing that has an identity but no properties.

Descartes compares our knowledge of substances to seeing people out his window, crossing the street in the dead of winter, completely bundled up in clothes: "But what do I see over and above the hats and clothing? Could not robots be concealed under these things? But I judge them to be men."[10] Similarly, "when I distinguish the wax from its external forms, as if having taken off its clothes, as it were, I look at the naked wax."[11] (How quaint Western philosophy is, with all its little similes and metaphors!) The problem, of course, is that we have seen people without their coats and hats on, and we know what they look like. In contrast, we have not seen wax without its "external forms." As Descartes admits, we know the wax in itself "neither by sight, nor touch, nor imagination."[12]

Descartes discusses space-occupying substances as a step toward understanding what a thinking substance is. However, his account of souls inherits all the problems that afflicted his account of material objects. Souls engage in mental acts like thinking, perceiving, and willing. But none of these acts are what the soul is. The soul is the underlying thing that does the thinking, perceiving, and willing. And your soul is supposed to be different from mine, even if you and I are thinking the very same thing. What makes one soul different from another if the acts of the soul are not what make it what it is?

The puzzles of personal identity are illustrated by the film *Regarding Henry* (1991), in which Harrison Ford plays an attorney who is shot in the head during a convenience store robbery. After brain surgery, Henry's memories are gone. He does not recognize his wife, his children, or his colleagues from work. Prior to his brain injury, Henry was a brilliant but also heartless lawyer. Afterward, he seems to have only average intelligence, but is kind and loving. Is he the same person before and after brain surgery or not? According to Descartes, there is a definitive answer: the same soul is attached to his body, so he is the same person. But this answer seems unsatisfying because all the qualities of the soul that seemed to make Henry who he was have changed. Perhaps it is the same Henry because he has the same *body*? However, Henry's body is actually *not* the same. His brain, the physical organ we probably associate the most with our identity, has suffered significant trauma. So perhaps we should say that Henry$_1$ (before brain trauma) and Henry$_2$ (after brain trauma) are different people? But our bodies (and our mental states) are changing all the time. My brain and my mind at birth are immensely different from my brain and mind today. Am I not the same person? Or do only sudden and significant changes in the brain or mind make us a new person? How significant must a change be in order to count as making someone a new person? If these questions seem vexing, perhaps it is because we started with the wrong assumption: that there *is* an unchanging self that persists through qualitative change.[13]

Descartes's only real argument that there must be individual substances distinct from all of their qualities is that "no one denies it; no one thinks otherwise."[14] Well, actually, some people have denied this. The Buddhist tradition argues that there are five kinds of states that exist: physical states (being hard or malleable, hot or cold, etc.), sensations (experiences of physical or mental states, which may be pleasant, unpleasant, or neutral), perceptions (conceptual identification of that which one senses), volitions (such as desiring, willing, and choosing), and consciousness. Buddhists call these the "Five Aggregates." A concrete example will clarify what sorts of things they are: Suppose I am in the presence of a plate of freshly baked chocolate chip cookies. The visual receptors in my eyes are stimulated by the light reflected off the cookies, while molecules liberated by the heat of the cookies stimulate the olfactory receptors in my nose. As a result of these *physical states*, I have a visual *sensation* of golden brown circles with dark brown spots against a white background, and the pleasant olfactory *sensation* of baked dough, brown sugar, and just a hint of vanilla. These sensations are followed by a *perception*: the identification of what I am sensing as chocolate chip cookies. At this point, I develop a *volition*, a desire to eat the cookies—all of them, right now, in one sitting. However, I also have consciousness, which allows me to be aware of and think critically about my mental states. I may remind myself that eating a couple of cookies is pleasant, but I will feel an unpleasant sugar rush if I eat all of them at once, thereby reconceptualizing my choice in a way that leads to moderate consumption. (In the case of cookies, this last step never happens for me, but you get the idea.)

[margin note:] outside descartes conceptual map/scheme

[handwritten note:] I love this author.

Of course, this simple example does not do justice to the complexity of the concept of the Five Aggregates. As Jay Garfield points out, Buddhist accounts of "consciousness" do not map neatly onto those in Western philosophy of mind (even though they are debated with the same level of subtlety).[15] What is important to grasp is that Buddhist metaphysics regards the world as composed of transient states and properties that are causally dependent on other states and properties. It does away with the notion of metaphysical substances or prime matter as explanatorily useless. This ontology of states rather than things has substantial (pardon the expression) implications for how we think about ourselves.

In the second century BCE, in what is now Pakistan, the Buddhist monk Nāgasena arrived for a royal audience with King Milinda. When Milinda asked him his name, the monk replied that he is called "Nāgasena," but "this 'Nāgasena' is only a designation, a label, a concept, an expression, a mere name because there is no person as such that is found."[16] Milinda and Nāgasena proceed to have a subtle philosophical debate over what it means to say that there is "no person." (At this same period in history, Descartes's and my ancestors in Europe were illiterate barbarians bashing one another with clubs.) They consider three suggestions about what a self would be: Is the self identical with one of the Five Aggregates? Is the self identical with *all* of the Aggregates? Is the self something distinct from all of the Aggregates? Nāgasena and Milinda are obviously both familiar with previous Buddhist arguments against the reality of the self, so they quickly agree on negative answers to all three questions. (1) The self cannot be identified with a person's nails, "teeth, skin, flesh, sinews, bones, bone marrow, kidneys, heart, liver . . . brain, bile, phlegm, pus, blood, sweat," or any physical thing.[17] As the Buddha himself had explained, nothing physical could plausibly be identified as the self because, qua physical thing, it has no experiences: "If, friend, no feeling existed, could there be the thought, 'I am'?"[18] In other words, identifying the self with any physical thing violates our intuition that the self is conscious. One of the other Aggregates might seem a better candidate for the self, since they each involve consciousness in some way. However, suppose we identified the self with a pleasant sensation. The Buddha explains why this is also unsatisfactory: "So anyone who, on feeling a pleasant feeling, thinks 'This is my Self,' must, at the cessation of that pleasant feeling, think, 'My self has departed!'" This violates our intuition that the self is something that persists over time. The same applies to any other kind of sensation, as well as to any instance of the other mental Aggregates. (2) What about the possibility that the self is identical with *all* of the Aggregates taken together? Upon reflection, we see that this will not work either. Since each of the Aggregates is changing individually, the combination of them taken together is also changing, and so cannot be a permanent self: "It is just like a mountain river, flowing far and swift, taking everything along with it; there is no moment, no instant, no second when it stops flowing, but it goes on flowing and continuing. So . . . is human life, like a mountain river. The world is in continuous flux and is impermanent."[19] This is very similar to the famous claim of the Greek philosopher Heraclitus, who "says that all things pass and nothing stays, and comparing existing things to the flow of a river, he says you could not step twice in the same river."[20] (Of course, some people seem to think that, when Heraclitus says this, it is philosophy, but when a Buddhist says the same thing, it is not philosophy.)

(3) Is the self then something different from the Aggregates? This would be something like Descartes's view. The king asks Nāgasena about a very similar position in another part of their extensive dialogue:

> "Revered Nāgasena, is there such a thing as an experiencer?"
>
> "What does this 'experiencer' mean, sire?"
>
> "A soul within that sees a visible form with the eyes, hears a sound with the ear, smells a smell with the nose, tastes a taste with the tongue, feels a touch with the body and discriminates mental states with the mind. Just as we who are sitting here in the palace can look out of any window we want to look out of, even so, revered sir, this soul can look out of any door it wants to look out of."[21]

Nāgasena argues that it is unclear how to understand the relationship between such a soul and the body that it is supposed to "look out of." If the soul sees, why does it need the eye at all, for example? Why can't the soul see as well, or even better, without the organ of the eye? Of course, the soul *does* use the eye to see, and does not see better when the eye is removed. But then, Nāgasena suggests, why not adopt a simpler alternative: "Because, sire, of the eye and visible form eye-consciousness arises. . . . The same applies to the ear and sound, nose and smell, tongue and taste, body and touch, and mind and mental states. These are things produced from a condition and there is no experiencer found here."[22] In other words, the Aggregate of consciousness is different for each kind of consciousness, and arises simply as a result of the interaction between the intentional object of consciousness (for example, a color) and the sense organ (for example, an eye). Reference to some mysterious "experiencer" beyond the interaction between the color and the eye adds nothing to the explanation.

The metaphysical arguments against a self seem unanswerable, but what concerns King Milinda is the problematic ethical implications that they appear to have. If there is no self, *who is it* who engages in virtuous or vicious conduct? *Who is it* who is ignorant or enlightened? As King Milinda notes, the doctrine of no-self seems to lead to ethical nihilism: "revered Nāgasena, if someone were to kill you there would be no murder."[23] It appears that there would be no self who murders and no self who is murdered, and hence no wrongdoing.

Nāgasena replies with the simile of the chariot. He asks the king, "did you come on foot or in a vehicle?"[24] The king replies that he came in a chariot. Nāgasena then applies the same anti-substantialist argument to the chariot that they had applied to Nāgasena himself. Is a chariot the same as its wheels? Clearly not, because you can repair the wheels and it will be exactly the same chariot. Is the chariot the axle? No, we would refer to it as the same chariot even if the axle were completely replaced. Is the chariot the yoke, reins, goad, or flagstaff? No, no, no, and no, for the same reasons. Nāgasena teasingly tells the king that he was obviously not telling the truth when he said he rode here in a chariot, since he can identify no thing that is the chariot: "You are king over all India, a mighty monarch. Of whom are you afraid that you speak a lie?"[25] Milinda protests that he is not lying, and that "'chariot' exists as a mere designation" based upon the various parts.[26]

"Even so it is for me, sire," Nāgasena explains. "'Nāgasena' exists as a mere designation," used in the presence of his physical form, consciousness, etc. "However, in the ultimate sense there is no person as such that is found." He then quotes some verses attributed to a Buddhist nun and praised by the Buddha himself:

> Just as when the parts are rightly set
> The word "chariot" is spoken,
> So when the there are the aggregates
> It is the convention to say "a being."[27]

It is easy to misunderstand Nāgasena's position here. He is *not* claiming that there is a thing that is the chariot (or a person) and that it is identical with the combination of the relevant Aggregates. (We saw earlier why this won't work.) Instead, he is suggesting that, in the presence of certain combinations of Aggregates, we follow social convention in using the word "chariot" (or "Nāgasena"). In other words, there is no *thing* that is oneself; the Cartesian thinking substance is an illusion. However, this does not mean that we can or should stop calling one another "Nāgasena," or "Milinda," or "Bryan," or "Barack." To do so is useful for practical purposes, and what guide us are social conventions about linguistic usage. Similarly, we can continue to say things like "Charles Manson is a bad person" or "Mother Teresa was very enlightened." But these claims do not require that there is some unique metaphysical entity that a proper name refers to that remains the same over time.

Returning to our earlier example from the film *Regarding Henry*, Nāgasena would say that there is no fact about whether Henry is the same person. It is a matter of social convention whether we regard him as such. There is a collection of changing physical and mental states prior to the shooting and there is a collection of transient psychophysical states after the shooting, and our social convention is to call them both "Henry." This is reflected in the fact that the family and colleagues of

"Henry" prior to the shooting welcome "him" back after the shooting (and prefer the way "he" is now). Notice that similar considerations could apply to abortion. For a Cartesian, there is a fact about when the fetus is "ensouled," and from that moment on it is the same person. To end the life of an ensouled body is the moral equivalent of murder. However, the problems with defining when human life begins suggest that an application of Nāgasena's view is more appropriate. We do not *discover* when human life begins; we *decide* when life begins, trying to do so in a way that is as humane as possible.[28]

The preceding view is characteristic of Theravāda, which nonsectarian historians regard as the earlier form of Buddhism. Mahāyāna Buddhism, the dominant form in East Asia, would not deny anything Nāgasena said, but extends it in a new direction. We might say that Theravāda argues that there is no self, while Mahāyāna claims that there is no *individual* self. The Tang-dynasty Chinese Buddhist philosopher Fazang (643–712) wrote a philosophical dialogue that is representative of one strand of the Mahāyāna position.[29] Fazang asks us to consider a building.[30] What makes a building a building? Surely it is nothing other than the parts that make it up. There is no thing in addition to its parts that constitutes the building. So what are the parts of the building? Consider an individual rafter: What makes it a rafter? Fazang argues that it is a rafter because of the role that it plays in constituting the building. One might object that the rafter would still exist even if the rest of the building did not. Fazang replies that then it would no longer be a rafter. (For example, a plank that had been a rafter might be repurposed as a bench. We might want to say, "This bench *used to be* a rafter," but it would not be plausible to say, "This bench *really* is a rafter, despite the appearance that it is a bench.") What makes a rafter a rafter (as opposed to a bench or a teeter-totter) is the role it plays in the building. So the rafter is dependent on the building for its identity, but we already saw that the building is identical with all its parts. Consequently, the rafter is dependent on all the other parts of the building for its identity: the rafter depends on each of the other rafters, each of the shingles, each of the nails, and so on. But what is true of the rafter in relation to the building is true of anything in relation to the entire universe.

Fazang summarizes his point with a slogan: "All is one, because all are the same in lacking an individual nature; one is all, because cause and effect follow one another endlessly."[31] "All is one," because the entire universe is nothing else beyond the particular configuration of transient physical and mental states in causal relationships that make it up. "One is all," because any one thing is what it is because of its relationships with all the other things that define it. The building is the building because of each of the parts that make it up ("all is one"), but the rafter is a rafter because it is a part of the building ("one is all"). As a matter of brute causal fact, the universe we live in would collapse like a house of cards if some malevolent higher power plucked out of the causal web the lowliest member of the army of Alexander the Great, or your third cousin twice removed. It is not poetry but the most relentless logic of cause and effect that demonstrates that the last breath of Julius Caesar is my morning cup of coffee; the entire universe is a speck of dust; and I am you. A universe without you, or even a universe without this particular grain of sand, is as completely fictional as Hogwarts or House Lannister.

Ray Bradbury's seminal short story "A Sound of Thunder" (1952) gives a colorful example of the way in which events separated by immense gulfs of space and time can be substantially connected. In the story, a time traveler goes back to the Jurassic era and accidentally steps on a butterfly. When he returns to the present, he finds that the course of history has been modified, in some ways that are trivial, but in some ways that are disastrous. Bradbury's story is more than speculation, because scientists have known since the nineteenth century that minute changes in the initial conditions of deterministic systems can lead to immense changes in the later states of that system: Henri Poincaré noted this in regard to "the three-body problem" in physics.[32] Then, in the twentieth century, Edward Lorenz helped bring about a minor revolution in science by showing a similar phenomenon in meteorology: extremely small atmospheric changes (like the beating of a butterfly's wings in Brazil) can have massive consequences (like a hurricane in Florida).[33] In honor of Bradbury, this scientific truth is now called "the butterfly effect." While the significance of causal connections may not always be as dramatic as in Bradbury's story, it seems undeniable that it is possible to trace relations between any two things in the universe. If it seems difficult to imagine what relation exists between Diego, my French bulldog, and Charon, the largest of the moons of Pluto, keep in mind that the two exert a gravitational pull on each other (gravity decreases as the inverse square of distance but never disappears) and both were created in the same Big Bang.

Consider how this understanding transforms our conceptions of ourselves. Who am I? I am a husband, a father, a teacher, an author, and a US citizen, among other things. But each of these properties is relational: I am a husband because I have a spouse, a father because I have children, a teacher because I have students, an author because I have a readership, a US citizen because of historical facts and institutional structures I participate in. But the things I am related to are also defined by me.[34]

[right margin handwritten note: Similarities with Communitarianism.]

POLITICAL PHILOSOPHY

Thomas Hobbes shared Descartes's radical metaphysical individualism, arguing that there is "nothing in the world universal but names, for the things named are every one of them individual and singular."[35] For this reason, Hobbes's political philosophy is in many ways the natural counterpart of Descartes's metaphysics. Just as Buddhism helped us see alternatives to individualistic metaphysics like that of Descartes, Confucianism will help us to see the limitations of individualistic political philosophies like that of Hobbes.

Hobbes's political project is to explain how government authority can be justified, on the assumption that each human is originally completely independent, metaphysically and ethically, from every other human. Hobbes also appears to assume that each human being is purely self-interested: "of the voluntary acts of every man, the object is some *good to himself*."[36] Consequently, "if any two men desire the same thing . . . they become enemies; and in the way to their end, which is principally their own conservation, and sometimes their delectation only, endeavor to destroy or subdue one another."[37] Given these assumptions, Hobbes concludes that the natural state of human beings is "a condition of war of every one against every one."[38] In this conflict, one individual may have some marginal physical or intellectual advantage over another. However, these do not make a significant difference, since even "the weakest has strength enough to kill the strongest, either by secret machination or by confederacy with others that are in the same danger with himself."[39] Consequently, life in the state of nature is "solitary, poor, nasty, brutish, and short,"[40] like the worlds portrayed in the film *Mad Max: Fury Road* (2015) and the television series *The Walking Dead* (2010–present).[41]

This situation might seem to make legitimate government authority impossible, but Hobbes argues that, on the contrary, it is precisely what makes government a rational necessity. In humans' natural state of merciless competition "there can be no security to any man, how strong or wise soever he be, of living out the time which nature ordinarily allows men to live." Consequently, it is a law of nature "that a man be willing, when others are so too, as far forth as for peace and defense of himself he shall think it necessary, to lay down this right to all things, and be contented with so much liberty against other men as he would allow other men against himself."[42] Humans therefore can and do enter into a "covenant" to renounce violence, dishonesty, and thievery against one another. Now, since "covenants without the sword are but words, and of no strength to secure a man at all,"[43] it is necessary that there "be some coercive power to compel men equally to the performance of their covenants by the terror of some punishment greater than the benefit they expect by the breach of there covenant."[44] This coercive power is provided by the government. In summary, humans naturally have a right to do anything, including harming and killing others, in the pursuit of their individual self-interests. However, everyone will suffer horribly in this situation. Consequently, humans agree to renounce most of their rights to the government in exchange for protection from other people. In order for this to succeed, government must have an exclusive and in principle unlimited right to use force to compel adherence to its laws. Although government restricts our natural liberty, we are better off under even the most authoritarian government than we are in the state of nature.

Hobbes's philosophy is ingenious, but it faces several insurmountable problems. In a passage that seems almost tailor-made as a response to Hobbes, Confucius (551–479 BCE) argues that "if you try to guide the common people with coercive regulations and keep them in line with punishments, the common people will become evasive and will have no sense of shame. If, however, you guide them with Virtue, and keep them in line by means of ritual, the people will have a sense of shame and will rectify themselves."[45] The Confucian critique of authoritarian positions like that of Hobbes is that, no matter how severe the punishments and how intrusive the government surveillance, people will endlessly devise ways to evade the laws so long as their only motivations for compliance are self-interested. In contrast, if humans can cultivate compassion and integrity ("Virtue") and respect for social conventions that they regard as sacred ("ritual"), the laws and punishments will be almost unnecessary.[46]

Mengzi, a philosopher of the fourth century BCE, defends Confucius's political thesis, arguing that a state can be prosperous in the long run only insofar as its citizens are motivated by benevolence (compassion for the suffering of others) and righteousness (disdain to do what is shameful, like lying and cheating). In contrast, being motivated by profit—even if it is the profit of a group to which one belongs—is self-undermining. Mengzi warns a ruler:

> Why must Your Majesty say "profit"? Let there be benevolence and righteousness and that is all. Your Majesty says, "How can my state be profited?" The Counselors say, "How can my family be profited?" The scholars and commoners say, "How can I be profited?" Those above and those below mutually compete for profit and the state is endangered. . . . There have never been those who were benevolent who abandoned their parents. There have never been those who were righteous who put their ruler last. Let Your Majesty say, "Benevolence and righteousness," and that is all. Why must you say "profit"?[47]

Mengzi demonstrates a further problem with Hobbes's philosophy: its vision of human nature is not just ugly; it is also demonstrably mistaken. Mengzi presents a thought-experiment aimed at an egoist in his own era, Yang Zhu, that is equally effective against Hobbes:

> The reason why I say that humans all have hearts that are not unfeeling toward others is this. Suppose someone suddenly saw a child about to fall into a well: everyone in such a situation would have a feeling of alarm and compassion—not because one sought to get in good with the child's parents, not because one wanted fame among their neighbors and friends, and not because one would dislike the sound of the child's cries. From this we can see that if one is without the heart of compassion, one is not a human.[48]

Every aspect of Mengzi's thought-experiment is carefully chosen. Notice the following points. (1) Mengzi asks us to imagine a case in which a *child* is in danger. Children, since they are innocent and nonthreatening, trigger our compassion more easily than adults. (2) We are supposed to imagine that a person *suddenly* sees the child. The suddenness is important, because it suggests that the reaction will be unreflective. There is no time to think about who the child's parents are, or what rewards might come from saving the child, or even whether it would be annoying to listen to the child cry all night as it struggled to stay afloat in the well. All that the instantaneous reaction can represent is one's feelings for the child in danger. (3) This passage is often misquoted as stating that any human would *save* the child at the well; however, Mengzi does not commit himself to anything as strong as that. He merely states that any human in such a situation would have a "a feeling of alarm and compassion." The feeling could be fleeting. Perhaps one's second thought would be about how one hates the child's parents and would love to see them suffer, or self-interested fear that one might fall into the crumbling well oneself if one attempted to save the child. All Mengzi is arguing for is the universal human capacity to feel genuine compassion in at least some circumstances. (4) Mengzi invites us to consider what we would say of someone who did not have at least a fleeting feeling of compassion when suddenly confronted with a child about to fall into a well. He suggests—plausibly, I think—that we would describe such a person as "inhuman." "Psychopath" is the technical term for beings who lack even this minimal compassion for others. We can quibble over whether they are technically not human, but we certainly agree that they lack something crucial to normal humanity.

In summary, Mengzi's child-at-the-well thought-experiment describes a reaction to a child (a paradigmatic object of compassion) that is sudden (so there is no time to formulate ulterior motives). Mengzi only claims that any human in this situation would at least have a momentary reaction of alarm and compassion (he does not claim that everyone would act to save the child), and he suggests that we would regard someone who lacked such a reaction as an inhuman beast (rather than a human being). Elsewhere, Mengzi expresses his view of human nature concisely as "Benevolence is what it is to be human."[49]

Contemporary developmental psychology supports Mengzi's view that normal humans have an innate but incipient disposition toward compassion.[50] Intuitively, we should not be surprised in the least that humans have evolved a disposition to care for the well-being of others. Like other primates (and like canids, cetaceans, and elephants), we humans are pack animals whose survival depends upon a mutual willingness to make sacrifices for others, typically without any certainty of payback. Darwin himself offered an account of the evolution of moral motivations,[51] and more formal demonstrations of how evolution selects for altruism have been provided by recent biologists.[52]

Mengzi's alternative conception of human nature leads to a very different view of humans in the state of nature. Humans naturally live in groups, and naturally work together to solve common problems. Government is important because it can harness the human tendency toward group loyalty for the benefit of all. Mengzi claims that, in ancient times, "the waters overflowed their courses, inundating the central states. Serpents occupied the land, and the people were unsettled. In low-lying regions, [people] made nests in trees. On the high ground, they lived in caves." In response to these problems, a sage arose who organized people who "dredged out the earth and guided the water into the sea, chasing the reptiles into the marshes."[53]

Mengzi does not hold some Pollyannaish vision of humans as never engaging in conflict. He recognizes that military and police force will sometimes need to be used. However, he thinks that crime is generally a product of poverty: if the people "lack a constant livelihood . . . [w]hen they thereupon sink into crime, to go and punish them is to trap the people."[54] Confucius was making the same point when he advised a ruler who was concerned about the prevalence of robbers in his state: "If you could just get rid of your own excessive desires, the people would not steal even if you rewarded them for it."[55]

In addition to the fact that controlling the people solely through appeals to narrow self-interest and the threat of violence is impractical, and the fact that Hobbes's psychology is unrealistic, there is a third major problem with Hobbes's political philosophy. As we saw in considering Buddhist critiques of

Descartes's view, it is implausible that humans are ultimately metaphysically distinct from one another. But what are the political implications of the Buddhist view? The movement known as "Neo-Confucianism" appropriated the insights of Buddhism in order to provide a metaphysical basis for its own distinctive political philosophy and ethics. Cheng Hao (1032–85) expressed the Neo-Confucian view clearly with a metaphor: "A medical text describes numbness of the hands and feet as being 'unfeeling.' This expression describes it perfectly. Benevolent people regard Heaven, Earth, and the myriad things as one Substance. Nothing is not oneself."[56] Cheng is comparing being numb or "unfeeling" toward one's own limb with being "unfeeling" toward another person. Something is wrong if we are numb in one of our feet because we might allow it to become damaged and not be motivated to do anything about it. Our numbness makes us fail to act appropriately toward what is a part of us. Similarly, being unfeeling toward the suffering of another is a failure to respond with appropriate motivation and action toward what is, ultimately, a part of ourselves.

But can we really accept the ethical and political implications of the view that there are *no* individual selves? This is the issue that divided the Buddhists and the Neo-Confucians. Their disagreement had a metaphysical aspect and an ethical aspect. Metaphysically, Buddhists like Fazang claim that we are all aspects of a transpersonal self. Because an enlightened being sees all humans as equally parts of one whole, he or she rejects selfishness and loves everyone equally. However, this view also leads the fully enlightened person to reject romantic love and filial piety, because each of these is an attachment of one (illusory) individual to other (illusory) individuals. (This is why Buddhist monks and nuns in most cultures are celibate.) As Fazang puts it: upon achieving enlightenment, "the feelings are extinguished, and the dharmas that are manifestations of Substance become blended into one."[57]

Neo-Confucians were drawn to the Buddhist view that benevolence is justified by the metaphysical fact that we form "one body" with others. However, they harshly criticized Buddhists for challenging the value of conventional familial relationships,[58] and argued that the Buddhists went too far in undermining the notion of the individual. When one of his disciples announced happily, "I no longer feel that my body is my own," Cheng Hao smiled and replied, "When others have eaten their fill are you no longer hungry?"[59] Consequently, Neo-Confucians tweaked the Buddhist metaphysics: they argued that, in order for things to be defined by their relationships to other things, there must be individual things that stand in those relationships. How can you have a relationship without *things* that are related by it? (More abstractly, a relationship is of the logical form aRb, where a and b are individuals that stand in the relationship R. Without the distinct individuals a and b to relate, there is no relationship R.) For example, if the rafter is defined by its relationship to other parts of the building, like the nails and shingles, there must be bits of wood, metal, and tile (these specific individual entities) in order for them to stand in the relationship of being-parts-of-the-building. Similarly, the relationship of motherhood does not exist unless there is at least one specific person who is a mother and another specific person who is her child; the property of being a student does not exist unless there is at least one individual who stands in the student-of relationship to one other individual. The great Neo-Confucian philosopher Zhu Xi (1130–1200) explained it like this, using the term "Pattern" to describe the web of relationships among entities: "It's like a house: it only has one Pattern, but there is a kitchen and a reception hall. . . . Or it's like this crowd of people: they only have one Pattern, but there is the third son of the Zhang family and the fourth son of the Li family; the fourth son of the Li family cannot become the third son of the Zhang family, and the third son of the Zhang family cannot become the fourth son of the Li family."[60] Consequently, romantic intimacy, filial piety, and other attachments are justified because there genuinely are individual husbands who love *their* individual wives, individual children who respect *their* individual parents, and so on.

I worry that the Neo-Confucians have fallen back into a paradoxical notion similar to a Cartesian substance or Aristotelian prime matter: the quality-less individual that stands in relationships but is not defined by them. However, there is something very appealing about the Confucian effort to do justice both to the fact that we are dependent upon others and to the fact that we are individuals with our own needs, goals, life histories, and attachments.

During his reelection campaign in 2012, President Barack Obama gave a speech in which he (unknowingly) expressed this Confucian perspective:

> If you were successful, somebody along the line gave you some help. There was a great teacher somewhere in your life. Somebody helped to create this unbelievable American system that we have that allowed you to thrive. Somebody invested in roads and bridges. If you've got a business—you didn't build that. Somebody else made that happen. . . . The point is, is that when we succeed, we succeed because of our individual initiative, but also because we do things together.[61]

This statement was widely criticized by conservatives, who saw it as an attack on the achievements of individual business owners and their right to profit from the fruit of their labor.[62] However, for those who have learned the lessons of Neo-Confucianism, Obama's statement is simple common sense.

I am not a businessman, but I too am proud of my accomplishments. I am proud of having taught generations of students, and of publishing a number of books and articles. I believe that my successes in teaching and publication would not have occurred without my hard work and ability. However, I suffer from no delusions that I am some sort of intellectual Robinson Crusoe.[63] I know that I did not single-handedly come up with every idea and methodology I have ever depended upon as a stepping-stone to developing my own original thoughts. I am indebted to my parents for giving me opportunities they did not have. My career is dependent on every teacher I have had from first grade through graduate school. And, of course, my roles as teacher and author are completely dependent upon my students and my readers. So you should look with pride upon your individual accomplishments, but you should also not lose sight of the fact that you did *not* do that alone.

Confucians are certainly not the only political theorists in China. Mozi argued two millennia before Hobbes that conflict in the state of nature necessitates the establishment of government. Moreover, Mozi's version of this argument is more plausible than that of Hobbes, because Mozi does not assume that humans are self-interested. He argues that the conflict in the state of nature arises from the fact that humans have different conceptions of right and wrong.[64] Legalists like Shen Dao and Hanfeizi argued that humans are largely (although perhaps not exclusively) self-interested, and so governments can only succeed through explicit and clear laws that are enforced with lavish rewards for compliance and severe punishments for transgression.[65] This chapter only scratches the surface of Chinese political thought.

ETHICS

Closely related to the issue of how society should be structured is the fundamental question of ethics: How should one live? In his seminal book *After Virtue*, Alasdair MacIntyre argued that modern Western ethics is fundamentally incoherent because it turned its back on the insights of Aristotelian thought. I am sympathetic to much of MacIntyre's critique. However, we shall see that Confucian views of ethical cultivation can provide plausible alternatives to the Aristotelian conception.

MacIntyre argues that modern ethics inherited an ethical framework from medieval Aristotelianism but dropped one of the parts necessary to make sense out of it.[66] According to the classical conception, humans are born with an *uncultivated nature* characterized by various drives, intellectual faculties, and most importantly ethical potentialities. Without cultivation, these drives lead to *immorality* (cruelty, dishonesty, etc.) as well as self-destructiveness. Through *ethical cultivation*, humans shape their drives, hone their faculties, and *actualize their potentialities*. For example, we have drives to satisfy our sensual desires, but we learn delayed gratification; we have some capacity for practical reasoning, but we improve it through education and practice; and we have a potential to become a virtuous person that we gradually actualize. Insofar as we fully actualize our potential, we develop a stable *virtuous character*, which leads to consistently *moral behavior*. In summary, *morality* is an expression of the *virtuous character* we develop as the result of *ethical cultivation that actualizes our potentiality*, thereby trans-

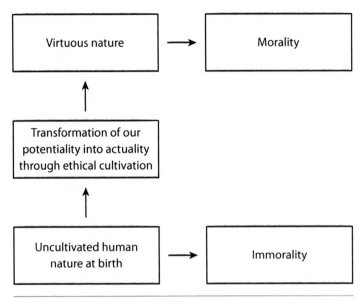

FIGURE 2.1

forming our *uncultivated nature at birth*, which would otherwise lead to immorality. Figure 2.1 gives us a visual representation of this framework.

However, an important part of the rise of modern science was the rejection of the classic Aristotelian distinction between potentiality and actuality. In a famous parody by Molière (1622–73), an Aristotelian medical student explains that the reason opium puts people to sleep is that it has a *virtus dormitiva*, a "sleep-inducing power."[67] The suggestion is that accounts of the universe in terms of *potentialities* that become *actualities* are nothing but pretentious pseudo-explanations. Both Descartes and Hobbes deny that there is any such thing as potentiality. Descartes asserted that "a merely potential being, . . . properly speaking, is nothing."[68] Hobbes complained that "There is no such word as potentiality in the Scriptures, nor in any author of the Latin tongue. It is found only in School-divinity, as a word of art, or rather as a word of craft, to amaze and puzzle the laity."[69] All that exists is purely and fully actual. As we shall discuss in chapter 4, Aristotelian science is more sophisticated than it is now given credit for. Ironically, the contemporary view that physical reality is composed of mass-energy, which has the potential to assume different forms, is closer to the Aristotelian view than it is to the atomism that was the scientific orthodoxy in the eighteenth and nineteenth centuries.[70] However, it is undeniable that early modern science achieved a revolution by attempting to explain reality quantitatively in terms of objects in motion rather than qualitatively in terms of things actualizing their potential.

What was a positive conceptual development for natural science was disastrous for ethics, though. The stricture against discussing the actualization of a potentiality made the relationship between our innate motivations and our moral practices incoherent. The vertical dimension of ethics—what we might call the ethics of aspiration—collapsed, leaving us with an image of human nature as savage, and a moral code with no intelligible relationship to that nature. Figure 2.2 is a visual representation of the fractured framework for ethics that modernity left us with.

The political philosophy of Hobbes is an example of the desperate effort to find some rational justification for morality that appeals only to human nature at its most unrefined. Ultimately, modern ethics was led to the existentialist view that ethics is a criterion-less choice between equally unjustified ways of life (some moral and some immoral).[71] Educational and spiritual practices, on this conception, are nothing but brainwashing.

Recognizing the insoluble problems that modern ethics created for itself, a host of recent Western philosophers have been

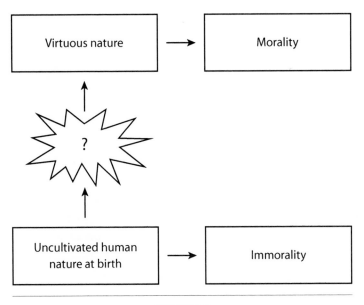

FIGURE 2.2

leading us "back to the future" by seeking to recover and mod-
ernize the insights of the Aristotelian tradition of *virtue ethics*.[72]
However, Aristotle's conception of ethical cultivation has serious problems of its own. Aristotle claims that "the virtues arise
in us neither by nature nor against nature, but we are by nature
able to acquire them, and reach our complete perfection through
habit."[73] In other words: "we become just by doing just actions,
temperate by doing temperate actions, brave by doing brave actions."[74] However, Aristotle thinks that the beginner in ethical
cultivation does not do virtuous actions "in the way in which
just or temperate people do them."[75] Specifically, the beginner
does not yet love virtue for its own sake, nor does he act out of
a settled state of character.[76] But this leaves us with a substantial theoretical problem: If we are not naturally virtuous, how
could any amount of habituation help us to develop the emotions

(handwritten margin note:) @ molto Return to past rather than seek new voices

and motivations that are distinctive of virtue? It seems that habituation can produce, at most, external behavioral compliance with virtue, rather than genuine virtue.

Consider an analogy. The behaviorist B. F. Skinner famously demonstrated that a pigeon can be taught to play ping-pong through conditioned response. By rewarding the pigeon with food for certain behaviors, it gradually becomes habituated to beating back a ping-pong ball thrown toward it, using its wings as paddles. This is a clear example of what habituation is like. However, it is a very unsatisfactory model of ethical cultivation. First, if we avoid stealing or lying simply because, like the pigeon, we have become habituated to certain *behavior*, we are not really virtuous, because we do not have the right *motive*. As Mengzi puts it, a virtuous person "*acts out of* benevolence and righteousness; he does not merely *act out* benevolence and righteousness."[77]

Perhaps even more importantly, humans are capable of more adaptive and reflective behavior than pigeons. As Skinner demonstrated, the pigeon will keep responding to ping-pong balls the same way for the rest of its life, long after you stop rewarding it with food. However, a human can come to realize that she is no longer being rewarded for virtuous behavior, or punished for vicious behavior. As soon as virtue seems inconvenient, a person who merely behaves virtuously out of habit is easily prone to succumbing to temptation. Aristotle knows that virtue requires acting out of the right motive. However, what he lacks is a coherent explanation of how to instill those motives, given that he regards human nature as morally indifferent.

Comparative philosophers have developed a useful framework for situating Aristotle's view of ethical cultivation in relation to various alternatives, both Anglo-European and Asian. This framework divides theories of cultivation into development, discovery, and re-formation models.[78] According to re-formation models, human nature has no active disposition toward virtue, so it must be reshaped through education and behavior to acquire whatever motivations, perceptions, or dispositions that are required for virtue. Aristotle has a re-formation model, as does the ancient Confucian Xunzi. Xunzi illustrates this model of ethical cultivation with a metaphor: "Through steaming and bending, you can make wood straight as a plumb line into a wheel. And after its curve conforms to the compass, even when parched under the sun it will not become straight again, because the steaming and bending have made it a certain way."[79] Human ethical transformation is just as radical: people "are born with desires of the eyes and ears, a fondness for beautiful sights and sounds. If they follow along with these, then lasciviousness and chaos will arise."[80] However, through ethical education and socialization, a person "makes his eyes not want to see what is not right, makes his ears not want to hear what is not right, makes his mouth not want to speak what is not right, and makes his heart not want to deliberate over what is not right."[81] Re-formation models are not antirational. The person who has been successfully cultivated is in a position to see *why* morality is justified. However, re-formation models tend toward an authoritarian view of education, because the beginner must simply have faith that she will eventually see the *why* behind the *what* that she is being habituated into.[82] The primary theoretical problem of re-formation models is that, as we have seen, they have trouble explaining how motivations like compassion, a sense of shame, and love of virtue develop out of a nature that is morally inert.

Developmental models have an easy answer to this challenge; they claim that humans innately have incipient dispositions toward virtuous feeling, cognition, and behavior. Ethical cultivation is a matter of nurturing these nascent dispositions into mature virtues. Part of what is fascinating about Mengzi is that there is no other philosopher, Chinese or European, who presents such a pristine version of a developmental model. (Rousseau is the closest Western analogue.)[83] We saw earlier that Mengzi presents a thought-experiment to show that normal humans have at least an incipient tendency toward compassion (the child at the well story). Using an agricultural metaphor, Mengzi describes our innate dispositions toward virtue as "sprouts." He claims that, in order to become fully virtuous, we have to "extend" these sprouts. There has been a vibrant debate, both in East Asia and in the West, about how precisely to understand extension. A famous dialogue between Mengzi and a king illustrates the issues.

The ruler's subjects suffer because he taxes them excessively to pay for wars of conquest and the luxurious lifestyle that he and other aristocrats enjoy. However, Mengzi says that he knows the king is capable of being a genuinely great ruler. When the king asks Mengzi how he knows this, Mengzi relates an anecdote he had heard: "The King was sitting up in his hall. There was an ox being led past below. The King saw it and said, 'Where is it going?' Someone responded, 'We are about to consecrate a bell with its blood.' The King said, 'Spare it. I cannot bear its frightened appearance, like an innocent going to the execution ground.'"[84] The king confirms that the story is true but asks Mengzi what the incident has to do with being a great ruler. Mengzi replies, "In the present case your kindness is sufficient to reach birds and beasts, but the benefits do not reach the commoners. Why is this case alone different? . . . Hence, Your Majesty not being a genuine king is due to not acting; it is not due to not being able."[85]

David Wong notes that there are three major lines of interpretation of this passage in recent Western discussions.[86] (1) As we saw earlier, there were egoists in Mengzi's era, so perhaps

Mengzi simply wants the king to recognize that he is *capable* of acting out of compassion. This interpretation is supported to the frequent references in the discussion to the king's capability or ability. (2) We could see Mengzi as giving the king what is a "quasi-logical" argument.[87] You showed compassion for the suffering of an ox being led to slaughter (case A). However, your subjects are also suffering (case B). Since case B is relevantly similar to case A, and you showed compassion for case A, you ought to, as a matter of logical consistency, also show compassion in case B. This interpretation is supported by the fact that the word Mengzi uses for "extend" here is used by another ancient Chinese philosopher as the name for a form of inference: "'Extending' is submitting it to him on the grounds that what he does not accept is the same as what he does accept."[88] (3) Wong himself has argued persuasively for a third interpretation. Mengzi is trying to help the king to conceptualize his subjects in a new way that allows his compassion for the ox to flow to his subjects: he should see not just the ox, but each of his suffering subjects, as "like an innocent going to the execution ground." One advantage of this interpretation is that it provides a psychologically plausible explanation of how ethical cultivation is a genuine *development* of preexisting motivations.

We have seen that the best metaphor to illustrate a re-formation model of ethical cultivation is carving or reshaping a recalcitrant material. In contrast, a development model goes well with the metaphor of a farmer cultivating a plant.[89] Discovery models, the third category of theories of ethical cultivation, often use visual metaphors: "The Pattern of the Way simply is right in front of your eyes."[90] As this metaphor suggests, discovery models hold that humans innately have the fully formed capacities necessary for virtue. All that is needed is to exercise them. Buddhists and Neo-Confucians tend toward discovery models, because they hold that everyone is capable, at least in principle, of achieving enlightenment, which is a matter of simply discovering the way the universe actually is. Discovery models are also extremely common in the West, particularly in the modern era. The two major trends in modern Western metaethics are naturalism and intuitionism. Naturalists, like Hobbes or David Hume (1711–76), see morality as grounded in human motivations or passions. In contrast, Western intuitionists think that morality is a matter of "seeing" nonnatural moral facts. However, for both, morality is not about developing a capacity or restructuring one's motivations, but simply discovering something, either about oneself or about the world. For example, H. A. Prichard (1871–1947) is representative of many intuitionists. He asserts that our knowledge of ethical truth is self-evident and infallible: "To put the matter generally, if we do doubt whether there is really an obligation to originate A in a situation B, the remedy lies not in any process of general thinking, but in getting face to face with a particular instance of the situation B, and then directly appreciating the obligation to originate A in that situation."[91] Notice the visual metaphor: "getting face to face with." The only concession Prichard makes to possible disagreements is that "the appreciation of an obligation is, of course, only possible for a developed moral being, and that different degrees of development are possible."[92] We can easily imagine what sort of person Prichard, an Englishman writing at the height of the British empire, imagines to be a less "developed moral being," and how convenient this was for imperialism.

[margin note: historical influence on phil]

What is striking from a comparative perspective is how remarkably primitive Western versions of discovery models are compared to their Buddhist and Neo-Confucian counterparts. This is so for at least two reasons: (1) Buddhist and Neo-Confucian versions of discovery models do not resort immediately to appeals to brute intuitions or emotions that one either has or does not have,[93] and (2) they offer guidance about how to deal with cases in which you know what you should do, but find yourself strongly tempted to do something else.

Suppose I am being an inattentive father: I do not make time for my children, nor do I make an effort to share their interests, nor do I ask them persistent but good-natured questions until they finally talk to me. You tell me I really ought to take a more active role as a father. I reply that I have my own needs and projects, I already provide my children with free room and board, and lots of other parents are positively abusive, so why are you giving me a hard time? You tell me, as Prichard might, that it is a self-evident truth that I have an obligation to be a better father. Do you actually expect anything other than a middle finger in reply?

Contrast the preceding with the Neo-Confucian response to the same challenge. The Neo-Confucian would ask me "Who are you?" Any answer I give will make reference, at least implicitly, to other people, who define who I am. Consequently, if I am an inattentive father, it is not just bad for my children, because being a father is part of what defines me. Being a bad father is being a bad me. Similarly, if I am a lazy teacher, it is not bad only for my students, because being a teacher is part of who I am. To fail at being a teacher is to fail at being me. Now, I am not suggesting that the Neo-Confucian approach is guaranteed to transform immoral people into moral people. There is no magic fix for ethical nihilism. The most we can hope for from *any* moral theory is that it helps a few people to be a little better, and prevents a few people from becoming worse. But the Neo-Confucian challenge at least has some kind of rational traction in convincing those who may be susceptible to conversion, as opposed to the schoolmarmish finger-waving of Western intuitionism or naturalism.

WEAKNESS OF WILL

In contrast to the preceding examples, suppose I already *know* that I should be a more attentive father or a more demanding teacher, but I give in to the temptation to fail in one or both areas. Western philosophers describe cases like these as "weakness of will": the phenomenon in which a person knows what she ought to do but gives into temptation and does something else. This is one of the most common and familiar phenomena of our moral experience. However, it raises two substantial problems: one theoretical and one practical. The theoretical problem is to explain how moral knowledge is related to moral action in a way that makes weakness of will possible. This problem is especially pressing for any discovery model. If all there is to morality is discovering something through the exercise of an innate capacity, then it seems that the discovery of this knowledge must be both necessary and sufficient for action. The practical problem is to provide guidance to those who succumb to weakness of will about how to overcome it. Neo-Confucian philosophers have fascinating contributions to make on both issues.

Neo-Confucian debates over weakness of will typically start from an evocative passage in the canonical ancient text, the *Great Learning*: "What is meant by 'making thoughts have Sincerity' is to let there be no self-deception. It is like hating a hateful odor, or loving a lovely sight. This is called not being conflicted."[94] What is the "it" that should be "like hating a hateful odor, or loving a lovely sight"? The passage means that a person with Sincerity will hate *evil* like she would hate a bad odor, and love *goodness* like she would love a lovely sight. What is distinctive about hating a bad odor is that cognition and motivation are combined. To recognize an odor as disgusting is to be repelled by it. If I smell the milk and recognize that it has gone bad, I do not have to try to muster the motivation to avoid putting it in my coffee. My hatred of evil should manifest the same unity of cognition and motivation. If I recognize that something is evil, I should be repulsed by it, viscerally and automatically. I should not have to force myself to avoid doing evil, any more than I have to force myself to avoid drinking spoiled milk.

"Loving a lovely sight" illustrates the same point, but it requires explanation to see why. The term I am translating as "sight" here is *sè*. In classical Chinese (the language in which the *Great Learning* is written), *sè* can mean color or appearance,[95] and some translations render it this way.[96] However, it more commonly means *lust*, or *the physical beauty that inspires lust*. Thus, Confucius once complained, "I have yet to meet someone who loves Virtue as much as he loves physical beauty (*sè*)."[97] Consequently, "loving a lovely sight" does not refer to our fondness for a particular shade of blue, or even our admiration for a beautiful sunset. It refers to being erotically attracted to physical beauty.[98]

So when the *Great Learning* tells us that we should hate evil "like hating a hateful odor" and we should love goodness "like loving a lovely sight," it means that we are to hate evil the same way we are repulsed by a disgusting odor, and we are to love goodness the same way we are erotically drawn to physical beauty. The substantive content of these similes is the claim that our hatred of evil and our love of goodness should be simultaneously cognitive and affective. When we recognize that an odor is disgusting, we do not have to *decide* to be repulsed by it, or *force* ourselves to treat it as disgusting. To recognize an odor as disgusting (a form of perception) is to be repulsed by it (a kind of motivation). Similarly, when we recognize something as evil (perception), we should be repulsed by it (motivation) just as automatically and viscerally. The visual simile makes the same point about cognition and affect. To find someone sexually attractive is to feel drawn to that person erotically. In a parallel manner, when we recognize something as good (perception), we should be drawn toward it (motivation), without the need for any strength of will. "Sincerity" is the term used to describe this state.

Now that we understand what Sincerity is, we are in a better position to see why the *Great Learning* characterizes it as the absence of self-deception. On a Neo-Confucian version of a discovery model, we have an innate capacity to recognize that we are individuals who are largely defined by our relationships to others. As Wang Yangming (1472–1529) states:

> Great people regard Heaven, Earth, and the myriad creatures as their own bodies. They look upon the world as one family and China as one person within it. Those who, because of the space between their own physical form and those of others, regard themselves as separate [from Heaven, Earth, and the myriad creatures] are petty persons. . . . How could it be that only the minds of great people are one with Heaven, Earth, and the myriad creatures? Even the minds of petty people are like this. It is only the way in which such people look at things that makes them petty. This is why, when they see a child [about to] fall into a well, they cannot avoid having a mind of alarm and compassion for the child. This is because their benevolence forms one body with the child.[99]

One who fully grasps that she "forms one body" with others can no more be indifferent to the suffering of her neighbor than she can be indifferent to an injury to her own limb. However, one can choose whether to attend to this knowledge or not. If one decides not to attend to his ethical knowledge, he is deceiving himself about who he really is. Hence, he is doubly engaging in self-deception: he is deceiving *himself* about what his *self* is. When we lie to ourselves in this way, we are "conflicted," as the *Great Learning* says, because there is a tension between one part of ourselves, our moral nature, and another part, our selfish desires.[100]

Interesting thought [handwritten marginal note]

Neo-Confucians in general would agree with the preceding account, both as an interpretation of the *Great Learning* and as a description of human moral psychology. However, there is a crucial disagreement on one detail. This ambiguity is suggested by a distinction drawn by Cheng Yi (1033–1107):

> Genuine knowledge is different from common knowledge. I once met a farmer who had been mauled by a tiger. Someone reported that a tiger had just mauled someone in the area and everyone present expressed alarm. But the countenance and behavior of the farmer was different from everyone else. Even small children know that tigers can maul people and yet this is not genuine knowledge. It is only genuine knowledge if it is like that of the farmer. And so, there are people who know it is wrong to do something and yet they still do it; this is not genuine knowledge. If it were genuine knowledge, they definitely would not do it.[101]

The fear of the farmer who had been mauled by a tiger is another example of the sort of visceral combination of cognition and motivation that the *Great Learning* illustrates with the examples of a "hateful odor" and a "lovely sight." Now, when Cheng Yi describes this as "genuine knowledge," this suggests that those who have not been mauled by the tiger do not *really* know how dangerous tigers are. However, Cheng Yi does not contrast the phrase "genuine knowledge" with "fake knowledge" or "so-called knowledge," as we might expect. He contrasts the knowledge of the farmer with "common knowledge," which suggests that others *do* know that tigers are dangerous, just not as profoundly as the farmer who was mauled. So which is the right way to understand the relationship between virtuous knowledge and motivation? Should we say that those who are not motivated to do what is right do not really possess knowledge in any sense at all, or should we say that they may have a kind of knowledge, but not the deep kind of knowledge that is ideal?

Zhu Xi argues that the simile from the *Great Learning* must be interpreted in the light of an earlier passage in the same text that reads: "Only *after* knowledge has reached the ultimate do thoughts have Sincerity."[102] For Zhu Xi, this suggests a two-part process of ethical cultivation: obtaining knowledge of what is good and bad, and then making that knowledge motivationally efficacious through continual attentiveness. The beginner in cultivation will find that this attentiveness requires constant effort. When he lapses at this effort, he will succumb to weakness of will: "When people know something but their actions don't accord with it, their knowledge is still shallow. But once they have personally experienced it, their knowledge is more enlightened, and does not have the same significance it had before."[103] This solves both the theoretical and the practical challenge that weakness of will poses. Weakness of will is possible through a failure to be attentive to the moral knowledge that we have. Our task as ethical agents is to avoid self-deception and be attentive to our moral knowledge, until doing so becomes second nature. Consequently, Zhu Xi understands the *Great Learning*'s similes of loving the good like loving a lovely sight and hating evil like hating a hateful odor as descriptions of the ultimate goal that each of us is working toward.

Zhu Xi's most incisive critic was Wang Yangming. He is famous for his doctrine of the "unity of knowing and acting," which is typically interpreted as a denial that weakness of will is possible.[104] Wang states: "There never have been people who know but do not act. Those who 'know' but do not act simply do not yet know."[105] One of Wang's disciples questions how this is possible: "For example, there are people who despite fully knowing that they should be filial to their parents and respectful to their elder brothers, find that they cannot be filial or respectful. From this it is clear that knowing and acting are two separate things." Wang responds with three arguments.

First, Wang argues that ethical knowing is intrinsically connected to ethical motivation, in the same way that knowledge and motivation are connected in "loving a lovely sight" or "hating a hateful odor":

> Smelling a hateful odor is a case of knowing, while hating a hateful odor is a case of acting. As soon as one smells that hateful odor, one naturally hates it. It is not as if you first smell it and only then, intentionally, you decide to hate it. Consider the case of a person with a stuffed-up nose. Even if he sees a malodorous object right in front of him, the smell does not reach him, and so he does not hate it. This is simply not to know the hateful odor. The same is true when one says that someone knows filial piety or brotherly respect. That person must already have acted with filial piety or brotherly respect before one can say he knows them.[106]

For Wang, the simile from the *Great Learning* does not describe the *goal* of cultivation, in which ethical knowledge and motivation are fully unified after years of effort; instead, it describes what genuine ethical knowledge is like from the very start. In the vocabulary of Western ethics, Wang is a motivational internalist, who holds that to know the good is intrinsically to be motivated to pursue it.[107]

Wang's second argument for the unity of knowing and acting is that merely verbal assent is insufficient to demonstrate knowledge: "One cannot say that he knows filial piety or brotherly respect simply because he knows how to *say* something filial or brotherly. Knowing pain offers another good example. One must have experienced pain oneself in order to know pain. Similarly, one must have experienced cold oneself in order to know cold, and one must have experienced hunger oneself in order to know hunger."[108] To understand the important epistemological and linguistic point Wang is making here, consider a variation on a classic example from Western philosophy. Imagine a hypothetical individual, "Mary," who is forced to perceive the world through a black and white television monitor. She becomes a brilliant neuroscientist specializing in vision, and eventually knows everything there is to know about the physics and neurology of color experiences. However, suppose she is finally released from her bondage to the black and white television monitor and can go and see the world as it is. Now she will learn something new. She will finally know what phenomenal colors are like. Previously, Mary knew more *about* color experiences than anyone else, but she did not know what phenomenal colors are.[109] Similarly, Wang says, you might know a lot *about* pain, hunger, feeling cold, and goodness, but you do not know pain, hunger, feeling cold, or goodness itself unless you

[handwritten margin note: This seems to be the same arg of sympathy ∨ empathy.]

have the right experience. One significant difference between Wang's example and that of Mary is that color experiences are not intrinsically motivating. It does seem plausible, though, that some experiences (among them pain) are intrinsically motivating.

Wang's disciple objects that we talk about knowing and acting separately, and that this verbal distinction is valuable because it reflects the fact that there are two distinct aspects to moral cultivation. Wang acknowledges that it can be useful for practical purposes to verbally distinguish between knowing and acting:

> there is a type of person in the world who foolishly acts upon impulse without engaging in the slightest thought or reflection. Because they always act blindly and recklessly, it is necessary to talk to them about knowing. There is also a type of person who is vague and irresolute; they engage in speculation while suspended in a vacuum and are unwilling to apply themselves to any concrete actions. Because they only grope at shadows and grab at echoes, it is necessary to talk to them about acting.[110]

[handwritten margin note: This audre Lorde agrees.]

However, Wang argues that verbally distinguishing "knowing" and "acting" is consistent with recognizing that they are two aspects of one unified activity: "I have said that knowing is the intent of acting and that acting is the work of knowing and that knowing is the beginning of acting and acting is the completion of knowing. Once one understands this, then if one talks about knowing [the idea of] acting is already present, or if one talks about acting, [the idea] of knowing is already present."[111] We might say that knowing and acting are like the concave and the convex sides of a curved line: conceptually but not meta-physically distinguishable.

Reviewing Wang's arguments, we can see why David S. Nivison remarked, "There are pages in Wang, sometimes, that could almost make acceptable brief notes in contemporary philosophy journals like *Analysis*."[112] However, it is important to recognize that Wang's point is not purely theoretical. What he is concerned about is the phenomenon of people who

> *Hypocrites also speak to Lorde*
>
> separate knowing and acting into two distinct tasks to perform and think that one must first know and only then can one act. They say, "Now, I will perform the task of knowing, by studying and learning. Once I have attained real knowledge, I then will pursue the task of acting." And so, till the end of their days, they never act, and till the end of their days, they never know. This is not a minor malady, nor did it arrive just yesterday. My current teaching regarding the unity of knowing and acting is a medicine directed precisely at this disease.[113]

Wang has in mind the followers of Zhu Xi, but his point has contemporary relevance. Eric Schwitzgebel has done empirical research on the relationship between studying or teaching ethics and actual ethical behavior. He acknowledges that the data is limited, but so far he has been unable to find any positive correlation between the theoretical study of ethics and being ethical.[114] Wang would argue that this proves his point: the abstract and theoretical study of ethics will not make you a better person. However, Wang would insist that what is wrong with Western ethics is not that it tries to make humans better people, but that it does not try in the right ways. If we have any interest in our courses in ethics and political philosophy making a difference, it is worth looking at what else thinkers like

Mengzi, the Buddhists, Zhu Xi, and Wang Yangming have to say on this topic.

Just to give a teaser: Confucians stress that, to provide a foundation for ethical development, it is the responsibility of government to make sure that the people's basic physical needs are met (for food, for freedom from fear, and for the possibility for communal life), that everyone gets an education that both teaches them basic skills and socializes them to be benevolent and have integrity, and that everyone who can benefit from advanced education has the opportunity to receive it (regardless of social class). Regarding the structure of ethical education, Confucius himself says, "If you learn without thinking about what you have learned, you will be lost. If you think without learning, however, you will fall into danger."[115] As Philip J. Ivanhoe notes, later Confucians agree with this saying, but argue vociferously about the relative emphasis to give to learning from classic texts and teachers as opposed to thinking independently.[116] As you might guess, philosophers with a discovery model of cultivation like Wang Yangming tend to emphasize thinking, while those with a re-formation model like Xunzi put more emphasis on learning.

Contemporary US philosophers will probably have the most difficulty in accepting two additional aspects of Chinese ethical education. (But perhaps these are the sine qua non for genuine ethical transformation?) First, Chinese philosophers think that practical activities—including meditation, communal ritual activities, and even what we might describe today as "work-study"—have as much of a role to play as intellectual ones in learning ethics. In addition, it is considered crucial to keep in mind that the ultimate point of studying ethics is to be a better person and transform society, not just to theorize. (I return to this latter point in chapter 5.)

OTHER VOICES

I hope readers of this chapter have found some things that they agree with or at least find intriguing conceptual possibilities. However, this chapter discusses subtle and complex issues in only a few pages, so I would be surprised if you found nothing you want to challenge. (In fact, if you have no questions or objections, I'm disappointed in you. As Zhu Xi said, "Those who don't have opinions simply have not read carefully enough to have any doubts!")[117] But there is one thing I believe I have established beyond any possible doubt. (And that is not a phrase I use very often.) Buddhist, Confucian, and Neo-Confucian texts can obviously be brought into productive dialogue with major Anglo-European philosophical works. It's fine to tell me that you don't agree with them, but philosophy is not about teaching only figures whom you agree with. (I regularly teach Descartes, Hobbes, Hume, Russell, and Sartre, each of whom I think is deeply and fundamentally wrong.) So after reading this chapter, don't try telling me that Buddhist, Confucian, and Neo-Confucian thinkers are not *really* philosophers.

Given limitations of space and of my own abilities, I have only talked about a few philosophers from outside the Anglo-European mainstream. However, any acquaintance with Indian philosophy reveals that, in terms of both methodology and subject matter, it is philosophical even according to the most narrow standards that Anglo-European philosophy might supply. Just open a book! (One place to start is my bibliography of readings on the less commonly taught philosophies at http://bryanvannorden.com.) African-American, feminist, Islamic, Jewish, Latin American, and LGBTQ philosophies are influenced by the mainstream Anglo-European traditions, so it should come as no surprise that they can easily be integrated into the curriculum of US colleges and universities. I know the least about African philosophies and the philosophies of the Indigenous peoples of the Americas. However, a few examples illustrate how easily they can be brought into dialogue. James Maffie's excellent *Aztec Philosophy* provides a philosophically sophisticated introduction to this form of pre-Columbian metaphysics, which is challengingly different from both the individualistic metaphysics characteristic of most of the West and the versions of monism that we find in Chinese Buddhism or Neo-Confucianism.[118] In *The Dance of Person and Place*, Thomas M. Norton-Smith uses the philosophy of Nelson Goodman (a leading twentieth-century analytic thinker) to understand Shawnee Native American thought.[119] From a more Continental perspective, *This Is Not a Peace Pipe* by Dale Turner uses the resources of Critical Theory to understand the political situation of Native Americans.[120] For an anthology of essays by Indigenous philosophers on a variety of topics, see *American Indian Thought*, edited by Anne Waters.[121] Turning to African philosophy, Kwame Gyekye's *An Essay on African Philosophical Thought* discusses the conceptual scheme of the Akan people, which he suggests offers a form of communitarian ethics distinct from any Western system.[122] Kwazi Wiredu's *Philosophy and an African Culture* deals with a variety of problems recognizable from the Anglo-European tradition, including critiques of Marxism and various theories of truth (including Ramsey's redundancy thesis and Dewey's conception of truth as warranted assertibility).[123] Even if you insist that Indigenous American or African thought is not philosophy, these books will at least give you a way to integrate examples drawn from these traditions into the philosophical curriculum. In summary, to paraphrase Mengzi:

> In the present case your philosophizing is sufficient to reach from Socrates to Sartre, but the benefits do not reach to Confucius

or the Buddha, to the Shawnee or the Akan. Why is this case alone different? Hence, your not being a multicultural philosopher is due to not acting; it is not due to not being able.

In the preceding two chapters, I have presented a number of rational arguments for a multicultural approach to philosophy. However, not all beliefs are rational, or are held for conscious reasons. In the next chapter, I try to show that the desire to draw a sharp boundary between Anglo-European philosophy and supposedly nonphilosophical thought is a manifestation of a broader pattern of xenophobic, chauvinistic, nationalistic, and racist efforts to separate "us" from "them."

3

TRUMP'S PHILOSOPHERS

I will build a great, great wall on our southern border.

—Donald J. Trump

If we do not make it to the Great Wall we are not real Chinese.

—Mao Zedong

I think that you would have to conclude that this is a great wall.

—Richard Nixon

Donald Trump repeatedly promised to build a wall between the United States and Mexico, and Ronald Reagan promised to protect "states' rights." President Xi Jinping has praised classical philosophers like Confucius for forging the "unique mental outlook of the Chinese."[1] Conservative intellectuals have warned of the dangers of higher education betraying "our Western heritage." And contemporary philosophers, including ones who identify as politically progressive, click their tongues about how everything outside the traditional canon that goes back to Plato and Aristotle is not *real* philosophy.

They are all in the business of building walls.

Although these camps disagree about many things, each is deploying an ethnocentric and chauvinistic view of culture to distinguish "us" from "them" in a way that makes clear that "we" are rational, self-controlled, just, and civilized, whereas "they" are illogical, impassioned, unfair, and barbaric. Sometimes they are explicit; other times they speak in code. Some of them are fully aware of what they are doing; others have absorbed subconsciously a worldview that they would reject if they could see it for what it is. Sometimes they try to make their views palatable by masking them in what are essentially myths of noble savages, quaint and childlike, untouched by the deformations of Western thought—but, for that very reason, excluded from dialogue with it. But all of them are building and maintaining walls.

BUILDING RACIAL WALLS IN AMERICAN POLITICS

Trump has compared his proposed US-Mexico wall to the Great Wall of China in terms of its grandeur and feasibility. He could stand to learn a bit more about Chinese history. The Great Wall was completed around 1570, and China was conquered by the Manchus in 1644. This is hardly a model of success. Why does Trump want to build a wall?[2] The supposed reason was to stop the flow of illegal immigrants from Mexico: "They're bringing drugs. They're bringing crime. They're rapists."[3] The reality is that the number of illegal immigrants from Mexico living in the United States has been steadily declining since 2007.[4] In other words, illegal immigrants from Mexico have been *leaving* the United States for years, so if a border wall would be good for anything, it would be for keeping illegal immigrants in. In addition, immigrants as a whole are substantially less likely to commit crimes than those born in the United States.[5] Since there is no genuine policy reason for building the wall, the only explanation for the immense popularity of the suggestion among Trump's supporters is that it is symbolic of the need to separate "us" from "them."[6] Trump's success in capturing the Republican nomination and then the presidency in 2016 was so shocking, and confounded so much conventional political wisdom, that it is tempting to think that he is some kind of aberration. In reality, Trump is merely appealing explicitly to ethnocentric rage and fear that previous mainstream politicians have encouraged implicitly, or at least benefitted from.[7]

When Reagan ran for president in 1980, one of his first campaign speeches was at the Neshoba County Fair. No presidential candidate has spoken at this event before or since, and there is no good reason to choose this as a site for a speech—except for one. The fairgrounds are a few miles from Philadelphia, Mississippi, where, in 1964, three civil rights workers were murdered, with the direct participation of local law enforcement officers, for the "crime" of registering African Americans to vote. In his speech in Neshoba, Reagan stated that he supported "states' rights." The official name of the openly segregationist "Dixiecrats" (the southern Democrats who opposed Truman because of his support for civil rights) was the "States Rights' Democratic Party," so the message was transparent to Reagan's audience.[8] I have no doubt that some people have voted Republican because they interpret "states' rights" as a principled commitment to limited government. But to do so is to be blind to what this phrase actually means for a substantial number of people.

If one has any remaining doubts about the racism underlying Reagan's appeal, they should be crushed by the admission of Lee Atwater, a top political strategist for both Reagan and G. H. W. Bush, and later Republican National Committee chairman. In an infamous but frank interview, Atwater admitted that the GOP had consciously decided to use coded language to appeal to racist voters:

> You start out in 1954 by saying, "Nigger, nigger, nigger." By 1968 you can't say "nigger"—that hurts you. Backfires. So you say stuff like forced busing, states' rights, and all that stuff. . . . I'm saying that if it is getting that abstract, and that coded, that we are doing away with the racial problem one way or the other. You follow me—because obviously sitting around saying, "we want to cut this," is much more abstract than even the busing thing, *and* a hell of a lot more abstract than "Nigger, nigger."[9]

If we consider the preceding facts, a clear picture emerges. The party of Lincoln made a deal with the Devil to win over voters who want to build walls between races.

Surprisingly, this sort of racial nationalism is not that different from certain forces at work in contemporary China.

BUILDING WALLS TO PROTECT CHINESE CIVILIZATION

In January 2011, a thirty-foot-tall bronze statue of Confucius was unveiled in Tiananmen Square. Just three months later, a scaffold went up around it. When the scaffold came down, the statue was gone.[10] Official sources were initially silent about the removal of the statue. Eventually, they explained that the plan all along had been to temporarily display the statue in Tiananmen Square, and then later move it to a courtyard in the nearby museum of antiquities, where the statue now sits. However, if this were the plan, why hadn't the authorities announced this in advance, or at least explained it immediately when questioned about the statue's disappearance?

Tiananmen Square is a sensitive location for many reasons. It is in front of the Forbidden City, the home of China's emperors in the Qing dynasty. It is the location of the mausoleum of Mao Zedong (1893–1976), the founder of the People's Republic of China.[11] And it is the site of what is discreetly referred to in China as "the incident of June 4, 1989," in which student protestors agitating for government reform were killed by the army. Consequently, the political significance of anything that happens there is magnified. The peek-a-boo of the Confucius statue reflects an ideological struggle for the soul of China between China's left and right. For China's left, Confucius is a symbol of feudalism, superstition, and exploitation of the people by the privileged. For China's right, Confucius is an example of the greatness of Chinese civilization, a guide to personal morality of contemporary relevance, and a symbol of what unifies all Chinese as a people. In order to understand the contours and significance of this debate, we need to take a quick look at recent Chinese history.

After leading the Chinese Communists to victory in the civil war against the Nationalists (1949), Mao Zedong instituted the radical agricultural and industrial "reforms" of the Great Leap Forward (1958–61). The results were disastrous. Tens of millions starved during the "Great Famine." Officials were initially reluctant to report the truth for fear of being persecuted, but when the extent of the disaster became known, moderates like Deng Xiaoping (1904–97) began to edge Mao out of power. Mao responded by launching the "Great Proletarian Cultural Revolution" (1966–76), in which students were encouraged to drop out of school and join the paramilitary Red Guards. With all the mercy of the Inquisition and all the objectivity of the Salem Witch Trials, the Red Guards humiliated, tortured, and killed whoever appeared to them to be a supporter of feudalism or capitalism. The temple of Confucius in his (supposed) hometown of Qufu was vandalized. Worse yet, many people (including Deng) were tortured on trumped-up charges. On a recent visit to China, I talked with a retired professor who showed me the scars left from when Red Guards drove nails into his hands, trying to get him to confess to being a foreign agent. The evidence against this professor? He had studied German literature abroad.

After Mao's death in 1976, Deng Xiaoping returned to power and led China in a much more moderate direction. A significant part of "Deng-ism" is acknowledging Mao's mistakes. The official slogan is that Mao was 70 percent right and 30 percent wrong. However, China continues to wrestle with Mao's legacy. Mao founded the People's Republic of China, so to completely repudiate him would be to disavow Communism. The Communist Party is woven too intimately into the very fabric of government to do that. (Recently a popular TV host got in serious trouble when a video of him making some sarcastic comments about Mao at a dinner party came to light.)[12] However, there is almost nothing recognizable as "Mao-Zedong-Thought" per se in the actual practices of Chinese society, culture, and economy.[13]

Professor Paul Gewirtz of Yale Law School describes the social and political problem that faces China:

> China today places great value on making money and on self-interested material success, long denied to the Chinese. But values in addition to individual materialism are needed to hold a country together and make it a good country. Where will these values continue to come from in China? The announced ideology of China's Communist Party no longer seems to be a source of moral values for Chinese society. Indeed, it is no longer clear what that ideology really is. China certainly has no equivalent to the United States' faith in its Constitution as a continuing source of our country's values, as almost a civic religion.
>
> Moreover, China does not have a strong conventional religious tradition that can be the source of values. Furthermore, the close family structures that were a traditional forum for the generational transfer of values have been weakened as Chinese society has become more mobile and, yes, more free.[14]

Why should we regard this situation as problematic for China? There are at least three issues. (1) First, as thinkers in the hermeneutic tradition have stressed, human beings are creatures who can only make choices against the "horizon of significance" that an ethical vocabulary supplies.[15] The seminal sociologist Emile Durkheim used the term "anomie" to describe the feeling of alienation that results when the individual lacks a horizon of significance and feels at sea in an amoral society. Anomie (which we might also describe as "alienation") is, at the very least, unpleasant, and it seems to be a serious issue for some in China. A recent mental health survey of students at Peking University reported that over 40 percent of freshmen feel that life is "meaningless."[16] In addition, there is some reason to think

that it is one of the causes of the second problem. (2) When individuals have no ethical vocabulary in which to articulate deep
values, they are easily prone to certain kinds of wrongdoing.
Everyone can see the force of satisfying immediate and superfi-
cial desires, such as desires for food, sex, wealth, prestige, and
power. There is nothing intrinsically wrong with any of these
motivations. However, if pursued without regard for other values, they can easily lead to corruption and cruelty.[17] (3) A third
problem is that, in the absence of an ethical vocabulary, it is far
too easy for those who wield power to do so in an arbitrary or
self-serving manner. I take this to be part of the point that Milan Kundera is making when he writes that "The struggle of
man against power is the struggle of memory against forgetting."[18] Insofar as we, as a community, remember our shared
ethical vocabulary, we can deploy that vocabulary to resist arbitrary exercises of governmental (or other) authority. For all
three of these reasons, post-Mao China needs new ethical vocabularies in which people can believe.[19]

The complexity of the intellectual situation in China was
brought home to me at a conference I attended in Wuhan,
China, in 2014.[20] Of the Chinese philosophers in attendance, I
would say that about 40 percent were Marxist philosophers,
approximately 40 percent were specialists in some kind of
Anglo-European philosophy (including Western political philosophy), and about 20 percent were specialists in traditional
Chinese philosophy (who seemed interested only in narrow
philological issues). Throughout the conference, the three groups
largely spoke past one another. I don't assume that these exact
percentages are representative of the state of the field in China
as a whole; however, the discipline of philosophy in China is
largely segregated along these lines, and dialogue across the
divides seems minimal.

This is the complex situation that China's President Xi Jin-ping has inherited. Xi was born into privilege: his father was a high-ranking official in the government and the Chinese Communist Party. However, during the Cultural Revolution, Xi's father was purged from power and jailed, and Xi himself was, like many young intellectuals, "sent down" to do farm work in the countryside. "Bullied" is far too weak a term to describe the physical, verbal, and psychological abuse Xi suffered at the hands of the Red Guards.[21] Reflecting later on his experience, Xi said: "I think the youth of my generation will be remembered for the fervor of the Red Guard era. But it was emotional. It was a mood. And when the ideals of the Cultural Revolution could not be realized, it proved an illusion."[22] Because of this background, what Xi and many other Chinese government officials see as particularly important today is to avoid the mob rule and violence of Cultural Revolution–era China.

Xi has also inherited a nation with numerous separatist movements. Most Westerners are aware of the unrest in Tibet. But many people in Hong Kong, which only rejoined the People's Republic in 1997, are also unsatisfied. Hongkongers are most comfortable speaking Cantonese or English, and angrily refer to the throngs of Mandarin-speaking shoppers from the Mainland as "locusts." Xinjiang, the huge and natural-resource-rich province in China's northwest, is largely populated by the Uighurs, a Muslim group, which sometimes chafes under Beijing's control. The island of Taiwan has had an independent government since 1949, but the People's Republic has made clear that it will go to war if it formally claims independence. The United States has regularly sent aircraft carrier strike forces to Taiwan as a show of strength whenever it has been threatened by the mainland. This happened as recently as 1995. This is why Trump's decision (while he was president-elect) to accept a congratulatory phone call from Taiwan's president was a serious and potentially dangerous strategic error, rather than a minor diplomatic faux pas.[23]

In order to give the Chinese people something to believe in that can unify them as a race, Xi has frequently praised the legacy of Confucius, something that would have been unthinkable under Mao.[24] I would classify Xi's appropriations of Confucianism into four groups: genuine, vacuous, confused, and nationalistic. One of Xi's exhortatory addresses to Communist Party members illustrates him genuinely understanding and correctly applying a Confucian saying. Xi stressed the importance of avoiding greed, being self-disciplined, and maintaining one's integrity. He appropriately illustrated this with one of the most famous lines from *Analects*: "One who rules through the power of Virtue is analogous to the Pole Star: it simply remains in its place and receives the homage of the myriad lesser stars."[25] Xi's message, prompted by the widespread corruption in China's government, is that citizens will not respect and obey the Party unless its members show genuine integrity.

Other times, classical allusions are simply empty window dressing, because Xi seems completely uninterested in what the passage he cites actually means. In a speech delivered to the Chinese Academy of Engineering praising technological innovation, Xi cites a line from a canonical Confucian text merely because the latter uses the word "new." However, the original Confucian classic is praising *moral* renewal, not new technology.[26] Xi shows a similar lack of interest in the original meaning of expressions when he quotes Confucius's famous autobiographical comment "at forty I became free of doubts" merely to note that it was the fortieth anniversary of the establishment of diplomatic relations between China and Brazil.[27]

Xi sometimes attempts to sincerely apply a phrase, but fails to understand it. In an address to the students of Peking University, Xi admonishes them with a phrase that he takes to be a description of an ideal person: "In his speech he insists on being trustworthy, and with regard to his actions he insists they bear fruit." However, in its original context, Confucius is *criticizing*, not praising, the "narrow, rigid little man" who insists on these rules.[28] In fact, the later Confucian Mengzi would explicitly state that "As for great people, their words do not have to be trustworthy, and their actions do not have to bear fruit. They rest only in righteousness."[29] Confucius and Mengzi are not advocating casual lying. They simply disagree with those who (like Kant in the West) claim that the obligation to tell the truth may not be broken in any circumstances, even to save an innocent life.[30] In denying that actions "have to bear fruit," they are suggesting that actions should be judged by their intentions and motivations, not by their actual consequences. (Hmm. These sound suspiciously like *philosophical* issues, don't they?)

In my opinion, what is most significant about Xi's appropriation of Confucianism is his use of it to inspire racial identity and nationalism. This comes out most clearly in an address he gave to students at Peking University:

> Chinese culture emphasizes that "the people are the foundation of the state," "the heavens and humans form a unity," "harmonize without forming cliques"; it emphasizes that "just as the actions of the heavens are reliable, the gentleman improves himself unceasingly"; "the great Way is to treat the whole world as one community"; it emphasizes that "whether the world rises or decays is every ordinary person's responsibility"; it stresses ruling the country by means of Virtue, transforming people through culture; it emphasizes that "the gentleman cares about righteousness," "the gentleman is magnanimous," "the gentleman takes righteousness as his substance"; it emphasizes that

"speech must be trustworthy, and actions must bear fruit," "if a person is not honest, how can he be acceptable?"; it emphasizes that "virtue is never alone, it is sure to have neighbors"; "the benevolent love others," "help others to do good," "that which one does not like, do not inflict upon others," "be friendly to one another whether coming or going, help one another in keeping watch," "treat the old and young of one's own family as you should and extend it to the old and young of other families," "support the poor and rescue those in difficulty," "do not be anxious over having little, be anxious about inequality," etc. These sorts of thoughts and ideals, both in the past and today, all clearly have the distinctive characteristic of our nation; they all have an unfading value for one's era. . . . Most fundamentally, what makes us Chinese at birth is that we have the unique mental outlook of the Chinese, that we have a perspective on value that the common people intuitively employ daily. The core values of socialism that we advocate have simply fulfilled and embodied the inheritance and refinement of the distinguished Chinese tradition.[31]

What is important here is not the undigested barrage of quotations. What is important is the inspiring feeling they leave his audience with: the feeling that they should be proud to be Chinese, that the Chinese have a unique perspective on the world, and that socialism is the way that this proud heritage will be preserved. In this respect, Xi's support of the Chinese classics is as insincere as the invocation of the Bible by US politicians who would bar refugees ("He loveth the stranger in giving him food and raiment, love ye therefore the stranger" [Deuteronomy 18:19, KJV]) or cut funding to the needy ("Inasmuch as ye have done it unto the least of these, my brethren, ye have done it unto me" [Matthew 25:40, KJV]), or as the violence done in the name of the Qur'an, a scripture that explicitly condemns harming noncombatants ("whosoever kills a human being, except (as punishment) for murder or for spreading corruption in the land, it shall be like killing all humanity; and whosoever saves a life, saves the entire human race" [5:32]) and preaches love of those who practice other religions ("all those who believe, and the Jews and the Sabians and the Christians, in fact any one who believes in God and the Last Day, and performs good deeds, will have nothing to fear or regret" [5:69]).[32]

President Trump's expressions of respect for the Bible are similarly hypocritical. He claimed that the Bible is his favorite book, but in a talk at Liberty University it became clear that he does not even know how to pronounce the name of one of the most commonly cited books of the Bible. (He referred to 2 Corinthians, which any Christian knows is read as "Second Corinthians," as "Two Corinthians.")[33] On another occasion, when pressed to name his favorite Bible verse, Trump said it was "never bend to envy"—a line that is not found in the Bible.[34] (Lest I be accused of hypocrisy, my own favorite Bible verse is Micah 6:8: "and what doth the Lord require of thee, but to do justly, and to love mercy, and to walk humbly with thy God?" [KJV])

Political figures who invoke philosophical or spiritual works for nationalistic purposes have no interest in the actual *content* of the classics they claim to revere. What is important in each case is that the classics are *symbols* of what is distinctive and superior about *us* as opposed to *them*. The distinction between an "idol" and an "icon" is helpful in understanding the deformed role that spiritual traditions often play in politics. As historian Jaroslav Pelikan explained, to treat something as an idol is to worship a finite worldly thing, regardless of whether that thing is a statue, a text, an institution, or a person. In contrast, to treat something as an icon is to regard it as an important gift to humanity, but one that points beyond itself to some higher truth that the icon can never fully reveal to us.[35] Nationalistic demagogues around the world are guilty of idolatry, of worshiping some limited product of human history as if were the truth that it guides us toward. There is a problem with encouraging idolatry, though. The classics are classics for a reason, and if you tell young people to revere the classics, they just might take you seriously. In other words, they might start reading the classics with care and understanding, so that they search for the great truths that the classics point toward. All great philosophies and religious traditions have sometimes been co-opted as ideologies to support the status quo, or to encourage nationalistic intolerance. But thinkers in every generation have been inspired by these same traditions to think for themselves, challenge injustice, and fight for the well-being of the common people, not just the elites. This is what gives us people like Martin Luther King, Jr., Mahatma Gandhi, Akbar the Great (1542–1605), and Kang Youwei (1858–1927).

As we shall see in the next section, there are those who genuinely treat the classics as icons rather than as idols, but nonetheless want to build walls between civilizations. However, I will argue that their views are ultimately incoherent. Once you are serious about seeking the truth, you cannot have any plausible reason for silencing other voices in that quest.

BUILDING WALLS TO PROTECT
WESTERN CIVILIZATION

In his recent book *Too Dumb to Fail*, conservative commentator Matt K. Lewis discusses "the dirty secret of the conservative movement in America today: everyone knows that it has lost its intellectual bearings."[36] Lewis states that, prior to the rise of the Tea Party, "the story of the rise of the conservative movement . . . is one of big, thoughtful ideas that address serious existential questions about human nature and the rise of civilization."[37] Specifically, "Conservatism is about conserving the good things about *Western* civilization. . . . It's the belief that *Western* civilization didn't merely happen, but was instead the result of the accumulated wisdom of our ancestors. It's about a realization that *Western* civilization and its institutions evolved naturally, and that long-standing traditions must be preserved."[38] The italics in the quotation are mine, but I don't think they unfairly distort the underlying message: there is something special about Western civilization as opposed to other civilizations, and the unique Western tradition is under threat by those who wish to dilute it with something else. Lewis warns that "almost every facet of the culture, from the music industry to the worlds of food writing and travel writing . . . are dominated by people of the Left."[39] The undermining of culture doesn't stop there: "conservatives worry about the 'feminization' of sports."[40] (True. Every time I watch the Super Bowl, I just shake my head and sadly mutter, "Butch it up, girls!")

Lewis traces the development of the sort of conservatism he represents to Aristotle's *Politics* (fourth century BCE) and Edmund Burke's *Reflections on the Revolution in France* (1790). Aristotle strikes me as an unlikely ally for a contemporary conservative, because he believes that the state is responsible for raising children in the right habits. Aristotle would have no tolerance for fundamentalist parents who want to home school their children to "protect" them from socialization, or for those who want to leave education to the uncertainties of the free market. Aristotle's position on the responsibilities of the state for the education of the young seems more like Hillary Clinton's slogan "It takes a village to raise a child." Moreover, the anti-intellectualism of contemporary conservatism (that Lewis laments and that we shall explore in chapter 4) is in direct opposition to Aristotle's view of a good life. Aristotle regards manual labor and trade as necessary to support a civilization, but unworthy of cultivated gentlemen, who should devote their time to purely intellectual pursuits. Wealth, for Aristotle, is not for gaudy individual displays of conspicuous consumption; wealth exists to educate people and to give them the leisure to think, to discuss, and to research. Unsurprisingly, Aristotle regards a plutocracy (in which the wealthy rule) as one of the worst forms of government, so he would be horrified by the level of influence of money in contemporary US politics.

Edmund Burke (1729–97) is a more promising inspiration for conservatism. Burke was horrified by the French Revolution, and showed considerable prescience in recognizing that it would turn into an orgy of anarchic violence. The lesson to learn, Burke claimed, was that human institutions have gradually evolved to meet human needs, and we do not always fully understand how or why they work. Consequently, to radically restructure society in the light of a utopian ideal will have unforeseeable and dangerous consequences. Burke was right about genuinely radical utopian schemes. As Lewis notes, the horrors of the Russian Revolution were as bad as those of the French. He might have added that a further vindication of Burke's thesis can be found in Mao's disastrous Great Leap Forward (discussed earlier).

However, there is a problem with trying to be both Aristotelian and Burkean. For many contemporary Aristotelians—from lay Catholic philosopher Alasdair MacIntyre to progressive secularist Martha C. Nussbaum—what is inspiring about

Aristotelianism is precisely that it is not a static catalogue of "a priori" truths (as Lewis describes it), but a framework that can adapt and improve in the light of new experiences, including exposure to new cultures.[41] As MacIntyre explains:

> We are apt to be misled here by the ideological uses to which the concept of a tradition has been put by conservative political theorists. Characteristically such theorists have followed Burke in contrasting tradition with reason and the stability of tradition with conflict. Both contrasts obfuscate. . . . Traditions, when vital, embody continuities of conflict. Indeed when a tradition becomes Burkean, it is always dying or dead.[42]

Moreover, it is simply a mistake to try to apply Burke to mainstream political disagreement in the United States. A woman who wants to be paid the same amount as a man for doing the same job, and doesn't want to be groped or ogled as a condition of her employment, is not Madame Defarge, gleefully condemning innocents to the guillotine. African Americans who want to exercise the right to vote, or receive the same treatment during a routine traffic stop that a white person expects, are not destroying the foundations of the rule of law: they are asking to fully participate in it. Hispanics and Latinos who want to have their citizenship and their ethics affirmed, not challenged, are not lining Czar Nicholas II and his family up against a wall and executing them. Gays and lesbians who can now marry and adopt children are not undermining the oldest human institution; they are happily integrated into it. And, to turn specifically to the main topic of this book, it is hard to see how giving students the opportunity to be inspired by Buddhism in addition to Platonism, or Confucianism in addition to Aristotelianism, will lead to (in the immortal words of Bill Murray's character from the original *Ghostbusters*) "human sacrifice, dogs and cats *living* together, mass hysteria."

For me, one of the most valuable lessons to learn from the French Revolution and Burke's insights about it is that a society that does not gradually evolve in response to changes and social pressures will eventually suffer sudden and disastrous upheaval. France, Russia, and China did not have violent revolutions because those in power agreed to moderate changes. They descended into violent chaos because change was denied for so long. Contemporary philosophy professors who insist that "We already get students of color in our classes. Remember that one last year?" are expressing the "Let them eat cake" of our era. (Remember the Stoic adage cited in chapter 1: "The Fates lead those who come willingly, and drag those who do not.")

Lewis is part of a long line of conservative US intellectuals whose thought emphasizes protecting Western civilization, including William F. Buckley, whose book *God and Man at Yale*, published in 1951, accused the professors of his alma mater of undermining their students' faiths in Christianity and laissez-faire capitalism.[43] Buckley expressed the outrage of a conservative undergraduate confronted by liberal professors, while Allan Bloom, in *The Closing of the American Mind*, published in 1987, vividly described the experience of a conservative professor who found the traditional canon to which he had devoted his life under siege by student agitators.[44] Both books were surprise best sellers, and Bloom's is particularly relevant to our topic.

I am not completely unsympathetic to Bloom's frustrations. I was a graduate student at Stanford when undergraduates occupied the president's office to chants of "Hey hey, ho ho! Western culture's got to go!" and used the acronym *DEWM* to describe a curriculum consisting only of the works of dead European white males.[45] Even though I am (obviously) completely supportive of broadening the curriculum, it is not because I do not also love the best of the Western tradition. And the comments and actions of the students did manifest a sort of contemptuous and uninformed dismissiveness that I found grating. I suppose in a parallel universe I am an educational fundamentalist with a goatee. (That's a Star Trek reference, in the unlikely event that anyone reading this is not a nerd at heart.)

However, I disagree with substantial aspects of Bloom's diagnosis of the problem. Bloom complains bitterly that nowadays

> One of the techniques of opening young people up is to require a college course in a non-Western culture. Although many of the persons teaching such courses are real scholars and lovers of the areas they study,* in every case I have seen this requirement . . . has a demagogic intention. The point is to force students to recognize that there are other ways of thinking and that Western ways are not better. . . . Such requirements are part of the effort to establish a world community and train its member—the person devoid of prejudice.[46]

Many readers will find themselves nodding and wondering what is *wrong* with any of this. Bloom's response is that a certain degree of ethnocentrism is necessary for the well-being of the individual and for society:

> Men must love and be loyal to their families and their peoples in order to preserve them. Only if they think their own things are

---

*Bryan waves.

good can they rest content with them. A father must prefer his child to other children, a citizen his country to others. That is why there are myths—to justify these attachments. And a man needs a place and opinions by which to orient himself. . . . The problem of getting along with outsiders is secondary to, and sometimes in conflict with, having an inside, a people, a culture, a way of life.[47]

In short, in order to continue to exist and to flourish, it is necessary for the members of a culture to believe that "their way of life is the best way, and all others are inferior," even if myths are needed to sustain this ethnocentrism.[48]

So Bloom's position on the importance of studying the classics of Western civilization is importantly different from that of traditional conservatives like Lewis or Buckley. Bloom is *not* committed to the specific value of the Bible, or the free market system, or even belief in God. What is important for Bloom is that we avoid spiritual shallowness and ethical nihilism by being educated into "our" cultural tradition, and respectfully participating in the great conversation that runs through classics like Plato's *Republic*, Aristotle's *Nicomachean Ethics*, Augustine's *Confessions*, Descartes's *Meditations on First Philosophy*, Pascal's *Penseés*, Hobbes's *Leviathan*, Locke's *Second Treatise of Civil Government*, Spinoza's *Theological-Political Treatise*, and Rousseau's *Émile* (each of which Bloom discusses in the book). Bloom is fully aware that there are competing voices in this conversation (like Nietzsche and Heidegger), and it *almost* doesn't matter to him which voice one prefers, as long as one (deferentially) adds one's own to it. But this brings out the fundamental incoherence in Bloom's view. He states that "the Bible is not the only means to furnish a mind, but without a book of similar gravity, read with the gravity of the potential believer, it will remain unfurnished."[49] I actually agree, but with an emphasis on the qualification "a book of similar gravity." If reading the Bible intently and seriously gives breadth and depth to one's mind (and it certainly does), why not also the *Mengzi*? or the *Bhagavad Gita*? or *Chūshingura*? There is more than one "great conversation" in the world, and more than one way to furnish a soul.

In addition to his call for a return to the reverential study of the classics of the Western tradition, many other things that Bloom said endeared him to US conservatives. He asserts that affirmative action led to colleges having "a large number of students who were manifestly unqualified and unprepared," and therefore facing a dilemma: "fail most of them or pass them without their having learned."[50] I have not experienced the dilemma Bloom alleges occurred. (And I suspect that it was a self-fulfilling prophecy for Bloom: if you don't expect a particular group of students in your class to do well, they probably won't.) Furthermore, what discussions of affirmative action typically miss is that, even if race ceased to be a factor in admissions tomorrow, no competitive college or university would admit students solely based on standardized tests and high school grades. It is well established that standardized tests like the SAT and ACT are weak predictors of academic success in college, and so many applicants with strong grades and test scores apply to competitive schools that colleges almost have to use some other criteria to select students. Moreover, at the undergraduate level, the influence of athletic affirmative action dwarfs that of racial affirmative action. Does this have a positive effect on education? Brock Turner was a championship swimmer and was attending Stanford University on an athletic scholarship when he sexually assaulted an unconscious woman in 2015.[51] Although his case attracted considerable media attention, he is hardly unusual. Fifty-four percent of student athletes *admit* to engaging in coercive sexual activities.[52] (How many more are less self-aware about what they have done?) Where are the calls to eliminate *athletic* affirmative action? In addition, elite schools continue to give preference to children of alumnae. For example, George W. Bush had poor grades and mediocre SAT scores. His admission to Yale was based almost solely on his being a "legacy" (the son and grandson of Yale graduates). Donald Trump was able to transfer to an Ivy League business school because his elder brother was high-school friends with the admissions officer of the Wharton School. Where is the outrage over this class-based affirmative action?[53]

The fact is that not everyone can afford to take the standardized tests multiple times; not everyone can afford test prep courses; not everyone can afford for an editor to go over their application essay. Most importantly, not everyone even knows these are *options*.[54] I have been fortunate over the years to have many students—of all races and social backgrounds—who were bright and passionate. But I have also taught a few of the George W. Bushes and Donald J. Trumps of the world: white, wealthy students whose writing and reading comprehension skills are mediocre at best, who show up for class smelling of "weed," and who put the bare minimum effort into their courses because they know their family connections will get them a good job after they graduate. Thanks, but I'll take the first-generation college students trying to make a better future for themselves and their families any day.

Bloom's defense of the Western canon, his criticisms of affirmative action, and his disdain for the supposedly lax morals of his colleagues and students made him a star in conservative circles. There is an ironic coda to Bloom's association with conservatism, though. The GOP has always taken a hard line against gay rights. Two decades before Bloom published *The Closing of the American Mind*, William F. Buckley had publicly denounced novelist Gore Vidal as a "queer" in a televised debate (long before the term was "owned" by gays).[55] In the early years of the AIDS crisis, Reagan's press secretary simply cracked jokes when asked what steps the administration was taking to address the disease that was rapidly spreading among members of the gay community.[56] In 2016, in the wake of the deadliest single incident of violence against LGBTQ people in US history (in which forty-nine people were murdered and fifty-three were injured by a shooter in an Orlando gay nightclub), the GOP approved what the Log Cabin Republicans condemned as "the most anti-LGBT Platform in the Party's 162-year history. Opposition to marriage equality, nonsense about bathrooms, an endorsement of the debunked psychological practice of 'pray the gay away'—it's all in there."[57] Trump's vice president, Mike Pence, supported a constitutional amendment to ban gay marriage, and said that same-sex marriage could lead to "societal collapse."[58] However, after Bloom passed away, he was outed as gay by his close friend Saul Bellow, who also suggested that Bloom died of AIDS.[59] As critic D. T. Max wondered, "How many members of the right will want their money back now?"[60]

JERICHO

Demagogues like Trump are explicit about wishing to build walls to separate races and religions; earlier politicians have made similar promises using coded language. Chinese nationalists like President Xi Jinping want to boost support for Confucius as a symbol of Chinese culture, to preserve a Chinese racial identity distinct from the West. Some intellectual US conservatives want to separate what they see as the individualistic, rational philosophy of the West from its decadent counterparts in the rest of the world.

Many Western philosophers have similarly built a wall between "real" philosophy and some "other." As we saw in chapter 1, this is sometimes done by claiming that "real" philosophy has the same kind of rigor that is characteristic of the natural sciences, while everything else is poetry or nonsense. Of course, the philosophers who assert this do not actually bother to read non-Western or other less commonly taught philosophies to see whether they are rigorous. Other times, the wall-building is done by stipulating that both philosophy and the overcoming of philosophy must be historical descendants of the Greek *philosophia*. This argument treats philosophy as if it is a hermetically sealed dialogue with one particular set of ancient canonical texts, and thereby both ignores and precludes the diversity and creativeness of philosophy. These sorts of shallow arguments are found among both analytic and Continental philosophers. Almost all philosophers would categorically reject *explicit* racism. But I ask my fellow philosophers to recognize whom you are implicitly aligning yourself with when you reject—without genuinely investigating—philosophy from outside the Anglo-European tradition. You are helping those who build and maintain walls: walls between races, walls between religions, walls between civilizations. These walls need to come down. Let us take inspiration from the Bible:

> So the people shouted when the priests blew with the trumpets: and it came to pass, when the people heard the sound of the trumpet, and the people shouted with a great shout, that

the wall fell down flat, so that the people went up into the city, every man straight before him, and they took the city. (Joshua 6:20, KJV)

Although I have criticized many different kinds of intellectuals in this chapter, all of us have one opponent in common: the anti-intellectualism that rejects *all* philosophy as pointless or impractical. I respond to this trend in the next chapter.

4

WELDERS AND PHILOSOPHERS

We need more welders and less philosophers.
—Marco Rubio

Whenever I hear "culture"—I cock my pistol.
—SS officer Hanns Johst

When Marco Rubio quipped, during one of the 2016 GOP presidential debates, "Welders make more money than philosophers. We need more welders and less philosophers," he was doing more than making a grammatical error.[1] He was also guilty of several factual errors. First, as any economist will tell you, the fact that profession X is paid more than profession Y does not mean that the economy needs more people to do X. The supply and demand for X and Y may have achieved equilibrium at different salary levels from each other. (Does Rubio think that in an ideal economy neurosurgeons would be paid the same as chimney sweeps?) More importantly, philosophy majors on average earn more than welders. The median starting salary for those who studied "welding technology" was $37,000 per year, while those with undergraduate degrees in philosophy earned on average $42,000 per year; after ten to twenty years of experience, welders can expect to earn $53,000 per year, while philosophy majors on average will earn $82,000 per year.[2] Ironically, the same data shows that those with a bachelor's degree in political science (like Rubio) earn almost exactly as much on average as philosophy majors upon graduation; however, the philosophy majors overtake the political science majors after a few years of job experience, and earn more on average over their lifetimes. But perhaps we are interpreting Rubio uncharitably. Maybe by "philosophers" Rubio meant only *professors* of philosophy. He is still wrong. The average starting salary for assistant professors of philosophy and religion is over $54,000 per year, already more than the salary a welder can expect after ten years of experience, and full professors earn an average of $86,000 per year.

My point is *not* that we need more philosophers and *fewer* welders. (Unlike Rubio, I believe in the free market system, and have faith that the invisible hand of supply and demand will determine how many philosophers and welders we need.) And I am certainly not trying to "stigmatize vocational education," as Rubio accused some unspecified group of doing. There is nothing intrinsically more noble about either being a philosophy professor or being a welder. But in this chapter I will insist on three points that Rubio's comment missed: (1) Studying philosophy is a legitimate career choice, even from a narrowly vocational perspective. (2) It is a false dichotomy that one must either study philosophy or become a welder. A liberal arts education is valuable to every citizen of a democracy, and to the maintenance of democracy itself. (3) Philosophy has made immense contributions to our civilization. Moreover, by its nature it is impossible for philosophy to ever become obsolete.

PHILOSOPHY AND
OCCUPATIONAL TRAINING

Philosophy majors earn more than those with any other humanities degree,[3] and my own students have gone on to success in a variety of different professions, including medicine, secondary teaching, social work, and law enforcement. For those considering a law degree, it is worth knowing that undergraduate philosophy majors on average score higher than any other major on the Law School Admission Test.[4] (As I am writing this, I currently have three former students attending top law schools: one at Columbia Law School, another at NYU Law School, and a third at the University of Michigan Law School. Their parents must be thinking: "Oh, if only they had majored in welding!") Philosophy majors also have the highest average score on the GRE Verbal and GRE Analytical Writing, and are among the highest-scoring majors for the GMAT, the business-school admissions test.[5] Perhaps most impressively, philosophy majors have the highest average probability of getting admitted to medical school, better on average than any other major, including biology and chemistry![6] We shouldn't be surprised that Darrell Kirch, MD, the CEO of the organization that administers the Medical College Admission Test, was an undergraduate philosophy major himself.[7]

What else do people who majored in philosophy do? A philosophy major can be president of Morgan Stanley (Robert Greenhill), founder and manager of a hedge fund (Don Brownstein), an investor (George Soros *and* Carl Icahn), CEO of Overstock.com (my former Stanford classmate Patrick Byrne), CEO of Time Warner (Gerald Levin), cofounder of PayPal (Peter Thiel), a Supreme Court justice (Stephen Breyer *and* David Souter), cofounder of Wikipedia (Larry Sanger), mayor of

Los Angeles (Richard Riordan), US secretary of education (William Bennett), chair of the Federal Deposit Insurance Corporation (Sheila Bair), political activist (left-wing Stokely Carmichael *and* right-wing Patrick Buchanan), prime minister of Canada (Paul Martin, Jr.), president of the Czech Republic (Vaclav Havel), a network television journalist (Stone Phillips), a Pulitzer Prize–winning author (Studs Terkel), a Nobel Prize–winning author (Pearl Buck *and* Bertrand Russell *and* Jean-Paul Sartre *and* Albert Camus *and* Alexander Solzhenitsyn), a Nobel Peace Prize winner (Albert Schweizer *and* Aung San Suu Kyi), host of an iconic game show (Alex Trebek), a comedian/actor/producer (Ricky Gervais *and* Chris Hardwick), an Academy Award–winning filmmaker (Ethan Coen), a four-star general in the US army (Jack Keane), a fighter in the French Resistance in World War II (Stephane Hessel), coauthor of the United Nations' Universal Declaration of Human Rights (P. C. Chang *and* Charles Malik), a martyr to German opposition to Nazism in World War II (Sophie Scholl), pope (John Paul II *and* Benedict XVI), or a seminal anthropologist (Claude Levi-Strauss *and* Clifford Geertz)—just to give a few examples.

The practical value of our discipline relates to the fact that philosophy courses typically do particularly well at teaching the "three Rs" of a humanities education: reading, writing, and reasoning. Harvard Medical School professor David Silbersweig, MD, explained that his undergraduate major in philosophy

has informed and provided a methodology for everything I have done since. If you can get through a one-sentence paragraph of Kant, holding all of its ideas and clauses in juxtaposition in your mind, you can think through most anything. If you can extract, and abstract, underlying assumptions or superordinate principles, or reason through to the implications of arguments, you can identify and address issues in a myriad of fields. It has helped me in immeasurable ways along my trajectory from philosophy to an academic medical career, which suggest that Rubio [has] a number of serious misconceptions about education.[8]

Philosophy is not unique among humanities fields in teaching reading, writing, and reasoning, but philosophy classes typically put a special emphasis on clarity of expression, accuracy of interpretation, and cogency of argumentation that is sometimes lacking in other disciplines.[9]

I certainly wouldn't say that *most* people should major in philosophy (any more than I would say most people should become welders). But some training in the reading, writing, and reasoning skills that are distinctive of philosophy courses is valuable to majors in a variety of different fields. I know an engineer who, as an undergraduate, fed me the line every humanities professor must have heard at some point: "Why should an engineer be required to take a humanities course instead of taking that one additional engineering course that would help him design a bridge that won't collapse?!" First, any engineer who is only one course away from designing a bridge that collapses should not be anywhere close to graduation! I expect my bridges to be designed by engineers who are well over the absolute minimum skill level required. More seriously, the fact is that, when you study a technical field, advanced knowledge is constantly changing. You always use the concepts that are taught to you in the basic courses your freshman and maybe your sophomore year. After that, the content of your courses is typically things that will be obsolete a few years after you graduate, or perhaps irrelevant to the particular job you end up in. You are still getting something out of them, but it is simply more practice in "thinking like an engineer" (or a businessperson, or a computer scientist, or whatever). This is certainly valuable. However, whatever sort of career you end up in, if you need a college degree for it, part of your job will be reading challenging texts with understanding and writing clearly and persuasively. If you end up in an advanced management position, your job may also involve understanding and discussing knowledgeably issues involving ethics.

How do I know all this? The engineer in question admitted it when I talked to him years later, after he had practical experience in his own profession.

Let us remind ourselves that the distinctive higher education system of the United States—which requires most students to take a liberal arts curriculum and, since World War II, has been increasingly open to people of all social classes—is the envy of the world. No wonder, because the system that makes natural scientists study poetry and philosophy has produced nuclear power, computers, supersonic flight, the polio vaccine, lasers, transistors, oral contraceptives, CDs, the Internet, email, and MRIs, and has put the first people on the moon. Ironically, as liberal arts education in the United States is increasingly under fire, governments in China, India, Japan, Singapore, and South Korea try to re-create in their own countries the liberal arts model that they recognize is one of the keys to US technological and economic dominance.[10]

PHILOSOPHY AND DEMOCRATIC CITIZENSHIP

If failing to appreciate the practical value of studying philosophy were the only problem with Rubio's comment, it would be gratuitously cruel to pair it with one by an SS officer as the epigraphs to this chapter. Rubio certainly did not intend to lead anyone toward anything that horrific. In fact, his speech suspending his 2016 presidential campaign after his loss to Trump in his home state of Florida included the most inspiring rhetoric of the Republican primaries and expressed the values that I believe are most important to him.[11] But what Rubio fails to grasp is that the anti-intellectualism he took part in during the early parts of his campaign is inconsistent with the democracy and justice that he honored at the end of his campaign.

Certainly, Rubio's comment was not a political misstep in the context of contemporary Republican politics. Had Carly Fiorina (who also took part in the debate that night) confessed to the fact that she majored in philosophy, her political ambitions would have been crushed faster than you can fall off a stage—which she later did.[12] Rubio was not even the last person to explicitly target philosophy during that debate. Senator Ted Cruz, apparently noticing that Rubio's line had gotten thunderous applause, criticized the "philosopher-kings" who run the Federal Reserve. (I somehow doubt that this is what Plato meant by "philosopher-kings.") Not wanting to be left out, Governor John Kasich made the blanket statement, "Philosophy doesn't work when you run something." (This sentence makes less sense to me every time I read it.)

Ben Carson, Trump's secretary of housing and urban development, expressed his disdain for philosophy in another context, when he opined that "political correctness" is a serious problem for the US because "it's the very same thing that happened to the Roman Empire. They were extremely powerful. There was no way anybody could overcome them. But these philosophers, with the long flowing white robes and the long white beards, they could wax eloquently on every subject, but nothing was right and nothing was wrong. They soon completely lost sight of who they were."[13] Let's try to take Carson's comment seriously. By "these philosophers" Carson may mean either Academic or Pyrrhonian Skeptics. Carson's reaction is much like that of Rome's own archconservative, Cato the Elder (234–149 BCE), who had the skeptic Carneades (214–129 BCE) expelled from Rome. But neither ancient nor modern skeptics advocate ethical anarchy. Hellenistic Skeptics generally claimed that, while we cannot know what the truth is, we can and should act upon what appears to us to be most plausible.[14] This position raises many delightful philosophical puzzles (is there a distinction between acting on what seems most plausible to us and believing in it?), but it hardly seems like something that would bring the greatest empire of the ancient West to its knees.

Moreover, as a Christian, Carson should also know that there was more to Hellenistic philosophy than Skepticism: the Book of Acts (17:18) reports that St. Paul debated the Epicureans and Stoics he met in Athens.[15] Presumably, Carson would disapprove of the Epicureans' materialistic conception of the universe and their view that good and evil are reducible to pleasure and pain. However, the Epicureans did not see either of these facts as entailing a sybaritic lifestyle: they advocated the moderate satisfaction of desire as most conducive to a happy life. In addition, it is hard not to admire Epicurus for admitting women and slaves to his school.

The Stoics actually had a fairly significant influence on the development of Christian thought, and Carson would approve of many of their teachings, if he had bothered to learn about them. Contrary to the Skeptics, the Stoics claimed that we can know the truth with certainty, and contrary to the Epicureans the Stoics argued that the only thing good in itself is virtue. The Stoics also believed that God exists and is identical with *logos* (reason). (We find similar language in the New Testament: "In the beginning was the Word, and the Word was with God, and the Word was God," where "Word" is *logos* [John 1:1, KJV].) The Stoics argued that the best way of life is to live in accordance with the natural law dictated by the reason that exists within each of us. (Compare this with Romans 2:14–15: "For when the Gentiles, which have not the law, do by nature the things contained in the law, these, having not the law, are a law unto themselves: Which shew the work of the law written in their hearts" [KJV].)

If the philosophers are not responsible for the fall of Rome, what is? Edward Gibbon (1737–94) argued in his classic *The Decline and Fall of the Roman Empire* that "the introduction, or at least the abuse of Christianity" was a contributing factor to the decline of the empire, because it preached "the happiness of a future life" over political activity in this life.[16] Indeed, Gibbon claimed that the preference for the afterlife was so extreme among Christians during the period of persecution that they actively sought martyrdom, going unsummoned to the tribunal to gratuitously confess their faith and demand to be executed.[17] Gibbon editorialized that, after Christianity was legalized by Emperor Constantine (r. 306–37), "the active virtues of society were discouraged . . . the last remains of military spirit were buried in the cloister" and the "sacred indolence of the monks was devoutly embraced by a servile and effeminate age." When the Church did encourage activity, it was often counterproductive: "the church, and even the state, were distracted by religious factions, whose conflicts were sometimes bloody and always implacable."[18] Of course, Gibbon is not the last word on later Roman history.[19] But almost all serious historians would agree with one point he makes: "instead of inquiring *why* the Roman empire was destroyed, we should rather be surprised that it had subsisted so long."[20] Rome fell for many complicated social, political, and economic reasons. Although it is a common conservative trope to compare the decadent United States to decadent Rome, there is no simplistic lesson to be learned from its fate.

To some extent, dismissals of philosophy by politicians simply reflect the anti-intellectualism that has been central to US culture for a very long time.[21] Presidents have to affect an everyman demeanor, dressing up like a cowboy (Ronald "The Gipper" Reagan) or maintaining the hint of an accent they normally would have lost some time at Yale or Oxford ("Bill" Clinton). One of the reasons that Al Gore lost to George W. Bush in 2000 is that Gore never learned the art of hiding his intelligence and erudition; in contrast, Americans correctly saw in G. W. Bush someone they could relate to. Although Bush and Gore each went to an Ivy League school, Bush could be forgiven because (in his own words) he didn't learn "a damn thing at Yale."[22] Gore reminded Americans of the smart kid in class, who's in debate club, and always gets an A, and uses big words. Nobody likes that kid. G. W. Bush, in contrast, is the friendly goofball who's on the cheerleading squad (which Bush actually was). Everyone likes him, and even though he barely got through school with Cs and Ds, he'll be fine because when he graduates he'll just join the family business (which Bush also did).

There is a big difference, though, between wearing a Stetson or playing a saxophone to show what a regular guy you are and actively condemning education. The latter is the direction the GOP has recently been taking. As conservative commentator Matt K. Lewis laments, "Too many of today's conservatives deliberately shun erudition, academic excellence, experience, sagaciousness, and expertise in politics."[23] In other words, the conservative movement has been "Palinized."[24] When former Republican vice presidential candidate Sarah Palin compared conservative women like herself to "Mama Grizzlies," who "kinda just know when something's wrong," the unfortunate implication is that innate and inarticulate intuition invalidates informed intelligence.[25] Historian Stacy Schiff agrees that "Moms 'do kinda just know when something's wrong'" but notes that "ideally that category includes monitoring unprotected teenage sex under one's own roof" (something that Palin failed to do with her daughter Bristol). Turning more specifically to the political implications of Palin's metaphor, she states: "I'm all for saluting the maternal sixth sense, though I'm not sure I want a government run by intuition. We had one of those recently," under G. W. Bush, who led our country to war because of imaginary weapons of mass destruction in Iraq.[26] But it was precisely Palin's anti-intellectualism that made her appealing to so many in the contemporary Republican base.

It used to be that the Democrats were the party of anti-intellectual populism. In the early nineteenth century, our first Democratic president, Andrew Jackson, dismantled America's successful central bank, and was responsible for the ethnic cleansing of Native Americans known as the "Trail of Tears." William Jennings Bryan was the face of the Democratic Party at the beginning of the twentieth century, running unsuccessfully three times for the presidency. When Republican Teddy Roosevelt invited African American leader Booker T. Washington to dine with him and his family at the White House, Bryan expressed outrage.[27] Bryan also famously opposed evolutionary theory, taking the stand for the prosecution in the Scopes Monkey Trial, where he was skewered by Clarence Darrow.

In contrast, the Republican Party was once the party of thoughtful intellectuals like Lincoln (who boasted of "having studied and nearly mastered" the ancient classic of geometry, Euclid's *Elements*, and whose Gettysburg Address was modeled on the Funeral Oration of the Athenian statesman Pericles),[28]

Teddy Roosevelt (Phi Beta Kappa and Magna Cum Laude graduate of Harvard), Hoover (who spoke Chinese and translated the Renaissance work of metallurgy *De Re Metallica* out of Latin),[29] Eisenhower (graduate of West Point, war hero, and president of Columbia University), Nixon (who earned a degree from a liberal arts college and then went on to law school), and George H. W. Bush (Phi Beta Kappa at Yale). However, the GOP has now become the party of B-movie actor Ronald Reagan (who confessed that *he could not remember* whether he had violated his administration's own policy by trading arms to Iran in exchange for hostages),[30] C-student George W. Bush ("They misunderestimated me"),[31] and D-list celebrity Donald Trump ("I'm very highly educated. I know words, I have the best words. I have the best, but there is no better word than stupid.").[32]

What happened?

In his book *Too Dumb to Fail*, Lewis does an excellent job of diagnosing some of the causes of the rising anti-intellectualism of the GOP, including the need to please evangelical voters in southern red states, who often believe, mistakenly, that Christianity is inconsistent with education and reflectiveness. In every presidential election since 1980 (the year Reagan was first elected), the Republican presidential candidate has won in the Bible Belt states of Alabama, Mississippi, Oklahoma, South Carolina, and Texas. But pleasing this constituency sometimes leads to embarrassing results. None of the GOP candidates in 2016 would admit to believing in evolution. When Gov. Scott Walker was in the running for the Republican presidential nomination and visited the United Kingdom, he was ridiculed by a BBC interviewer for evading a question about whether he believed in evolutionary theory: "Any British politician, right- or left-wing, would laugh and say, 'Yes, of course evolution is true.'"[33] Ted Cruz also evaded questions about his views on the topic. However, even though "the son will not bear the punishment for the father's iniquity" (Ezekiel 18:20, KJV), it is difficult not to quote Cruz's father on this topic: "Communism and evolution go hand and hand. Evolution is one of the strongest tools of Marxism because if they can convince you that you came from a monkey, it's much easier to convince you that God does not exist."[34] Finally, Rubio, when asked how old he thought the Earth is, sounded like a student trying to bluff when he had not done the reading:

> I'm not a scientist, man. . . . At the end of the day, I think there are multiple theories out there on how the universe was created and I think this is a country where people should have the opportunity to teach them all. I think parents should be able to teach their kids what their faith says, what science says. Whether the Earth was created in 7 days, or 7 actual eras, I'm not sure we'll ever be able to answer that. It's one of the great mysteries.[35]

In reality, there is no good reason to assume that the Bible is inconsistent with evolutionary theory. The notion that parts of the Bible should be read metaphorically is quite orthodox. No less an authority than St. Augustine explained that he was initially reluctant to embrace Christianity because parts of the Bible seemed implausible. However, St. Ambrose explained to him that many passages were to be read not literally, but as metaphors for a higher truth.[36] Ambrose argued that this is part of the point St. Paul was making when he said, "for the letter killeth, but the spirit giveth life" (2 Corinthians 3:6, KJV). Augustine would himself provide an extensive metaphorical interpretation of the creation story in Genesis in the appendix to his spiritual autobiography, the *Confessions*.[37] But the ultimate authority for metaphorical interpretations of the Bible is Jesus, who warned his disciples against literalism:

> And when his disciples were come to the other side, they had forgotten to take bread. Then Jesus said unto them, Take heed and beware of the leaven of the Pharisees and of the Sadducees. And they reasoned among themselves, saying, *It is* because we have taken no bread. *Which* when Jesus perceived, he said unto them, O ye of little faith, why reason ye among yourselves, because ye have brought no bread? . . . How is it that ye do not understand that I spake *it* not to you concerning bread, that ye should beware of the leaven of the Pharisees and of the Sadducees? Then understood they how that he bade *them* not beware of the leaven of bread, but of the doctrine of the Pharisees and of the Sadducees. (Matthew 16:5–12, KJV)

Jesus was using the metaphor of yeast ruining what should be unleavened bread to warn the disciples not to be influenced by the self-righteousness of the Pharisees or the Sadducees (two sects that opposed Jesus). He chastises his disciples for their overly literal reading, and he would do the same for those who assume we must read the book of Genesis as if it were a newspaper instead of scripture.

In general, there is no intrinsic conflict between being a Christian (or any kind of theist) and being an intellectual. St. Paul said, "Beware lest any man spoil you through philosophy and vain deceit" (Colossians 2:8), but most Christians historically have taken this to mean only that philosophy—if practiced in a shallow or specious way—*can* be destructive of faith, not that it *must* be, or must be avoided intrinsically. Francis Bacon (1561–1626), whose works were a major influence on empiricist philosophy of science, stated, "It is true that a little philosophy inclineth man's mind to atheism; but depth in philosophy bringeth men's minds about to religion."[38] The plausibility of Bacon's claim is reflected in the impressive list of seminal philosophers who were theists (including Plato, Aristotle, Augustine, Anselm, Maimonides, Avicenna, Averroes, Aquinas, Descartes, Leibniz, Spinoza, Berkeley, and Kierkegaard). In the twentieth century, there have been many profound theologians,[39] and a number of highly influential philosophers who are theists.[40] This cuts in two directions. If those who believe in God are anti-intellectual, it is due to laziness, not religious principle. However, philosophers who are atheists should engage those with religious beliefs as seriously and respectfully as they engage those who disagree with them about the mind/body problem or consequentialism vs. deontology.

A mistaken conception of religion as incompatible with science or intellectual sophistication is one factor in the rise of political anti-intellectualism. And this became especially significant when the Moral Majority, a conservative Christian religious group, helped Reagan win the presidency in 1980. However, Reagan's politics had an anti-intellectual slant long before then. Part of Reagan's successful campaign for governor of California was predicated upon open disdain for the faculty and students of the state's public universities. (Students were protesting in favor of the hair-brained ideas that the Vietnam War was a bad idea, and that desegregation and ensuring the voting rights of African Americans were good ideas. Kids today!) Soon after being elected, Reagan complained that, by funding higher education, the state was "subsidizing intellectual curiosity."[41] It seems not to have occurred to Reagan that, as the *Los Angeles Times* editorialized, "If a university is not a place where intellectual curiosity is to be encouraged and subsidized then it is nothing."[42]

Anti-intellectualism grew even stronger in the GOP during the presidency of Bush the Younger. After writing an article critical of the administration, journalist Ron Suskind was summoned to a meeting with Karl Rove (who was Bush's campaign director and later senior advisor and deputy chief of staff in the White House). According to Suskind, Rove told him that

> guys like me were "in what we call the reality-based community," which he defined as people who "believe that solutions emerge from your judicious study of discernible reality." I nodded and murmured something about enlightenment principles and empiricism. He cut me off. "That's not the way the world really works anymore," he continued. "We're an empire now, and when we act, we create our own reality. And while you're studying that reality—judiciously, as you will—we'll act again, creating other new realities, which you can study too, and that's how things will sort out. We're history's actors . . . and you, all of you, will be left to just study what we do."[43]

This stunningly Nietzschean rejection of truth and evidence was followed, less than a year later, by the US invasion of Iraq, which was justified by the pursuit of imaginary weapons of mass destruction for which there was never any compelling evidence. (I still remember watching with incredulity as Secretary of State Colin Powell argued in favor of the war before the UN Security Council by waving a vial of what anthrax would look like—if we had any samples produced in Iraq, which we did not—and a drawing of what a mobile weapons lab would look like—if we had any photos of one, which we did not.) The Republican Party's turn away from evidence and facts, which began with Reagan and accelerated under G. W. Bush, has now reached its climax in the "alternative facts" of the Trump administration.

In fairness, the GOP has also fielded some impressive candidates for the presidency since Reagan. George H. W. Bush, Bob Dole, and John McCain were all intelligent, eloquent, pragmatic war heroes with distinguished careers in public service. But notice the common thread here: George H. W. Bush lost to Clinton in 1992; Bob Dole lost to Clinton in 1996; and McCain lost to Obama in 2008. There were certainly complex reasons for these losses, including Bush reneging on his pledge to tell Congress "read my lips: no new taxes" and the surge in new young voters and voters of color who supported Obama. However, I think thoughtful, sophisticated statesmen like Bush the Elder, Dole, and McCain had two insurmountable weaknesses: they don't ignite the Republican base like candidates who offer simplistic solutions, and they don't seem different enough from their Democratic counterparts to win over swing voters.

The serious ethical problem here is that anti-intellectualism is actually the worst kind of elitism, because it suggests that one must choose between being a welder and learning about philosophy. Why shouldn't welders study philosophy too? After all, Socrates was a bricklayer and Spinoza was a lens grinder. If they were alive today, they'd work at Home Depot and LensCrafters. (The Stoic philosopher Epictetus was a slave, so he'd be working at WalMart.)

Consider the following. Seven of the eight people on the stage when Rubio made his sneer had college degrees.[44] Rubio and John Kasich both majored in political science; Carly Fiorina majored in philosophy and medieval history; Ben Carson has an undergraduate degree in psychology; Jeb Bush majored in Latin American studies; Ted Cruz studied public policy.

These are all liberal arts majors. Why would anyone think that other liberal arts majors are more practical or employable or economically valuable than philosophy? Do we imagine a businesswoman at the office confiding to a coworker: "That was close. My son was going to be major in *philosophy*. Can you imagine?! Thank God he switched his major to public policy. He's going to be raking in the big bucks now!" The only person on the stage that night with a conventionally "practical" major was Donald Trump, who studied economics (and subsequently led multiple companies to bankruptcy and lost almost a billion dollars during an economic boom).

When Rubio stood on a stage with a group of people who, between them, have seven bachelor's degrees (six of them in the liberal arts), two JDs, an MBA, and two MDs, yet denigrated liberal arts education, it sent a clear message to the electorate: "*We* are highly educated; *you* should not be. *We* will get the education and training that will allow us to effectively pursue our goals; *you* don't need information or practice in thinking objectively or critically about the world. *We* will study something that opens our minds and helps us to choose our own futures; *you* should study something that makes you useful to the economic system that we run." A century ago, John Dewey warned of the dangerous political implications of publicly funding only a narrow vocational education: "This movement would continue the traditional liberal or cultural education for the few economically able to enjoy it, and would give to the masses a narrow technical trade education for specialized callings, carried on under the control of others."[45] This would make the educational system nothing but "an instrument in accomplishing the feudal dogma of social predestination" and for "transferring the older division of . . . directed and directive class into a society nominally democratic."[46]

There is an even more dangerous aspect of anti-intellectualism: it is fascistic. Stuart Hampshire was a leading British philosopher who served in military intelligence during World War II and participated in the debriefing of Nazi officers. Hampshire came to recognize that

> below any level of explicit articulation, hatred of the idea of the Jews was tied to hatred of the power of intellect, as opposed to military power, hatred of law courts, of negotiations, of cleverness in argument, of learning and of the domination of learning: and in this way anti-Semitism is tied to hatred of justice itself, which must set a limit to the exercise of power and to domination. . . .[47]

> The Nazi fury to destroy had a definite target: the target encompassed reasonableness and legality and the procedures of public discussion, justice for minorities, the protection of the weak, and the protection of human diversity.[48]

It is not coincidental that anti-Semitic themes are characteristic of every kind of American and European nativist and nationalist movement.

Consequently, in a democracy, philosophy courses are not an "intellectual luxury" (as Reagan suggested).[49] They should not be a privilege of the wealthy. Philosophy belongs to whoever has the intelligence and the willingness to appreciate it, whether it be the child of the welder or the child of the CEO. Studying philosophy makes people more informed and more thoughtful citizens, more comfortable with the fact that others disagree with them, less vulnerable to manipulation and deception, and more willing to resort to discussion rather than violence.

It should come as no surprise, then, that making a broad education widely available to the populace is part of what is most distinctive about the United States. As Martha Nussbaum explains:

> Unlike virtually every nation in the world, we have a liberal arts model of university education. Instead of entering college/university to study a single subject, students are required to take a wide range of courses in their first two years, prominently including courses in the humanities. . . . Nor is the emphasis on the liberal arts a vestige of elitism or class distinction. From early on, leading U.S. educators connected the liberal arts to the preparation of informed, independent, and sympathetic democratic citizens.[50]

Thomas Jefferson illustrates that Nussbaum's view of the value of a liberal arts education is not some trendy, liberal conceit. Jefferson argued that the best way to combat tyranny is

> to illuminate, as far as practicable, the minds of the people at large; . . . whence it becomes expedient for promoting the publick happiness that those person, whom nature hath endowed with genius and virtue, should be rendered by liberal education worthy to receive, and able to guard the sacred deposit of the rights and liberties of their fellow citizens, and that they should be called to that charge without regard to wealth, birth or other accidental condition or circumstance; but the indigence of the greater number disabling them from so educating, at their own expence, those of their children whom nature hath fitly formed and disposed to become useful instruments for the public, it is

better that such should be sought for and educated at the common
expence of all, than that the happiness of all should be confided
to the weak or wicked.[51]

Consequently, despite their claim to revere the wisdom of
America's Founding Fathers, the disdain of many contemporary conservatives for publicly funded liberal arts education is
in opposition to a significant part of what has made America
"exceptional" and a "shining city upon a hill," among other
nations.

PHILOSOPHY'S VALUE TO CIVILIZATION

As I noted in chapter 1, some contemporary scientists take a
dim view of philosophy. Noted edu-tainer Neil deGrasse Tyson
warned that majoring in philosophy "can really mess you up."
This is ironic, because Tyson has a PhD, which stands for doctor of philosophy, reflecting the fact that all the sciences grew
out of philosophy. The pre-Socratic philosophers were the first
to experiment and speculate about the physical world and provide naturalistic explanations for phenomena, setting the stage
for all later science. Anaxagoras (fifth century BCE) correctly
surmised that the Sun was not a god but actually a hot physical
object much larger than it appeared, that the Moon only shined
because of light reflected from the Sun, and that eclipses were
caused when objects came between the Earth and the Sun.
Leucippus (fifth century BCE) and Democritus (460–370 BCE)
developed the first version of the atomic theory, later confirmed
by chemist John Dalton (1766–1844 CE). Galileo (1564–1642)

famously said that "philosophy," which for him included physics and astronomy,

> is written in this grand book, the universe, which stands continually open to our gaze. But the book cannot be understood unless one first learns to comprehend the language and read the letters in which it is composed. It is written in the language of mathematics, and its characters are triangles, circles, and other geometric figures without which it is humanly impossible to understand a single word of it; without these, one wanders about in a dark labyrinth.[52]

In saying this, Galileo was consciously echoing Plato (428?–348? BCE), who had argued that the universe can only be comprehended in mathematical terms.[53]

Plato's student Aristotle (384–22 BCE) perhaps did more than anyone else to lay the foundations of Western science. He was a keen observer of the natural world, who described the development of chicken embryos that he observed by opening a series of eggs on successive days in between laying and hatching.[54] Carl Linnaeus (1707–78) is rightfully praised for elaborating the contemporary biological categorization of living things according to kingdom, phylum, class, order, family, genus, and species. However, his system is based on Aristotle's method of definition by genus and differentia.[55]

It is a party game among shallow intellectuals to mock Aristotle for his hypotheses that turned out to be mistaken, like his claim that the Sun goes around the Earth. However, it does not make someone a bad scientist that she turned out to be mistaken about something. If it did, Galileo would be a bad scientist because he believed that comets were optical illusions,[56]

Lavoisier (the founder of modern chemistry) would be a bad scientist because he denied that meteorites came from space,[57] and Einstein would be a bad scientist because he never accepted quantum mechanics.[58] A good scientist is someone who theorizes based upon the best empirical evidence and most plausible assumptions available to him or her. Aristotle's geocentric hypothesis made sense of the evidence available: the Sun does appear to move, and the Earth does not feel as if it is moving. Even more importantly, a good scientist lays the groundwork for later scientific advances by offering a theory that can be refined, tested, and even refuted. As Nietzsche noted, "It is certainly not the least charm of a theory that it is refutable; it is precisely thereby that it attracts subtler minds."[59]

Those ignorant of history accuse Aristotle and his later followers of an inflexible dogmatism that held back the development of science. The reality is much more complex. As historian of science Thomas Kuhn explained: "Men who agreed with Aristotle's conclusions investigated his proofs only because they were proofs executed by the master. Nevertheless their investigations often helped to ensure the master's ultimate overthrow."[60] The phenomenon that Aristotelian physics had the most trouble accounting for was the motion of projectiles, like an arrow (or, later, a cannonball). Aristotle offered some tentative explanations for projectile motion, but acknowledged that none of them was fully satisfactory. In response to these problems, Aristotle's medieval followers developed "impetus theory," which laid the foundation for Galileo's concept of inertia. In addition, as Jaroslav Pelikan observed, "By constructing the telescope and using it to observe empirically, Galileo was a more faithful Aristotelian than were those who quoted Aristotle's *Physics* against his observations."[61] For synthesizing many earlier theories and starting science on a research program that would eventually transcend his own insights, Aristotle is one of the greatest scientists ever.

Even computers, the most revolutionary scientific achievement of our era, are a gift of the philosophers. (You're welcome!) Binary arithmetic, which is the basis of all computers, was invented by G. W. Leibniz (whose Sinophilia we discussed in chapter 1). Leibniz had several acrimonious debates with Newton. One thing they quarreled over was who discovered calculus. The answer is that Newton discovered it first in time, but Leibniz announced his discovery first, and we use Leibniz's symbolism for the calculus nowadays. They also argued over whether location in space is relative or absolute. Newton argued for the latter, but Einstein would later prove Leibniz right. It's tempting for the humanist to crow that the philosopher won that argument. However, Newton described himself as a "natural philosopher," and he would have been genuinely offended at the suggestion that he was not *really* a philosopher. Of course, most scientists nowadays are not philosophers. As Bertrand Russell (1872–1970) explained, this is because, once we know the proper methodology for solving problems on a certain subject, "this subject ceases to be called philosophy, and becomes a separate science." Only the questions "to which, at present, no definite answer can be given remain to form the residue which is called philosophy."[62] So could science completely replace philosophy? Some people think so. Stephen Hawking recently pronounced that "philosophy is dead," and that "scientists have become the bearers of the torch of discovery in our quest for knowledge."[63]

Wrong.

There are at least three reasons why it is impossible that all of philosophy will be replaced by natural science, or that philosophy will become obsolete. First, the history of science alternates between long periods of "normal science" and brief periods of "revolutionary science."[64] During periods of normal science, scientists largely agree about the way the world works and the proper methodology for studying it. Normal science is an impressive activity, and those who do it, like Tyson and Hawking, deserve our utmost respect and admiration. However, revolutionary science is what the true geniuses of science do: people like Aristotle, Galileo, Newton, John Dalton, Darwin, Erwin Schrödinger, and Einstein. During scientific revolutions, scientists realize that their previous worldview and methodology do not do justice to some aspect of reality. Consequently, they have to radically restructure their concepts. For example, Einstein had to fundamentally rethink what space, time, and gravity were in order to formulate the Special and General Theories of Relativity. During periods of scientific revolution, scientists become philosophers, and draw on the work of other philosophers to help inform their views (for example, Galileo was influenced by Plato, Dalton drew on Democritus, and Einstein's approach to science was shaped by Pierre Duhem). Consequently, when another scientist asked him about the importance of physicists learning about philosophy, Einstein replied:

> I fully agree with you about the significance and educational value of methodology as well as history and philosophy of science. So many people today—and even professional scientists—seem to me like somebody who has seen thousands of trees but has never seen a forest. A knowledge of the historic and philosophical background gives that kind of independence from prejudices of his generation from which most scientists are suffering. This independence created by philosophical insight is—in my opinion—the mark of distinction between a mere artisan or specialist and a real seeker after truth.[65]

The second reason that natural science will never replace philosophy is that sciences like physics are successful precisely because they limit their inquiry to particular aspects of reality using particular methods. If someone argues that there is nothing to reality besides what is studied by physics, we can legitimately ask her why she thinks this. However, the answer to the question of whether there is anything beyond physics cannot be provided from within physics. Physics uses a particular methodology, M, to study reality insofar as it is physical, P. But the question we are asking is whether there is a reality that is not-P. Since M is the methodology we use to study reality only insofar as it is P, we cannot use that same methodology to explore whether there is anything that is not-P. More generally, you cannot show from within the limits of something that there is nothing outside that limit. You have to straddle a limit, conceptually speaking, in order to define it. So if you try to show that there is nothing beyond the factual and methodological limits of physics, you have already transcended the limits of physics.

The final reason that philosophy will never be obsolete is that it includes ethics, political philosophy, and philosophical theology. These topics are intrinsically controversial but also inescapable. As I am fond of telling my students, whatever opinions you have in these areas have their origins, at least in part, in philosophical thought. Do you think that the purpose of life is to make the most out of your intelligence and contribute to your community? You're an Aristotelian. Do you think that there is no purpose to life except for the one each of us chooses for herself? You're an existentialist. Do you think that morality has to be explained psychologically, by our emotions and other motivations? You're a Humean. Do you think that what is right is to do *whatever* produces the greatest happiness of the greatest number of people? You're a utilitarian. Do you think that there are some actions that are intrinsically wrong and must never be done, even if they would result in desirable consequences? You're a Kantian. Do you think that government is designed to protect our inalienable rights to life, liberty, and property? You're a Lockean. Do you think that government must protect our freedoms, but wealth inequality is justifiable only insofar as it benefits those most in need? You're a Rawlsian. Do you think that much of religious belief can be justified by philosophy? Please say hello to my friend Thomas Aquinas. Do you think we can legitimately have religious belief even though most of it must be accepted on faith? Go hang out with my buddies Pascal and Kierkegaard. Do you believe that religion is superstition that has had a largely negative influence on the world? Read Bertrand Russell or J. L. Mackie. Or do you dismiss philosophy as nothing but rationalizations for the will to power or structures of domination? Enjoy Nietzsche, Marx, Freud, and Foucault. (Oops! They're philosophers too!) The question is not *whether* philosophy is important to you. It already is. The only question is whether you choose to become self-aware and critically reflective about the philosophical beliefs that you hold.

Erwin Schrödinger, one of the founders of quantum mechanics and a noted cat lover/hater, was expressing similar views about the limitations of science when he said that

> the scientific picture of the real world around me is deficient. It gives a lot of factual information, puts all our experience in a magnificently consistent order, but it is ghastly silent about all and sundry that is really near to our heart, that really matters to us. It cannot tell us a word about red and blue, bitter and sweet, physical pain and physical delight; it knows nothing of beautiful and ugly, good or bad, God and eternity. Science sometimes pre-

tends to answer questions in these domains, but the answers are very often so silly that we are not inclined to take them seriously.[66]

It is tempting to point out that the two scientists I have quoted who praise philosophy, Einstein and Schrödinger, each won the Nobel Prize in physics, while neither of the two scientists I quoted who disparage philosophy has won one. However, that would be a snarky observation to make, so I won't do it.[67]

We have seen that philosophy is a valuable part of vocational training for many careers. Beyond that, philosophy is important to the maintenance of democracy itself: those who have been trained to argue rationally and constructively have learned to value discussion over violence, and pluralism over intolerance. Finally, philosophy is responsible for so much that we view as valuable in Western civilization, from natural science to the various formulations we use to talk about ethics, politics, and spirituality. For all these reasons, the anti-intellectualism that delights in degrading philosophy is both unwarranted and unfortunate. The value of philosophy was summed up nicely by John Cleese (who obtained a law degree from Cambridge University before becoming one of the founders of the legendary comedy troupe Monty Python):

> Philosophy seems so harmless, and yet, among dictatorships, philosophers have always been among the first people to be silenced. Why have dictators bothered to silence philosophers? Maybe because ideas really matter: they can transform human lives.[68]

But what distinguishes philosophy from other fields in the humanities and social sciences that discuss similar topics? And to what extent are philosophers to blame for their discipline's bad reputation in contemporary society? We turn to these questions in the final chapter.

5

THE WAY OF CONFUCIUS AND SOCRATES

For our discussion is not about some ordinary matter, but the way one should live.

—Socrates

Set your heart upon the Way.

—Confucius

PHILOSOPHY'S SPECIAL ROLE AMONG THE HUMANITIES

To paraphrase Frost, I have a lover's quarrel with academic philosophy. Although the narrow-mindedness of many contemporary philosophers infuriates me, I love philosophy itself: I love teaching it, and I love discussing it with students and colleagues. I also recognize that academic philosophy has a very distinctive role to play in higher education, especially today. I've mentioned in earlier chapters that philosophy teaches reading, writing, and reasoning, but in a way that is distinctive from other disciplines. Let me explain more clearly what I mean.

In many institutions, philosophy is one of the few humanities disciplines, and sometimes the only humanities discipline, that still reads classic texts with what is known as a "hermeneutic of faith." Those who use a hermeneutic of faith read texts in the hope of discovering truth, goodness, and beauty. They are open to the possibility that other people, including people in very different times and cultures, might know more about these things than we do, or at least they might have views that can enrich our own in some way. Of course, if you take seriously the possibility that others are right, you also have to take seriously the possibility that they are wrong. (It's a hermeneutic of faith, not a hermeneutic of blind faith.) And if you are torn between which of two options is right, or at least better than the other, you have to discuss what reasons you have for believing in one or the other. It might seem that this is the obvious or only way to read philosophical, literary, and religious texts, but it is not. There are two major alternative approaches to a hermeneutic of faith: hermeneutics of suspicion and relativism.

Many contemporary humanists and social scientists emphasize a hermeneutic of suspicion. Those using a hermeneutic of suspicion look for motives for the composition of a text that are unrelated to its truth or plausibility. Instead, they ask how the text serves ulterior motives like economic interests and relations of dominance and oppression, as well as sexist, racist, or imperialist conceptions of the world. Many of those who use a hermeneutic of suspicion reject as naïve a hermeneutic of faith. I once gave a presentation to a multidisciplinary program in which I outlined different philosophical perspectives one can take on cross-cultural ethical disagreements. The first comment after my talk was from an anthropologist who began, "The fact *is*, Bryan, . . . " and proceeded to explain to me that everything I said was absolutely irrelevant because the only thing that is really important is how cultural relations are dictated by economic interests. I replied that, while I agree that the issues she brought up are very important, this does not mean we shouldn't also be interested in what we *ought* or *ought not* to do, or at least in understanding more clearly what our options are. She merely stared at me with the look of condescension and disgust one might use on an adolescent who should know better than to be picking his nose at the dinner table.

Those who completely reject a hermeneutic of faith do not only have a narrow perspective; their position is simply incoherent. If you give an interpretation of a text using a hermeneutic of suspicion, you are asking your readers to take what *you* are saying about that text as a candidate for truth. In other words, the very act of interpretation assumes the validity of a hermeneutic of faith. I am not saying that it is wrong to use a hermeneutic of suspicion. The varieties of hermeneutics of suspicion are indispensable parts of our contemporary scholarly toolkit. You'll notice that I have used a hermeneutic of suspicion at a number of points in this book. My objection is only to the exclusive use of hermeneutics of suspicion. I am concerned that hermeneutics of suspicion have become hegemonic in the humanities and social sciences. Philosophy departments are often the last refuge of the hermeneutics of faith.

The other alternative to a hermeneutics of faith is a sort of relativism, which suggests that if you believe something then it is "true for you." While hermeneutics of suspicion deserve to be taken seriously, relativism does not. There are two forms of relativism, cognitive and ethical.[1] According to cognitive relativism, the truth or falsity of all claims depends upon the perspective from which they are evaluated. (For the cognitive relativist, "true" and "false" are like "front" and "back," in that they implicitly make reference to a point of view.) As Plato demonstrated in ancient Greece and the Mohists demonstrated in ancient China, we can see why this doctrine is incoherent by trying to apply it to itself.[2] Is cognitive relativism itself objectively true or only relatively true? If you say that relativism is objectively true, then not all claims are relative, so cognitive relativism is false. (And if cognitive relativism is objectively true, why can't other claims be objectively true too?) If you say that relativism is only relatively true, then from the perspective of those of us who deny it, relativism is false, and we may safely ignore it. (In fact, those of us who deny cognitive relativism believe that it is objectively false, so the cognitive relativist must agree that his view *is* objectively false.)

Ethical relativism asserts that the truth or falsity of evaluative claims (and only evaluative claims) depends upon the perspective from which they are evaluated. Ethical relativism is not intrinsically incoherent. (Since ethical relativism itself is *not* an evaluative claim—it is a purely semantic claim *about* evaluative claims—it does not apply to itself, so it is not self-undermining the way cognitive relativism is.) However, ethical relativism is a banal dead end in philosophy. Suppose you are unsure about whether capital punishment can be justified for some crimes. One kind of ethical relativism tells you that it depends on what *you* individually think. Does that help? Imagine you are torn about whether drones should be used to kill suspected terrorists. It depends upon what your *culture* thinks, says another kind of ethical relativism. Since Americans disagree about whether drones should be used to kill suspected terrorists, you now have to decide which "subculture" you belong to. Are you any closer to a decision now? Students often think that there is something more tolerant about relativism. This is simply a conceptual confusion. According to relativism, whether you should be tolerant of others depends upon the point of view you adopt.

If you adopt the point of view of xenophobic nationalists, then you ought to be *intolerant*. If it seems that I am grumpy about relativism, it's because I am. In my more than thirty years of experience as a teacher, I have found that *every single time relativism comes up* it is invoked by those who wish to insulate their opinions from criticism, not those who wish to bring new voices into the conversation or discuss issues in a more open-minded way. In short, when the conversation gets challenging, the challenged turn relativist.

SO WHAT IS PHILOSOPHY?

It is important that philosophy is one of the last bastions of the hermeneutic of faith, and a discipline that is willing to challenge relativism. But of course this is not what is definitive of philosophy. Other disciplines in the humanities can and occasionally do use a hermeneutic of faith. If we look at the broad sweep of activities that have been called "philosophy" (and its cognate terms) in Western history, there is no common methodology they employ, nor any set of topics they all discuss. In other words, there are no necessary and sufficient conditions for defining what has been called "philosophy" across all of history, even if we limit the discussion to the West.[3] However, I am foolhardy enough to propose a definition of what philosophy is for us *now*. We are doing philosophy when we engage in dialogue about problems that are important to our culture but we don't agree about the method for solving them.[4] In game theory, a game is said to be "solved" once there is an algorithm that determines the best move in each situation. Using the notion of a "solved game" as an analogy, we could say succinctly that "philosophy is dialogue about important *un*solved problems."

Once we do agree about the method for solving a problem, the problem gets kicked out of philosophy and into its own discipline. Consequently (as we noted in chapter 4), astronomy, biology, chemistry, mathematics, and physics began as parts of philosophy, but are now separate fields because in each case there is (generally) agreement about what counts as reliable evidence, good arguments, and well-established conclusions. Viewing it in this way, we can see why philosophy is like a glacier: it moves so slowly that it appears to be going nowhere, but in the long run it radically transforms the world you live in. *Interesting*

The fact that philosophy deals with problems that we are unsure how to solve is part of what makes it tempting to "build walls" around it.[5] We may be seduced into simplifying seemingly intractable philosophical problems by narrowing the number of solutions we consider and the premises we entertain. However, a moment's reflection shows that this sort of strategy is counterproductive. You cannot have confidence in the accuracy of your conclusions, or even the usefulness of your method, if you rule out in advance alternative perspectives on the problems under discussion. As Alasdair MacIntyre has stressed, "any claim to truth involves a claim that no consideration advanced from *any* point of view can overthrow or subvert that claim. Such a claim, however, can only be supported on the basis of rational encounters between rival and incommensurable points of view."[6] Consequently, it is a fundamental failure of rationality to rule out multicultural critiques a priori. *undermine the discipline*

I want to stress again that "dialogue about methodologically unsolved but important questions" is what philosophy is for us now (in extension if not in intension). Philosophers of earlier eras or different cultures typically categorize what they are doing differently.[7] This is something we need to keep continually in mind so that we have a genuinely sympathetic and accurate understanding of their projects as a whole. However, we can (without injustice) describe what they are doing as philosophy, in our sense, if we recognize what they are discussing as potential answers to similar questions to the ones we philosophers discuss today. And, as we have seen repeatedly in this book, we frequently do find thinkers in other cultures addressing the important unsolved problems in ethics, metaphysics, political philosophy, logic, and the philosophy of language that we still wrestle with. Consequently, it is both legitimate and productive to treat them as philosophers in our sense, and bring them into the dialogue.

What I mean by "dialogue" can take various forms. Philosophers sometimes provide arguments in favor of philosophical claims. Nonphilosophers often have trouble grasping what philosophers mean by an "argument." An argument is not simply a disagreement or a quarrel. In an argument, you try to convince someone of a particular claim (your conclusion) by drawing her attention to other claims (your premises) that you think she will agree with, and that give a good reason to accept your conclusion. What counts as a "good reason"? And are there some premises that everyone ought to agree about? Well, if we all agreed about the premises and what counts as a good reason, we wouldn't be doing philosophy anymore; we'd be doing astronomy, or biology, or mathematics, or some other methodologically "solved" discipline.

Providing arguments is undoubtedly an important part of philosophical "dialogue." However, I think philosophers in the English-speaking world sometimes make one of two mistakes about philosophical argumentation. First, there are many ways to express and construct an argument. The structure of some arguments is very clear. For example, Wang Chong (first century CE) presents the following argument against survival after death:

> Humans are animals. Even if exalted as a king or lord, one's nature is no different from an animal. There are no animals that do not die, so how could humans be immortal?[8]

Contrast Wang Chong's syllogistic argument with the more discursive and poetic style that Plato uses when he constructs the allegory of the cave in book 7 of *The Republic*. In this dialogue, Socrates invites his interlocutor Glaucon to

> compare the effect of education and of the lack of it on our nature to an experience like this: Imagine human beings living in an underground, cavelike dwelling, with an entrance a long way up, which is both open to the light and as wide as the cave itself. They've been there since childhood, fixed in the same place, with their necks and legs fettered, able to see only in front of them, because their bonds prevent them from turning their heads around. Light is provided by a fire burning far above and behind them. Also behind them, but on higher ground, there is a path stretching between them and the fire. Imagine that along this path a low wall has been built, like the screen in front of puppeteers above which they show their puppets.
>
> I'm imagining it.
>
> Then also imagine that there are people along the wall, carrying all kinds of artifacts that project above it—statues of people and other animals, made out of stone, wood, and every material. And, as you'd expect, some of the carriers are talking, and some are silent.
>
> It's a strange image you're describing and strange prisoners.

They're like us. Do you suppose, first of all, that these prison-ers see anything of themselves and one another besides the shadows that the fire casts on the wall in front of them?

How could they, if they have to keep their heads motionless throughout life. . . .

Then the prisoners would in every way believe that the truth is nothing other than the shadows of those artifacts.

They must surely believe that.

Consider, then, what being released from their bonds and cured of their ignorance would naturally be like. When one of them was freed and suddenly compelled to stand up, turn his head, walk, and look up toward the light, he'd be pained and dazzled and unable to see the things whose shadows he'd seen before. . . . And if someone dragged him away from there by force, up the rough, steep path, and didn't let him go until he had dragged him into the sunlight, wouldn't he be pained, and irritated at being treated that way? And when he came into the light, with the sun filling his eyes, wouldn't he be unable to see a single one of the things now said to be true?[9]

Socrates describes how the person would gradually adjust his eyes to the sunlight and come to recognize that the things he had taken to be real in the cave were just shadows of things that were themselves merely copies of the real things that existed outside the cave.

What about when he reminds himself of his first dwelling place, his fellow prisoners, and what passed for wisdom there? Don't you think that he'd count himself happy for the change and pity the others?

Certainly.

This whole image, Glaucon, must be fitted together with what we said before. The visible realm should be likened to the prison dwelling, and the light of the fire inside it to the power of the sun. And if you interpret the upward journey and the study of things above as the upward journey of the soul to the intelligible realm, you'll grasp what I hope to convey.[10]

Plato uses this elaborate allegory to explain how a proper education leads students to question their common-sense beliefs (represented by the shadows in the cave) and gradually rise to an understanding of reality through reason and mathematics. Aristotle argues in a similarly poetic mode that pleasure cannot be the goal of life, because pleasure is not itself a complete activity, but rather "completes the activity . . . like the bloom on [the cheek of] youths."[11] As we can see from these examples, Western philosophy largely consists of quaint myths and poetry, in contrast with the precise argumentation that is characteristic of Chinese philosophers.

My mainstream philosophical colleagues are champing at the bit to point out that I have taken these selections from Plato and Aristotle out of context. The allegory of the cave is part of a complex and subtle epistemological and ethical project. Aristotle's poetic comment about pleasure comes at the end of a tightly argued discussion, and must be interpreted in the light of his nuanced view of properties. You're quite right. But perhaps now you can understand my frustration with those who treat Chinese philosophy as nothing but context-less kōans or fortune-cookie platitudes. Reading philosophy requires an effort to think about the text holistically, constructively, and charitably. We are used to doing this with Western texts that we identify as philosophical. The fact that Aristotle, or Descartes, or Kant, or Russell is often hard to understand, or is seemingly contradictory, or occasionally gives what appear to be unpersuasive arguments only inspires us to read more carefully, interpret creatively, and reconstruct or even supply arguments. But many philosophers, when they come to non-European philosophy, simply roll their eyes and throw up their hands in frustration at the first knotty passage or unfamiliar technical term, like a petulant freshman confronting Plato for the first time. I cannot prevent anyone from being narrow-minded or intellectually lazy. But I would much prefer you did not excuse your intellectual vices by ignoring the fact that reading philosophy—any philosophy from any tradition—is always hard work.

I have noted that one common mistake in Anglophone philosophy is to pretend that all philosophical arguments (at least in the Western tradition) are in tight syllogisms or are transparent at first glance, when in reality almost none are. A second common mistake is the tendency to overemphasize argumentation, as if that were the only thing that philosophers do in dialogue. Another important aspect of philosophical dialogue is the classification and clarification of alternatives. Gilbert Ryle was doing this when he distinguished between "knowing how" and "knowing that."[12] The Confucian Mengzi (fourth century BCE) was doing this when he gave three different paradigms of what courage is (aggressive behavior, fearlessness, and action in accordance with a strong sense of righteousness).[13]

In addition to presenting arguments and clarifying alternatives, a third goal of philosophical dialogue is providing substantially new perspectives or answers to questions. Even if one did nothing else, this is a significant contribution to philosophical discussion. This can involve a narrow suggestion on a specific topic. Karl Popper is largely remembered now for his claim that science is distinguished from nonscience because we know what kinds of tests would falsify a scientific claim. Although this is merely a suggestion for an answer to the question of "What is science?" (and a demonstrably mistaken one at that), it is a contribution to philosophical dialogue. Similarly, when Confucius's disciple Youzi suggests that the virtue of benevolence develops out of love for family members, this is in itself a valuable contribution to philosophical discussion in ethics.[14]

Among the less commonly taught philosophies (LCTP), the ones that I know the most about are the Three Teachings of the Chinese tradition: Buddhism, Confucianism, and Daoism; I also have some familiarity with the Advaita Vedanta school of the Indian tradition. It is absolutely indisputable to anyone who actually bothers to learn about these traditions that they discuss the sort of "important unsolved topics" that we recognize as philosophical, and engage in all three of the methodologies characteristic of philosophical dialogue. In regard to other non-European traditions, I do not wish to make the same mistake I have criticized others for making and pontificate about them in ignorance. However, based on what little I know about African philosophies and the philosophies of the Indigenous peoples of the Americas, they at the very least provide substantial new perspectives on how to understand the world, and for this reason have earned their place in the philosophical dialogue.[15] The other LCTP (including African American, Christian, feminist, Islamic, Jewish, Latin American, and LGBTQ philosophy) are historically related to the Greco-Roman tradition, so they are transparently philosophical.

Philosophers in the Western hermeneutic tradition—including Heidegger, Gadamer, Habermas, Ricoeur, and Rorty—recognize the centrality of dialogue not just to philosophy but to all of human existence. However, many of them have failed to appreciate another of the key ethical requirements of dialogue: to be open to new voices, alternative solutions, fresh vocabularies, and different formulations of the same or similar problems from outside the Anglo-European tradition. In some cases, as with Gadamer, this can perhaps be forgiven as part of the limited cultural "horizon" in which the philosopher came to maturity. In other cases, as with Heidegger, hermeneutics became mistakenly fused with a dangerously nativist rejection of cosmopolitanism. Whatever the reason or rationalization, anyone who shuts down possible avenues of dialogue in advance is failing to be a philosopher. And when the dialogue is blocked by the exercise of institutional power, it becomes what Jean-François Lyotard rightly called "terror":

> By terror I mean the efficiency gained by eliminating, or threatening to eliminate, a player from the language game one shares with him. He is silenced or consents, not because he has been refuted, but because his ability to participate has been threatened (there are many ways to prevent someone from playing). The decision makers' arrogance, which in principle has no equivalent in the sciences, consists in the exercise of terror. It says: "Adapt your aspirations to our ends—or else."[16]

The most horrifying forms of terror are physical: murder, imprisonment, and assault. But there are also insidious forms of terror that are dangerous precisely because they are more subtle. Recall (from chapter 1) what doctoral student Eugene Park was told by one of his professors when he questioned why philosophy couldn't include works by noncanonical thinkers: "This is the intellectual tradition we work in. Take it or leave it."

RECOVERING THE WAY OF CONFUCIUS AND SOCRATES

One aspect of my characterization of philosophy may seem particularly problematic. I have argued that philosophy is dialogue over important unsolved problems. Some will object that this is far too broad, as different things will seem important to different people. But there is one question that is most important in every form of philosophy: What way should one live? Bernard Williams referred to this as "Socrates' question," and identified it as central to ethical philosophy.[17] I would expand upon this and say that it is the ultimate motivating question behind philosophy in every tradition. Furthermore, it is the question that gives sense and importance to even the most abstract topics in metaphysics, epistemology, and semantics. So if I may be forgiven one further tweaking of my definition: philosophy is dialogue about problems that we agree are important, but don't agree about the method for solving, where "importance" ultimately gets its sense from the question of the way one should live. - Action

I worry that contemporary academic philosophers often lose sight of this issue of importance, and are thus partly to blame for the perception that philosophy is nothing but intellectual masturbation. Consider some of the topics that many philosophers consider central to their discipline and often use in teaching introductory philosophy courses. If you were a disembodied brain in a vat being electronically stimulated to believe that you have a body, could you know this fact?[18] Suppose there were teleporters like in science fiction, but the way they worked was by disintegrating you completely, and then building an exact atom-by-atom duplicate of you somewhere else: Would this new person be you or not?[19] What is the right thing to do if you are confronted with a runaway train that will kill five people if you do nothing, but will only kill one person if you pull a lever redirecting the train?[20] Should we explain the fact that some sentences must be true (like "$1 + 1 = 2$") while others only happen to be true (like "Obama won in 2012") by postulating that there are an infinite number of alternative possible universes, each of them just as real as the one we inhabit, and that some sentences are true in all of them, while other sentences are only true in some of them?[21] What evidence do we have that emeralds are green rather than grue, where "grue" refers to anything we observed up until today that is green, or to anything we did not observe before today and is blue.[22] The examples I have drawn so far are from analytic philosophy, the style that is dominant in the English-speaking world. However, Continental philosophy is not immune to degrading into intellectual onanism. I think that Martha Nussbaum's comment about Jacques Derrida could be applied to many other recent Continental thinkers:

> Once one has worked through and been suitably (I think) impressed by Derrida's perceptive and witty analysis of Nietzsche's style, one feels, at the end of all the urbanity, an empty longing amounting to a hunger, a longing for the sense of difficulty and risk and practical urgency that are inseparable from Zarathustra's dance. . . . Nietzsche's work is profoundly critical of existing ethical theory, clearly; but it is, inter alia, a response to the original Socratic question, "How should one live?" Derrida does not touch on that question. . . . After reading Derrida, and not Derrida alone, I feel a certain hunger for blood; for, that is, writing about literature that talks of human lives and choices as if they matter to us at all.[23]

Some students find purely intellectual puzzles fun, and there will always be a trickle of students who want to devote their lives to wrestling with them. This trickle will be enough to keep elite philosophy departments staffed with people who, generation after generation, will keep the same puzzles alive. But it is not unreasonable for thoughtful students to wonder whether the intellectual games played in philosophy classrooms are a better use of their minds than crossword puzzles or Sudoku.

I am not arguing that philosophers should avoid thorny technical questions. Sometimes we are led to quite subtle issues by the dogged effort to construct a comprehensive answer to the challenge "What way should one live?" (I have myself written an entire article on grammatical and interpretive problems involving two sentences in the *Analects* of Confucius.)[24] If given the right context, even the abstract problems I mentioned earlier can assume a deep human significance. The teleporter thought-experiment was originally part of a challenge to our ordinary individualistic conception of ethics. The runaway train example was introduced to illustrate the difference between *doing* something that harms another person and *allowing to happen* something that harms another person. But my experience is that many philosophers end up fixating upon these examples as if they were self-contained intellectual games. Let us never lose sight of *why* the technical issues that we study matter, and let us always make sure that our students see why they matter.

Consider Nobel Laureate Bertrand Russell (1872–1970). Russell was the coauthor of *Principia Mathematica*, a three-volume book that uses logic and set theory to prove that $1 + 1 = 2$. (In case you weren't sure.) *Principia Mathematica* made significant contributions to formal thought, but Russell was not simply playing a pointless intellectual game when he worked on it. He had a powerful and moving view of the purpose of human life and how it is connected to philosophy:

The impartiality which, in contemplation, is the unalloyed desire for truth, is the very same quality of mind which, in action, is justice, and in emotion is that universal love which can be given to all, and not only to those who are judged useful or admirable. Thus contemplation enlarges not only the objects of our thoughts, but also the objects of our actions and our affections: it makes us citizens of the universe, not only of one walled city at war with all the rest. In this citizenship of the universe consists man's true freedom, and his liberation from the thraldom of narrow hopes and fears.[25]

After writing these lines, Russell would go on to become an advocate for women's suffrage, be imprisoned for his opposition to the pointless bloodshed of World War I, get fired from a job at the City College of New York for advocating sexual liberation, speak out against Stalin when many intellectuals looked the other way from his crimes, and become a leading advocate of nuclear disarmament. Russell's relentless search for objective truth no doubt played a role in preparing his mind for his activism.

However, readers of Russell's own *Autobiography* know that another factor shaping his ethics was a specific experience he had in 1901. Russell witnessed a close friend undergoing intense, unrelievable suffering due to an illness:

She seemed cut off from everyone and everything by walls of agony, and the sense of the solitude of each human soul suddenly overwhelmed me. . . . Suddenly the ground seemed to give way beneath me, and I found myself in quite another region. . . . At the end of those five minutes, I had become a completely different person. For a time, a sort of mystic illumination possessed me. . . . Having been an Imperialist, I became during those five minutes a pro-Boer and Pacifist.

Russell turns to the language of Asian philosophy to describe his transformation: "Having for years cared only for exactness and analysis, I found myself filled with semi-mystical feelings about beauty, with an intense interest in children, and with a desire almost as profound as that of the Buddha to find some philosophy which would ·make human life endurable."[26] It seems unlikely that Russell would have become such a forceful advocate for others had it not been for the compassion that this Zen-like experience taught him.[27] How many students who have read Russell's seminal essay "On Denoting" (about the semantics of the word "the") know the passion that lies behind his work?

Russell was deeply influenced by Plato. Plato explained that he was motivated to pursue philosophy because he was horrified by the corruption and vice that he saw in the government of Athens, regardless of whether those in power happened to represent the aristocratic or democratic faction: "So I was compelled, praising true philosophy, to declare that she alone enables men to discern what is justice in the state and in the lives of the individuals. The generations of mankind, therefore, would have no cessation from evils until either the class of those who are true and genuine philosophers came to political power or else the men in political power, by some divine dispensation, became true philosophers."[28] John Rawls, the most important mainstream Western political philosopher of the twentieth century, was a decorated soldier in World War II. As a member of the Occupation Force in Japan, he saw firsthand the devastation rendered by the atomic bomb on Hiroshima, and he said this affected him deeply.[29] The bombings of Hiroshima and Nagasaki were supposedly justified by utilitarian considerations: they saved more lives, on balance, than would have been lost by invading the Japanese home islands. However, Rawls's classic *A Theory of Justice* argued that, contrary to utilitarianism, each individual possesses intrinsic rights that cannot be sacrificed for the sake of the well-being of others. On this basis, Rawls would later argue explicitly that "both Hiroshima and the fire-bombing of Japanese cities were great evils"[30] because they specifically targeted civilians, who cannot be held morally responsible for the actions of their authoritarian government.

R. M. Hare, a leading British philosopher, developed a form of philosophy called Prescriptivism, according to which there are no objective moral facts, but only prescriptions that one is willing to universalize and to actually live by. Many philosophers are familiar with his work, but few know that he was led to this philosophy by his horrific experiences in a Japanese prisoner-of-war camp in World War II.[31] In this context, morality was reduced to the absolute bare bones conceptually required by the minimal meaning of moral terms.

So deeply meaningful life experiences often drive one to study philosophy; studying philosophy can also prepare one to face challenging life experiences. One of the most persuasive and moving accounts of the value of philosophy and a liberal arts education was offered by Admiral James Stockdale.[32] Stockdale was a POW in the Vietnam War. Prior to the war, he had taken a philosophy course at Stanford in which he studied the thought of the Stoic Epictetus. Epictetus teaches that maintaining one's integrity is more important than anything else, certainly more important than avoiding pain. He also argues that we must learn to accept our fate, and that hatred of our opponents is a trap. Stockdale said that philosophical lessons he learned from Epictetus helped him to survive years of torture with his character intact. (Epictetus was one of those Roman "philosophers, with the long flowing white robes and the long white beards," that Ben Carson warned us about.)[33] Upon his return to the

United States, Stockdale was awarded the Congressional Medal of Honor, the highest award given by the US military, for his courage and leadership as a POW.

Many people seem to think that education should only involve studying authors you agree with. (More realistically, authors *they* agree with. Recall Buckley's complaint that his professors at Yale were undermining students' faith in Christianity.)[34] However, Stockdale said that it was a great benefit to him that he had taken a course in which he read systematically and charitably the works of Marx and Lenin: "In Hanoi, I understood more about Marxist theory than my interrogator did. I was able to say to that interrogator: 'That's not what Lenin said; you're a deviationist.'"[35] Stockdale explained that among the soldiers most vulnerable to being "turned" by their interrogators were those who had never been exposed to criticisms of their own country, and had never gotten the opportunity to think carefully about why they rejected Marxism.

Stockdale isn't the only heroic figure who learned from and admired philosophy. Rev. Martin Luther King, Jr., said that his favorite book after the Bible was Plato's *Republic*: "it brings together more of the insights of history than any other book. There is not a creative idea extant that is not discussed, in some way, in this work. Whatever realm of theology or philosophy is one's interest—and I am deeply interested in both—somewhere along the way, in this book you will find the matter explored."[36] The influence of Plato's thought is evident in King's own philosophy. In his historic "Letter from Birmingham Jail," King invokes the allegory of the cave in order to explain taking actions (like civil disobedience) that were contrary to the conventional values of his era: "Just as Socrates felt that it was necessary to create a tension in the mind so that individuals could rise from the bondage of myths and half-truths to the unfettered realm of creative analysis and objective appraisal, we must see the need of having nonviolent gadflies to create the kind of tension in society that will help men to rise from the dark depths of prejudice and racism to the majestic heights of understanding and brotherhood."[37] In other writings, King makes reference to moral lessons he learned from Plato's *Symposium* and *Phaedrus*.[38]

As the preceding examples show, the greatest philosophy is inspired by and inspires passionate engagement with the problems important to human life. Western philosophers are the heirs to Socrates, who stated that "the unexamined life is not a life fit for a human."[39] Yet you would be stunned at how often contemporary philosophers are flummoxed or merely annoyed if you ask them what difference their philosophical research makes to the world, or even to their own lives. We should make clear to ourselves and to our students *why* what we are studying is important. And if we have trouble seeing the connection between our philosophy and any real-life concerns, we should focus our energies on something different.

Socrates and Confucius are seminal philosophical figures in their respective cultures, and also paradigms of what philosophy is in any culture. The differences between them are substantial, but the similarities are sometimes overlooked. For both Socrates and Confucius, philosophy is far from an intellectual parlor game: it has a significant ethical purpose. For both Socrates and Confucius, philosophy is conducted through dialogue. For both Socrates and Confucius, dialogue begins in shared beliefs and values, but is unafraid to use our most deeply held beliefs to challenge the conventional opinions of society. For both, to engage in dialogue is to only assert what one sincerely believes. For both, dialogue involves charitably interpreting and constructively responding to one's interlocutor. For the traditions that grow out of each thinker, the goal of dialogue is twofold: truth and personal cultivation. For both traditions, we do not fully understand at the beginning of the dialogue what truth and personal cultivation are. For both traditions, dialogue is an endless striving toward perfection. Fundamentally, dialogue is an attempt to persuade rather than coerce. We find the same values in the best philosophy of every era and every culture. Contemporary philosophy needs to recover these ideals.

The thesis of this book is not that mainstream Anglo-European philosophy is bad and all other philosophy is good. There are people who succumb to this sort of cultural Manicheanism, but I am not one of them. This book is about broadening philosophy by tearing down barriers, not about building new ones. I too desire to bask in the lunar glow of Plato's genius, and walk side by side with Aristotle through the sacred grounds of the Lyceum. But I also want to "follow the path of questioning and learning" with Zhu Xi, and discuss the "Middle Way" of the Buddha. I'm sure you and I will not agree about which is the best way for one to live.

Let's discuss it . . .

NOTES

FOREWORD

1. Thomas Babington Macaulay, "Minutes on Education in India," in *Selected Writings*, ed. John Clive and Thomas Pinney (Chicago: University of Chicago Press, 1972), 241.
2. Nicholas Tampio, "Not All Things Wise and Good Are Philosophy," *Aeon*, September 13, 2016, https://aeon.co/ideas/not-all-things-wise-and-good-are-philosophy.
3. Suzy Q. Groden, trans., *The Symposium of Plato* (Amherst: University of Massachusetts Press, 1970), 61 (Stephanus 189e–190b).
4. Wilfred Sellars, "Philosophy and the Scientific Image of Man" (1962), quoted in "Wilfrid Sellars," by Willem deVries, *Stanford Encyclopedia of Philosophy*, ed. Edward N. Zalta, http://plato.stanford.edu/archives/win2016/entries/sellars/.

1. A MANIFESTO FOR MULTICULTURAL PHILOSOPHY

The epigraphs to chapter 1 are from Immanuel Kant, *Physical Geography*, translated in Julia Ching, "Chinese Ethics and Kant," *Philosophy East and West* 28, no. 2 (April 1978): 169; and Martin Luther King, Jr., "Address Delivered at Poor People's Campaign Rally" (March 19, 1968; Clarksdale, Mississippi), cited in James Cone, *Risks of Faith* (Boston: Beacon, 1999), 152*n*20 (original transcript of speech archived at the King Center, Atlanta, GA, document 680323-02).

1. Tyson made this comment in an interview with Chris Hardwick (who majored in philosophy) on *Nerdist Podcast*, episode 139, uploaded November 11, 2011, http://nerdist.com/nerdist-podcast-139-neil -degrasse-tyson/. Rubio made his assertion during the Republican candidates' debate in Milwaukee, Wisconsin, on November 10, 2015, which is available at *The American Presidency Project*, www.presidency.ucsb.edu /ws/index.php?pid=110908.

2. For the sources to these claims and a more detailed response to critics of the study of philosophy, see chapter 4.

3. Ranking philosophy departments is, of necessity, a controversial matter. My ranking here follows the 2014–15 Philosophical Gourmet Report (PGR), www.philosophicalgourmet.com/. (Full disclosure: I am on the advisory board for the PGR.) For critiques of the PGR, see Katherine S. Mangan, "175 Philosophy Professors Blast Ranking of Graduate Programs," *Chronicle of Higher Education*, January 18, 2002, http://chronicle .com/article/175-Philosophy-Professors/34484/.

4. CUNY Graduate Center (Hagop Sarkissian), Duke University (David Wong), University of California, Berkeley (Kwong-loi Shun), University of California, Riverside (Eric Schwitzgebel), University of Connecticut (Alex McLeod), and University of Michigan (Sonya Ozbey). An additional two top-fifty institutions deign to allow members of another department to cross-list their courses in philosophy: Georgetown University (Erin Cline) and Indiana University at Bloomington (Aaron Stalnaker). (Departments often cross-list courses reluctantly and under pressure. And the fact that a course in another department is cross-listed does not ensure that students in philosophy with an interest in that topic are supported and encouraged.) In Canada, Edward Slingerland teaches in the philosophy department at the University of British Columbia.

5. University of Hawaii (Franklin Perkins), University of Oklahoma (Amy Olberding), and University of Utah (Eric Hutton). European philosophy departments are not much better. See Carine Defoort, "'Chinese Philosophy' at European Universities: A Threefold Utopia," *Philosophy East and West* (forthcoming). See also Defoort, "Is There Such a Thing as Chinese Philosophy? Arguments of an Implicit Debate," *Philosophy East and West* 51, no. 3 (2001): 393–413.

6. Indian philosophy is taught at the CUNY Graduate Center (Graham

Priest), State University of New York, Buffalo (Nic Bommarito), University of Texas at Austin (Stephen Phillips), University of New Mexico (John Bussanich and John Taber), Binghamton University (Charles Goodman), and University of Hawaii (Arindam Chakrabarti). At Harvard, Parimil Patil teaches a cross-listed course on Indian philosophy. The phrase "less commonly taught philosophies (LCTP)" is modeled on "less commonly taught languages (LCTL)," an expression used to refer conveniently to the otherwise heterogeneous collection of languages that are outside the "mainstream" languages taught in most US secondary and postsecondary schools.

7. Michigan State University (Kyle Powys Whyte) and University of Oregon (Scott L. Pratt).

8. Top philosophy doctoral programs with specialists on some area in Africana philosophy (which includes both African and African American philosophy) include Binghamton, Columbia, CUNY Graduate Center, Emory, Harvard, Michigan State, New York University, Purdue, Rutgers, Pennsylvania State, Stony Brook, Texas A & M, University of Connecticut, and Vanderbilt.

9. Richard D. McKirahan and Patricia Curd, trans., *A Presocratics Reader: Selected Fragments and Testimonia*, 2nd ed. (Indianapolis: Hackett, 2011), 58, no. 6 (B6). Although I tease Parmenides here, he is undeniably a great thinker. For a discussion, see Vishwa Adluri, *Parmenides, Plato, and Mortal Philosophy* (New York: Bloomsbury Academic, 2012).

10. See Bertrand Russell, "Descriptions" (from *Introduction to Mathematical Philosophy*), in *Classics of Analytic Philosophy*, ed. Robert R. Ammerman (Indianapolis: Hackett, 1990), 15–24; and Peter F. Strawson, "On Referring," in Ammerman, *Classics of Analytic Philosophy*, 315–34. For an entire book devoted to the debate, see Stephen Neale, *Descriptions* (Cambridge: MIT Press, 1990).

11. Javier C. Hernández, "China's Tech-Savvy, Burned-Out and Spiritually Adrift, Turn to Buddhism," *New York Times*, September 7, 2016, http://nyti.ms/2bTGFPG; Ian Johnson, "The Rise of the Tao," *New York Times*, November 5, 2010, http://nyti.ms/1ABiTcq. On President Xi's interest in Confucianism, see chapter 3.

12. Daniel Bell, *The China Model: Political Meritocracy and the Limits of Democracy* (Princeton: Princeton University Press, 2015); Joseph Chan,

Confucian Perfectionism: A Political Philosophy for Modern Times (Princeton: Princeton University Press, 2013); Jiang Qing, *A Confucian Constitutional Order: How China's Ancient Past Can Shape Its Political Future*, ed. Daniel Bell and Ruiping Fan, trans. Edmund Ryden (Princeton: Princeton University Press, 2012). I discuss Xi's use of Confucius in chapter 3.

13. I discuss what is distinctive about philosophy in chapter 5.

14. Lee H. Yearley, *Mencius and Aquinas: Theories of Virtue and Conceptions of Courage* (Albany: State University of New York Press, 1990).

15. Later books that have developed virtue ethics interpretations of Confucianism include May Sim, *Remastering Morals with Confucius and Aristotle* (New York: Cambridge University Press, 2007); Bryan W. Van Norden, *Virtue Ethics and Consequentialism in Early Chinese Philosophy* (New York: Cambridge University Press, 2007); Jiyuan Yu, *The Ethics of Confucius and Aristotle: Mirrors of Virtue* (New York: Routledge, 2007); and Stephen Angle, *Sagehood: The Contemporary Significance of Neo-Confucian Philosophy* (New York: Oxford University Press, 2012).

16. Erin Cline, *Confucius, Rawls, and the Sense of Justice* (New York: Fordham University Press, 2013). See also my review in *Notre Dame Philosophical Reviews*, review no. 38 of July 2013, http://ndpr.nd.edu/news/41386-confucius-rawls-and-the-sense-of-justice/.

17. Erin Cline, *Families of Virtue: Confucian and Western Views on Childhood Development* (New York: Columbia University Press, 2015).

18. Eric Schwitzgebel, "Human Nature and Moral Development in Mencius, Xunzi, Hobbes, and Rousseau," *History of Philosophy Quarterly* 24 (2007): 147–68. See also Schwitzgebel, "Zhuangzi's Attitude Toward Language and His Skepticism," in *Essays on Skepticism, Relativism, and Ethics in the "Zhuangzi,"* ed. Paul Kjellberg and Philip J. Ivanhoe (Albany: State University of New York Press, 1996), 68–96.

19. Aaron Stalnaker, *Overcoming Our Evil: Human Nature and Spiritual Exercises in Xunzi and Augustine* (Washington: Georgetown University Press, 2009).

20. David Wong, *Natural Moralities: A Defense of Pluralistic Relativism* (New York: Oxford University Press, 2006); and Owen Flanagan, *The Geography of Morals: Varieties of Moral Possibility* (New York: Oxford University Press, 2016).

21. Martha Nussbaum, "Golden Rule Arguments: A Missing Thought," in *The Moral Circle and the Self*, ed. Chong Kim-chong and Tan Sor-hoon (LaSalle, IL: Open Court, 2003); Nussbaum, "Comparing Virtues," *Journal of Religious Ethics* 21, no. 2 (1993): 345–67; Alasdair MacIntyre, "Incommensurability, Truth, and the Conversation Between Confucians and Aristotelians About the Virtues," in *Culture and Modernity*, ed. Eliot Deutsch (Honolulu: University of Hawaii Press, 1991), 104–22; MacIntyre, "Once More on Confucian and Aristotelian Conceptions of the Virtues," in *Chinese Philosophy in an Era of Globalization*, ed. Robin R. Wang (Albany: State University of New York Press, 2004), 151–62.

22. See Yasuo Deguchi, Jay L. Garfield, and Graham Priest, "The Way of the Dialetheist: Contradictions in Buddhism," *Philosophy East and West* 58, no. 3 (July 2008): 395–402, and the special issue of *Philosophy East and West*—63, no. 3 (July 2013)—devoted to discussion of their work. See also Graham Priest, *One: Being an Investigation Into the Unity of Reality and Its Parts, Including the Singular Object Which Is Nothingness* (New York: Oxford University Press, 2014), 167–235; and my review in *Dao* 15 (2016): 307–10.

23. For an accessible presentation, see A. C. Graham, *Disputers of the Tao* (La Salle, IL: Open Court, 1989), 150–55. Christoph Harbsmeier gives what is perhaps the definitive overview of ancient Chinese philosophy of language: Harbsmeier, *Language and Logic*, vol. 7, pt. 1, in *Science and Civilisation in China*, ed. Joseph Needham (New York: Cambridge University Press, 1998).

24. Myisha Cherry and Eric Schwitzgebel, "Like the Oscars, #PhilosophySoWhite," *Los Angeles Times*, March 4, 2016, www.latimes.com/opinion/op-ed/la-oe-0306-schwitzgebel-cherry-philosophy-so-white-20160306-story.html.

25. Kyle Whyte, "Indigenous Research and Professional Philosophy in the US," *Philosopher*, blog, February 3, 2017, https://politicalphilosopher.net/2017/02/03/featured-philosopher-kyle-whyte/.

26. Bryan W. Van Norden, "Three Questions About the Crisis in Chinese Philosophy," *APA Newsletter on the Status of Asian and Asian-American Philosophers and Philosophies* 8, no. 1 (Fall 2008): 3–6, https://c.ymcdn.com/sites/www.apaonline.org/resource/collection/2EAF6689-4B0D-4CCB-9DC6-FB926D8FF530/v08n1Asian.pdf.

27. Jay Garfield and Bryan Van Norden, "If Philosophy Won't Diversify, Let's Call It What It Really Is," *The Stone*, blog, *New York Times*, May 11, 2016, www.nytimes.com/2016/05/11/opinion/if-philosophy-wont-diversify-lets-call-it-what-it-really-is.html.

28. "What's Your Take on the Recent NYTimes Article Advocating Diversification in Philosophy Departments in the West?" www.reddit.com/r/askphilosophy/comments/4joun6/whats_your_take_on_the_recent_nytimes_article/. An especially insightful online response to critics of our piece is Amy Olberding, "When Someone Suggests Expanding the Canon," http://dailynous.com/2016/05/13/when-someone-suggests-expanding-the-canon/. Other interesting online discussions (pro and con) include Brian Leiter, "Anglophone Departments Aren't 'Departments of European and American Philosophy,'" *Leiter Reports: A Philosophy Blog*, May 11, 2016, http://leiterreports.typepad.com/blog/2016/05/anglophone-departments-arent-departments-of-european-and-american-philosophy.html; John Drabinski, "Diversity, 'Neutrality,' Philosophy," http://jdrabinski.com/2016/05/11/diversity-neutrality-philosophy/; Meena Krishnamurthy, "Decolonizing Analytic Political Philosophy," *Philosopher*, blog, June 3, 2016, https://politicalphilosopher.net/2016/06/03/meenakrishnamurthy/; and Justin Smith, "Garfield and Van Norden on Non-European Philosophy," www.jehsmith.com/1/2016/05/garfield-and-van-norden-on-non-european-philosophy-.html.

29. Patricia McGuire, comment on Jay Garfield and Bryan Van Norden, "If Philosophy Won't Diversify, Let's Call It What It Really Is," *New York Times*, www.nytimes.com/2016/05/11/opinion/if-philosophy-wont-diversify-lets-call-it-what-it-really-is.html#permid=18491745.

30. Shawn (no last name supplied), comment on Jay Garfield and Bryan Van Norden, "If Philosophy Won't Diversify," *New York Times*, www.nytimes.com/2016/05/11/opinion/if-philosophy-wont-diversify-lets-call-it-what-it-really-is.html#permid=18491934.

31. George Joseph, *The Crest of the Peacock: Non-European Roots of Mathematics*, 3rd ed. (Princeton: Princeton University Press, 2010).

32. Josh Hill, comment on Jay Garfield and Bryan Van Norden, "If Philosophy Won't Diversify," *New York Times*, www.nytimes.com/2016/05/11/opinion/if-philosophy-wont-diversify-lets-call-it-what-it-really-is.html#permid=18495750.

33. Anthony Kennedy, Majority Opinion in *Obergefell v. Hodges* 576 U.S. 3 (2015).

34. Antonin Scalia, Dissenting Opinion in *Obergefell v. Hodges* 576 U.S. 8n22 (2015).

35. Ibid., 9. For a discussion of Kennedy's invocation of Confucius, Scalia's dissent, and Chinese reactions, see Bryan W. Van Norden, "Confucius on Gay Marriage," *Diplomat*, July 13, 2015, http://thediplomat.com/2015/07/confucius-on-gay-marriage/.

36. "The East Pediment: Information Sheet," www.supremecourt.gov/about/eastpediment.pdf.

37. Masimo Pigliucci, "On the Psuedo-Profundity of Some Eastern Philosophy," *Rationally Speaking*, May 23, 2006, http://rationallyspeaking.blogspot.com/2006/05/on-pseudo-profoundity-of-some-eastern.html.

38. Philip J. Ivanhoe and Bryan W. Van Norden, eds., *Readings in Classical Chinese Philosophy*, 2nd ed. (Indianapolis: Hackett, 2005), 65–66.

39. Ibid., 145.

40. Ibid., 223.

41. Ibid., 327–32, 339–51.

42. Justin Tiwald and Bryan W. Van Norden, *Readings in Later Chinese Philosophy: Han Dynasty to the 20th Century* (Indianapolis: Hackett, 2014), 101.

43. Ibid., 80–86. Discussed in chapter 2.

44. Ibid., 266–68. Discussed in chapter 2.

45. Ibid., 321–27.

46. Ibid., 375–85.

47. Ibid., 370–75.

48. For the relevant portion of *The Sutra of the Teaching of Vimalakirti*, see Robin R. Wang, ed., *Images of Women in Chinese Thought and Culture: Writings from the Pre-Qin Period Through the Song Dynasty* (Indianapolis: Hackett, 2003), 272–77. For Li Zhi and Li Dazhao, see Tiwald and Van Norden, *Readings in Later Chinese Philosophy*, 300–4 and 359–61, respectively.

49. John Maynard Keynes, *Two Memoirs* (London: Kelly Hart-Davis, 1949), 243–44. This passage was brought to my attention by Sarah Mattice.

50. Surama Dasgupta, *An Ever-Expanding Quest of Life and Knowledge* (New Delhi: Orient Longman, 1971), 74.

51. D. Kyle Peon, "Yes—Let's Call Philosophy What It Really Is," *Weekly Standard*, May 19, 2016, www.weeklystandard.com/yes-lets-call -philosophy-what-it-really-is/article/2002458.

52. Nicholas Tampio, "Not All Things Wise and Good Are Philosophy," *Aeon*, https://aeon.co/ideas/not-all-things-wise-and-good-are -philosophy. See Jay Garfield's foreword to this book for a detailed dissection of Tampio's essay.

53. Christopher Cullen, *Astronomy and Mathematics in Ancient China: The Zhou Bi Suan Jing* (New York: Cambridge University Press, 1996).

54. *Encyclopedia Britannica*, 11th ed., s.v. "Siger De Brabant" (Cambridge: Cambridge University Press, 1911).

55. Peter K. J. Park, *Africa, Asia, and the History of Philosophy: Racism in the Formation of the Philosophical Canon, 1780–1830* (Albany: State University of New York Press, 2013), 76.

56. Even if it turns out that, as a matter of historical fact, Greek philosophy developed in complete isolation from Indian and African philosophy, this would not demonstrate that the latter was not philosophy. The important point to learn from Park is that it is not an a priori truth that "all philosophy begins in Greece."

57. David E. Mungello, *The Great Encounter of China and the West, 1500–1800*, 3rd ed. (New York: Rowman and Littlefield, 2009), 100–4.

58. Leibniz, Introduction to *Novissima Sinica* (1697), cited in Franklin Perkins, *Leibniz and China: A Commerce of Light* (Cambridge: Cambridge University Press, 2007), 146.

59. For discussions, see Robert Louden, "'What Does Heaven Say?' Christian Wolff and Western Interpretations of Confucian Ethics," in *Confucius and the "Analects": New Essays*, ed. Bryan W. Van Norden (New York: Oxford University Press, 2002), 73–93; and Donald F. Lach, "The Sinophilism of Christian Wolff (1679–1754)," *Journal of the History of Ideas* 14, no. 4 (October 1953): 561–74.

60. Mungello, *The Great Encounter of China and the West*, 128.

61. Derk Bodde, "Chinese Ideas in the West," unpublished essay prepared for the Committee on Asiatic Studies in American Education (March 9, 1948), http://afe.easia.columbia.edu/chinawh/web/s10/ideas.pdf. (I am indebted to Mark Csikszentmihalyi for bringing Quesnay's interest in China to my attention.) On king Shun, see *Analects* 15.5.

62. Ronald Reagan quoted *Daodejing* 60 in his State of the Union Address on January 25, 1988, archived at *The American Presidency Project*, www .presidency.ucsb.edu/ws/index.php?pid=36035.

63. Park, *Africa, Asia, and the History of Philosophy*, 69–95.

64. Edward Said, *Orientalism* (New York: Vintage, 1994), 73–92.

65. Kant AA xxv.2 1187–1188, cited in Mark Larrimore, "Sublime Waste: Kant on the Destiny of the 'Races,'" *Canadian Journal of Philosophy*, supplemental volume 25 (1999): 111–12. I learned of Kant's discussion of race in his lectures on anthropology from an excellent talk by Peter K. J. Park, "Kant's Colonial Knowledge and His Greek Turn," American Philosophical Association, Baltimore, MD, January 6, 2017.

66. Immanuel Kant, *Observations on the Feeling of the Beautiful and the Sublime*, ed. Patrick Frierson and Paul Guyer (New York: Cambridge University Press, 2011), 61. If you really want to be horrified, see the passage from Hume that Kant approvingly quotes, ibid., 58*n*82.

67. Kant AA xxv.2 843, cited in Larrimore, "Sublime Waste," 111.

68. Immanuel Kant, *Physical Geography*, translated in Ching, "Chinese Ethics and Kant," 169. All of us interested in Kant's views on China are deeply indebted to Helmuth von Glasenapp, ed., *Kant und die Religionen des Ostens, Beihefte zum Jahrbuch der Albertus-Universität Königsberg/Pr.* 5 (Kitzingen-Main: Holzner, 1954).

69. Immanuel Kant, *Physical Geography*, cited in Gregory M. Reihman, "Categorically Denied: Kant's Criticism of Chinese Philosophy," *Journal of Chinese Philosophy* 11, no. 1 (March 2006): 63*n*22.

70. David E. Mungello, *Drowning Girls in China: Female Infanticide Since 1650* (New York: Rowman and Littlefield, 2008), 3. Infanticide by drowning (*never* hanging) was the preferred method in China, and it resulted in a quick death, as opposed to the European preference for infanticide by abandonment, which resulted in a slow, lingering death.

71. Ibid.

72. Mungello, *The Great Encounter of China and the West*, 134–39. For a more detailed discussion see Mungello, *Drowning Girls in China*, 14–62. Christian missionaries and Chinese Christian converts also took part in charitable efforts to save children (99–115).

73. G. W. F. Hegel, *Lectures on the History of Philosophy: Greek Philosophy to Plato*, trans. E. S. Haldane (Lincoln: University of Nebraska Press,

1995), 121. In their brilliant *The Nay Science: A History of German Indology* (New York: Oxford University Press, 2014), Vishwa Adluri and Joydeep Bagchee note that Hegel was also seminal in expelling Indian philosophical texts from the philosophical canon and relegating them solely to philology and social history.

74. G. W. F. Hegel, *Lectures on the Philosophy of History*, trans. Ruben Alvarado (Aalten, Netherlands: WordBridge, 2011), 124.

75. Theodor Mommsen, *The History of Rome*, trans. William Dickson, vol. 4 (New York: Scribner's, 1887), 726.

76. Alston Hurd Chase, *Time Remembered* (San Antonio: Parker, 1994), 2.1, www.pa59ers.com/library/Chase/time2–1n2.html.

77. Herbert Fingarette, *Confucius—the Secular as Sacred* (New York: Harper, 1972), vii.

78. Martin Heidegger, *What Is Philosophy?* trans. William Kluback and Jean T. Wilde (New York: Twayne, 1958), 29–31, cited in Park, *Africa, Asia, and the History of Philosophy*, 4. Heidegger's views on Asian philosophy varied over the course of his career. At one point, he began to collaborate on a translation of the *Daodejing*, which he said had anticipated his own philosophical views. However, his final view of philosophy was ethnocentric. See Taylor Carman and Bryan W. Van Norden, "Being-in-the-Way: A Review of *Heidegger and Asian Thought*," *Sino-Platonic Papers* 70 (February 1996): 24–34.

79. Du Xiaozhen and Zhang Ning, *Delida zai Zhongguo jiangyanlu* [Lectures by Derrida in China] (Beijing: Zhongyang Bianyi, 2002), 139, cited in Carine Defoort and Ge Zhaoguang, "Editors' Introduction," *Contemporary Chinese Thought* 37, no. 1 (Fall 2005): 3 and 9n14.

80. Gayatri Spivak, "Translator's Preface," in *Of Grammatology*, by Jacques Derrida, rev. ed. (Baltimore: Johns Hopkins University Press, 1998), lxxxii. For a detailed critique of Derrida's Orientalism, see Jin Suh Jirn, "A Sort of European Hallucination: On Derrida's 'Chinese Prejudice,'" *Situations* 8, no. 2 (2015): 67–83.

81. Eugene Park, "Why I Left Academia: Philosophy's Homogeneity Needs Rethinking," November 3, 2014, www.huffingtonpost.com/hippo-reads/why-i-left-academia_b_5735320.html.

82. Said, *Orientalism*, 40.

83. Ibid., 38.

84. Eric Schwitzgebel, "Why Don't We Know Our Chinese Philosophy?" *APA Newsletter on the Status of Asian and Asian-American Philosophers and Philosophies* 1, no. 1 (2001): 27.

85. Joel J. Kupperman, *Classic Asian Philosophy: A Guide to the Essential Texts* (New York: Oxford University Press, 2001), 58.

86. When you do read the *Analects* and *Daodejing*, I recommend translations that contextualize the texts for you. For the sayings of Confucius, I recommend Edward Slingerland's translation, *Analects: With Selections from Traditional Commentaries* (Indianapolis: Hackett, 2003). For the *Daodejing* (also written *Tao Te Ching*, the *Classic of the Way and Virtue*, attributed to Laozi), I strongly recommend you first read *carefully* the "Outline Introduction to the *Laozi*," by Wang Bi (226–249) in Richard John Lynne, trans., *The Classic of the Way and Virtue: A New Translation of the "Tao-te Ching" of Laozi as Interpreted by Wang Bi* (New York: Columbia University Press, 2004), and only then read the *Daodejing* itself. My bibliography of "Readings on Less Commonly Taught Philosophies" at http://bryanvannorden.com lists some anthologies of secondary essays that will also help with the *Analects* and the *Daodejing*. There are actually only a handful of passages in the *Changes* (*Yijing*, also written *I Ching*, the *Classic of Changes*) that are philosophically important. Just read the selections in Tiwald and Van Norden, *Readings in Later Chinese Philosophy*, 42–54.

87. Schwitzgebel, "Why Don't We Know Our Chinese Philosophy?" 26.

88. For selections from the *Analects*, *Daodejing*, *Mozi*, *Mengzi*, *Zhuangzi*, *Xunzi*, and *Hanfeizi*, see Ivanhoe and Van Norden, *Readings in Classical Chinese Philosophy*. On Shen Dao, see Eirik L. Harris, *The Shenzi Fragments: A Philosophical Analysis and Translation* (New York: Columbia University Press, 2016).

89. For selections, see Tiwald and Van Norden, *Readings in Later Chinese Philosophy*. In chapter 2, I discuss more specifically the philosophical interest of several Confucian, Buddhist, and Neo-Confucian philosophers.

90. Justin E. H. Smith, *The Philosopher: A History in Six Types* (Princeton: Princeton University Press, 2016), 2.

91. Ibid., 9.

92. Personal communication from Robin R. Wang, President of the SACP, June 4, 2016.

93. See www.mapforthegap.com/about.html.
94. Leiter, "Anglophone Departments Aren't 'Departments of European and American Philosophy.'"
95. Augustine (*City of God*, bk. 5, chap. 8) attributes the quoted phrase to Seneca (c. 4 BCE–65 CE), but Seneca (letter 108) is quoting a poem by Cleanthes (fl. 300 BCE).

2. TRADITIONS IN DIALOGUE

The epigraphs to chapter 2 are from Terence, *The Self-Tormentor*, act 1, scene 1, and Confucius, *Analects*, 12.5.

1. Machiavelli (1469–1527) is also a defensible choice as the founding figure of modern political philosophy.
2. See Descartes, "Third Set of Objections, by a Famous English Philosopher, with the Author's Replies," in *Philosophical Essays and Correspondence*, ed. Roger Ariew (Indianapolis: Hackett, 2000).
3. Thomas Hobbes, *Leviathan: Parts One and Two*, ed. Herbert W. Schneider (New York: Macmillan, 1958), "Of Darkness from Vain Philosophy and Fabulous Traditions," 9. (For the sake of readability, I omitted a parenthesis present in the original quotation.)
4. David Hume (1711–76) has a particularly interesting critique of substantialist views of the self that has been compared to Buddhist views. For what I think is a decisive critique of Buddhist interpretations of Hume, see Ricki Bliss, "On Being Humean About the Emptiness of Causation," in *The Moon Points Back*, ed. Yasuo Deguchi, Jay Garfield, Graham Priest, and Koji Tanaka (New York: Oxford University Press, 2015), 67–96.
5. More precisely, Descartes argued that both souls and physical objects are dependent for their existence on a third substance, God.
6. Aristotle, *Categories*, 1.5.
7. Aristotle wrestles with the notion of substance, seemingly without reaching any resolution, in *Metaphysics*, book 6.
8. René Descartes, *Meditations on First Philosophy*, trans. Donald A. Cress, 3rd ed. (Indianapolis: Hackett, 1993), second meditation, 21.
9. Aristotle, *Metaphysics*, 7.3.
10. Descartes, *Meditations*, 22. Yes, he says "robots" (*automata*). Simple

mechanical automata existed in seventeenth-century Europe, and were much discussed.

11. Ibid.

12. Ibid., 21.

13. For a very readable survey of some major approaches to this topic, see John Perry, *A Dialogue on Personal Identity and Immortality* (Indianapolis: Hackett, 1978).

14. Descartes, *Meditations*, 21.

15. Jay Garfield, *Engaging Buddhism: Why It Matters to Philosophy* (New York: Oxford University Press, 2015), 122–74.

16. N. K. G. Mendis, trans., *The Questions of King Milinda: An Abridgement of the Milindpañha* (Kandy, Sri Lanka: Buddhist Publication Society, 1993), 29. Cf. Peter Harvey, trans., *Questions of King Milinda*, in *Buddhist Philosophy: Essential Readings*, ed. William Edelglass and Jay Garfield (New York: Oxford University Press, 2009), 272.

17. Mendis, *Questions of King Milinda*, 30.

18. Peter Harvey, trans., "Extract from the *Mahā-nidāna Sutta*, the 'Great Discourse on Causal Links,'" in Edelglass and Garfield, *Buddhist Philosophy*, 271. The Buddha's position does not need to reject the mind-body identity thesis (that our mental states are somehow identical with physical states). Instead, his argument can be interpreted as a dilemma: the claim that the self is identical with physical states as we ordinarily understand them violates our intuition that the self is conscious; the claim that the self is identical with physical states that are also conscious states is vulnerable to the arguments given in the body of the text against identifying the self with conscious states.

19. Devamitta Thera, ed., *Aṅguttara-nikāya* (Colombo, Sri Lanka: Pali Text Society, 1929), 700, quoted in Walpola Rahula, *What the Buddha Taught*, rev. ed. (New York: Grove Weidenfeld, 1974), 25–26.

20. Plato, *Cratylus* 402a, quoted in Daniel W. Graham, "Heraclitus," *Stanford Encyclopedia of Philosophy* (Fall 2015 ed.), ed. Edward N. Zalta, http://plato.stanford.edu/archives/fall2015/entries/heraclitus/.

21. Mendis, *Questions of King Milinda*, 47–48.

22. Ibid., 48–49.

23. Ibid., 29. Cf. Harvey, *Questions of King Milinda*, 272.

24. Mendis, *Questions of King Milinda*, 30.

25. Ibid., 31. Cf. Harvey, *Questions of King Milinda*, 273.

26. Mendis, *Questions of King Milinda*, 31.

27. Ibid.

28. I am expressing my own opinion about how the doctrine of no-self should be applied to abortion. Buddhist clergy, philosophers, and laity do not have a unified stance on this topic. For a sampling of perspectives, see Damien Keown, *Buddhism and Bioethics* (New York: Macmillan, 1995); Michael G. Barnhart, "Buddhism and the Morality of Abortion," *Journal of Buddhist Ethics* 5 (1998): 276–97; William R. LaFleur, *Liquid Life: Abortion and Buddhism in Japan* (Princeton: Princeton University Press, 1994); Damien Keown, ed., *Buddhism and Abortion* (Honolulu: University of Hawaii Press, 1998).

29. The two major philosophical schools of Mahāyāna are Madhyamaka and Yogacara. Fazang is a figure in Huayan Buddhism, which is largely Madhyamaka, but (like Chinese Buddhism in general) tends to be syncretic. See Jay L. Garfield and Jan Westerhoff, *Yogacara and Madhyamaka: Allies or Rivals?* (New York: Oxford University Press, 2015).

30. Fazang, "The Rafter Dialogue," in *Readings in Later Chinese Philosophy: Han Dynasty to the 20th Century*, ed. Justin Tiwald and Bryan W. Van Norden (Indianapolis: Hackett, 2014), 80–86.

31. Fazang, "Essay on the Golden Lion," in Tiwald and Van Norden, *Readings in Later Chinese Philosophy*, 88. "Cause" here is often translated as "condition," because the notion is broader than our concept of efficient causation. As the example of the rafter and the building suggests, "condition" includes conceptual dependence.

32. See James Gleick, *Chaos: Making a New Science* (New York: Penguin, 2008), 321–22.

33. Ibid., 9–31.

34. As Francis C. Cook explains, "my 'fatherness' is completely dependence [*sic*] on the 'sonness' of my son to the same extent that his 'sonness' is dependent on my 'fatherness.'" *Hua-yen Buddhism: The Jewel Net of Indra* (State Park: Pennsylvania State University Press, 1977), 83.

35. Hobbes, *Leviathan*, chap. 4, 39.

36. Ibid., chap. 14, 112 (italics in original). It has been disputed whether Hobbes is a strict psychological egoist. At the least, Hobbes thinks human benevolence and sympathy, if they do exist, are so weak that they

cannot play any substantial role in justifying or maintaining a political system.

37. Ibid., chap. 13, 105.

38. Ibid., chap. 14, 110.

39. Ibid., chap. 13, 105.

40. Ibid., chap. 13, 107. The phrase "state of nature" was coined by John Locke (1632–1704), but it is also used to describe other positions that appeal to the state of humans prior to government.

41. This is only a partial analogy, since what makes *The Walking Dead* interesting is that it explores the ways in which benevolence, integrity, and loyalty can find a place even in the most desperate situations. However, the primary characters repeatedly encounter people who have been reduced to a genuinely Hobbesian state, like the citizens of Terminus. (Sorry for the spoiler, but, come on, you *knew* Terminus was going to be a bad place. It's called "Terminus," after all.) The classic *Twilight Zone* episode "The Shelter" (1961) gives a brief and chilling expression of a Hobbesian view of human nature, suggesting what would happen among suburban neighbors during a nuclear attack if there were not enough room in the fallout shelter for all of them.

42. Hobbes, *Leviathan*, chap. 14, 110 (this entire passage is in italics in the original).

43. Ibid., chap. 17, 139.

44. Ibid., chap. 15, 120.

45. *Analects* 2.3 in Philip J. Ivanhoe and Bryan W. Van Norden, eds., *Readings in Classical Chinese Philosophy*, 2nd ed. (Indianapolis: Hackett, 2005), 5.

46. "Ritual" (or "rites") is one of the most intriguing concepts that Confucianism can offer Western philosophy. For discussions, see Herbert Fingarette, *Confucius: The Secular as Sacred* (New York: HarperCollins, 1972); Kwong-loi Shun, "*Ren* and *Li* in the *Analects*," in *Confucius and the "Analects": New Essays*, ed. Bryan W. Van Norden (New York: Oxford University Press, 2002), 53–72.

47. *Mengzi* 1A1, in Ivanhoe and Van Norden, *Readings in Classical Chinese Philosophy*, 117–18.

48. *Mengzi* 2A6, in Ivanhoe and Van Norden, *Readings in Classical Chinese Philosophy*, 129.

49. *Mengzi* 7B16, in Ivanhoe and Van Norden, *Readings in Classical Chinese Philosophy*, 155. More literally, the Chinese states "humaneness [rén 仁] is human [rén 人]."

50. Martin L. Hoffman, *Empathy and Moral Development* (New York: Cambridge University Press, 2001).

51. Charles Darwin, *The Descent of Man* (Amherst, NY: Prometheus, 1998), pt. 1, chaps. 4–5, 100–38.

52. A classic essay on this topic is Robert L. Trivers, "The Evolution of Reciprocal Altruism," *Quarterly Review of Biology* 46 (1971): 35–57. Trivers's paper is often misinterpreted as arguing that seemingly altruistic actions are actually self-interested; however, his actual view is that *"the emotion of sympathy has been selected* to motivate altruistic behavior; . . . crudely put, the greater the potential benefit to the *recipient*, the greater the sympathy and the more likely the altruistic gesture, even to strange or disliked individuals" (49, emphasis mine).

53. *Mengzi* 3B9, in Ivanhoe and Van Norden, *Readings in Classical Chinese Philosophy*, 134–35.

54. *Mengzi* 1A7, in Ivanhoe and Van Norden, *Readings in Classical Chinese Philosophy*, 122.

55. *Analects* 12.18, in Ivanhoe and Van Norden, *Readings in Classical Chinese Philosophy*, 37.

56. Tiwald and Van Norden, *Readings in Later Chinese Philosophy*, 201. "Substance" here is literally "body." It is not being used in quite the same sense as "substance" in the Western tradition, but the differences are not important for grasping the basics of the argument.

57. Tiwald and Van Norden, *Readings in Later Chinese Philosophy*, 88. "Dharma" here refers to an instance of one of the Five Aggregates.

58. For the Confucian critique, see Han Yu, "A Memorandum on a Bone of the Buddha," and Lu Xiangshan, "Letter to Wang Shunbo"; for a Buddhist response, see Huiyuan, *On Why Buddhist Monks Do Not Bow Down Before Kings*, all in Tiwald and Van Norden, *Readings in Later Chinese Philosophy*.

59. Tiwald and Van Norden, *Readings in Later Chinese Philosophy*, 152.

60. Ibid., 174.

61. President Barack Obama, "Remarks by the President at a Campaign Event in Roanoke, VA," White House Office of the Press Secretary,

July 13, 2012, www.whitehouse.gov/the-press-office/2012/07/13/remarks
-president-campaign-event-roanoke-virginia.

62. Some of the outraged businessmen that Republicans paraded before
the media had benefited extensively from government contracts. See
Andrew Rosenthal, "You Didn't Build That," *New York Times*, July 27,
2012, http://takingnote.blogs.nytimes.com/2012/07/27/you-didnt-build
-that/.

63. Although *Robinson Crusoe* has become a symbol for the possibilities of
individual achievement, those who have actually read the novel know
that it is more about how very dependent we are upon the civilization
we have inherited (symbolized by the things Crusoe salvages from the
shipwreck he survived) and faith in God. (There is also an imperialistic
subtext in the work.)

64. On the similarities and differences between Hobbes and the Mohists,
see Bryan W. Van Norden, *Virtue Ethics and Consequentialism in Early
Chinese Philosophy* (New York: Cambridge University Press, 2007), 163.
See also Angus C. Graham, *Disputers of the Tao* (La Salle, IL: Open
Court, 1989), 45–46.

65. Eirik L. Harris, trans., *The Shenzi Fragments: A Philosophical Analysis
and Translation* (New York: Columbia University Press, 2016).

66. My formulation differs in its details from MacIntyre, *After Virtue*, 3rd
ed. (Notre Dame: University of Notre Dame Press, 2007), 51–61. However, I think he would recognize my version.

67. Jean Baptiste Molière, *The Hypochondriac*, trans. A. R. Waller, in *The
Plays of Molière* (Edinburgh: John Grant, 1907), vol. 2, section 5, 235.
Molière's play premiered 1673. In 1651, Hobbes had applied the same
critique to the Aristotelian explanation of "heaviness": "But if you ask
what they mean by *heaviness*, they will define it to be an endeavor
to go to the center of the earth. So that the cause why things sink
downward is an endeavor to be below—which is as much as to say
that bodies descend or ascend because they do." Hobbes, *Leviathan*,
chap. 46, 13.

68. Descartes, *Meditations*, third meditation, 31.

69. Thomas Hobbes, "An Answer to Bishop Bramhall's Book," in *The English Works of Thomas Hobbes of Malmesbury*, ed. William Molesworth,
vol. 4 (London: John Bohn, 1840), 299.

70. Patrick Suppes, "Aristotle's Concept of Matter and Its Relation to Modern Concepts of Matter," *Synthese* 28 (1974): 27–50. See chapter 4 for more on Aristotle's contributions to the development of science.

71. See Jean-Paul Sartre, "The Humanism of Existentialism," in *Existentialism: Basic Writings*, ed. Charles Guignon and Derk Pereboom (Indianapolis: Hackett, 2001), 290–308. For an alternative formulation of a very similar position, see R. M. Hare, "A Moral Argument," from *Freedom and Reason*, 1963, reprinted in *Twentieth Century Ethical Theory*, ed. Steven M. Cahn and Joram G. Haber (Upper Saddle River, NJ: Prentice-Hall, 1995), 386–99.

72. The literature on this topic is already immense, but in addition to MacIntyre's *After Virtue*, some of the seminal works include Elizabeth Anscombe, "Modern Moral Philosophy," *Philosophy* 33 (1958): 1–19; Philippa Foot, *Virtues and Vices* (Hoboken, NJ: Blackwell, 1978); Rosalind Hursthouse, *On Virtue Ethics* (New York: Oxford University Press, 1999); John McDowell, "Virtue and Reason," *Monist* 62 (1979): 331–50; Iris Murdoch, *The Sovereignty of Good*, 2nd ed. (London: Routledge, 2001); Martha Nussbaum, "Non-Relative Virtues: An Aristotelian Approach," in *The Quality of Life*, ed. Martha C. Nussbaum and Amartya Sen (New York: Oxford University Press, 1993), 242–70; Michael Slote, *From Morality to Virtue* (New York: Oxford University Press, 1992); and Christine Swanton, *Virtue Ethics* (New York: Oxford University Press, 2003).

73. Aristotle, *Nicomachean Ethics*, trans. Terence Irwin (Indianapolis: Hackett, 1985), 33–34 (ii.1, 1103a).

74. Ibid., 34 (ii.1, 1103a–b).

75. Ibid., 40 (ii.4, 1105b).

76. Ibid. (ii.4).

77. *Mengzi* 4B19, translation slightly modified from Ivanhoe and Van Norden, *Readings in Classical Chinese Philosophy*, 140.

78. See Lee H. Yearley, *Mencius and Aquinas: Theories of Virtue and Conceptions of Courage* (Albany: State University of New York Press, 1990), 59–61; Philip J. Ivanhoe, *Confucian Moral Self Cultivation*, 2nd ed. (Indianapolis: Hackett, 2000), 17–18, 32–33, 59–60, 101–102; and Jonathan Schofer, "Virtues in Xunzi's Thought," in *Virtue, Nature, and Agency in the "Xunzi,"* ed. Thornton Kline and Philip J. Ivanhoe (Indianapolis: Hackett, 2000), 71–72.

79. *Xunzi*, "An Exhortation to Learning," cited in Ivanhoe and Van Norden, *Readings in Classical Chinese Philosophy*, 256. I think Confucius himself viewed moral cultivation as re-formation, but this would be heatedly disputed by many interpreters.

80. *Xunzi*, "Human Nature Is Bad," cited in Ivanhoe and Van Norden, *Readings in Classical Chinese Philosophy*, 298.

81. *Xunzi*, "An Exhortation to Learning," cited in Ivanhoe and Van Norden, *Readings in Classical Chinese Philosophy*, 260.

82. See Eric Schwitzgebel, "Human Nature and Moral Development in Mencius, Xunzi, Hobbes, and Rousseau," *History of Philosophy Quarterly* 24 (2007): 147–68. I borrow the terminology of "the what" and "the why" of ethics from Myles Burnyeat, "Aristotle on Learning to Be Good," in *Essays on Aristotle's Ethics*, ed. A. O. Rorty (Berkeley: University of California Press, 1980), 69–92.

83. See Jean-Jacques Rousseau, *Émile: Or On Education*, trans. Allan Bloom (New York: Basic, 1979); and Martha C. Nussbaum, *Not for Profit: Why Democracy Needs the Humanities* (Princeton: Princeton University Press, 2012), 27–46 (passim).

84. *Mengzi* 1A7, in Ivanhoe and Van Norden, *Readings in Classical Chinese Philosophy*, 119.

85. *Mengzi* 1A7, in Ivanhoe and Van Norden, *Readings in Classical Chinese Philosophy*, 120.

86. David Wong, "Reasons and Analogical Reasoning in Mengzi," in *Essays on the Moral Philosophy of Mengzi*, ed. Xiusheng Liu and Philip J. Ivanhoe (Indianapolis: Hackett, 2002), 187–220.

87. This is suggested by the seminal essay on this passage, David S. Nivison, "Motivation and Moral Action in Mencius," in *The Ways of Confucianism*, ed. Bryan W. Van Norden (La Salle, IL: Open Court, 1996), 91–119.

88. *Mozi* 45, "Lesser Selections," translation mine but see Nivison, "Motivation and Moral Action in Mencius," 97–98, for the comparison of Mengzi's use of the term and the Mohist one.

89. Edward Slingerland argues plausibly that "In order to engage in or guide an abstract process such as education or self-cultivation, we must *inevitably* make reference to some sort of metaphorical schema, and the schema we invoke will have entailments that will serve as important determinants of our practical behavior." Slingerland, *Effortless Action:*

Wu-Wei as Conceptual Metaphor and Spiritual Ideal in Early China (New York: Oxford University Press, 2003), 270 (emphasis in original).

90. Lu Xiangshan, *Recorded Sayings*, cited in Tiwald and Van Norden, *Readings in Later Chinese Philosophy*, 253.

91. Prichard, "Does Moral Philosophy Rest on a Mistake?" in Cahn and Haber, *Twentieth Century Ethical Theory*, 47.

92. Ibid., 43n7.

93. Fans of modern Western ethics will no doubt argue that I have given short shrift to more subtle intuitionists like Henry Sidgwick (1838–1900) or naturalists like Hume, who argue that practical reasoning has a substantial role to play in regard to means-end reasoning and clarifying the nature of potential objects of our intuitions or emotions. I agree that I need to say more to explain why I don't find accounts like theirs satisfactory. However, as I note at the end of this chapter, the point is not whether we agree about who is right in the philosophical debate among Buddhists, Confucians, Aristotelians, intuitionists, and naturalists. What is important is to admit that it is a *philosophical* debate.

94. *Great Learning*, commentary 6, in Tiwald and Van Norden, *Readings in Later Chinese Philosophy*, 191–92. The commentary section of the *Great Learning* is traditionally attributed to Confucius's disciple Zengzi (early fifth century BCE); however, more recent scholarship suggests that it is of unknown authorship and dates from the late third century BCE.

95. See *Analects* 10.8 and *Analects* 1.3, 2.8, respectively.

96. For example, Wing-tsit Chan has "love a beautiful color." *A Source Book in Chinese Philosophy*, trans. Wing-tsit Chan (Princeton: Princeton University Press, 1963), 89. Chan's *Source Book* was a great achievement for its era. However, his translations have largely been superseded. Similar comments apply to Yu-lan Fung, *A History of Chinese Philosophy*, trans. Derk Bodde, 2 vols. (Princeton: Princeton University Press, 1952). See my bibliography of readings on the less commonly taught philosophies at http://bryanvannorden.com for better choices.

97. *Analects* 9.18. The orthodox commentary of Zhu Xi explicitly links this passage to the *Great Learning*: "Loving a lovely sight and hating a hateful odor are Sincerity. Loving Virtue like one loves sex—this is to Sincerely love Virtue. However, people are seldom able to do this." Zhu

Xi, *Lunyu jizhu*, commentary on *Analects* 9.18, cited in Tiwald and Van Norden, *Readings in Later Chinese Philosophy*, 191*n*44.

98. One might argue that this example is intrinsically sexist. It certainly assumes what critic Laura Mulvey referred to as "the male gaze," in her classic essay "Visual Pleasure and Narrative Cinema," *Screen* 16, no. 3 (1975): 6–18. The authors of the *Great Learning* and over two millennia of Confucian commentators typically envisioned the "lovely sight" in question as a beautiful woman, a woman who was excluded from higher education and public office, and whose sexuality was a potentially dangerous distraction from Virtue. However, the situation is more complex than it appears at first. Generations of Confucians were quite aware that many an emperor was led to disaster by the influence of a handsome *male* lover. Furthermore, both male and female readers today can sympathize with the example of being drawn to someone erotically, even though they will conceptualize it according to their own tastes.

99. Wang Yangming, "Questions on the *Great Learning*," cited in Tiwald and Van Norden, *Readings in Later Chinese Philosophy*, 241–42 (glosses in original translation).

100. There is a classic debate in ethics over unity vs. conflict as ideals of psychological health. When Jesus demands that a demon name itself, it replies, "My name *is* Legion: for we are many" (Mark 5:9, KJV). This suggests that the evil are divided within themselves. On the other hand, Walt Whitman celebrates psychic conflict when he asks, "Do I contradict myself? / Very well then I contradict myself, / (I am large, I contain multitudes.)" "Song of Myself."

101. Cheng Yi, *Er Chengji* (Beijing: Zhonghua shuju, 2004), 1:16, cited in Tiwald and Van Norden, *Readings in Later Chinese Philosophy*, 159.

102. *Great Learning*, classic, in Tiwald and Van Norden, *Readings in Later Chinese Philosophy*, 189 (emphasis mine).

103. Zhu Xi, *Zhuzi yulei* (Beijing: Zhonghua shuju, 1986), 1:148, cited in Tiwald and Van Norden, *Readings in Later Chinese Philosophy*, 181.

104. David S. Nivison was the first to note the significance of weakness of will as an issue in Chinese philosophy. See especially "The Philosophy of Wang Yangming," in *The Ways of Confucianism*, by David S. Nivison, ed. Bryan W. Van Norden (Chicago: Open Court, 1996), 249–60.

105. Wang Yangming, *A Record for Practice* (*Chuan xi lu*), §5, cited in Tiwald and Van Norden, *Readings in Later Chinese Philosophy*, 267.

106. Wang Yangming, *A Record for Practice*, §5, cited in Tiwald and Van Norden, *Readings in Later Chinese Philosophy*, 267.

107. One of the classic Western essays on internalism is Donald Davidson, "How Is Weakness of the Will Possible?" in *Essays on Actions and Events*, 2nd ed. (New York: Clarendon, 2001), 21–42. Intriguingly, Davidson thanks David S. Nivison, a leading scholar of Chinese philosophy, in the acknowledgments to this anthology (xx).

108. Wang Yangming, *A Record for Practice*, §5, cited in Tiwald and Van Norden, *Readings in Later Chinese Philosophy*, 267 (italics in original translation).

109. Frank Jackson, "Epiphenomenal Qualia," *Philosophical Quarterly* 32, no. 127 (1982): 127–36.

110. Wang Yangming, *A Record for Practice*, §5, cited in Tiwald and Van Norden, *Readings in Later Chinese Philosophy*, 268.

111. Wang Yangming, *A Record for Practice*, §5, cited in Tiwald and Van Norden, *Readings in Later Chinese Philosophy*, 268 (glosses in original translation).

112. Nivison, "The Philosophy of Wang Yangming," 218.

113. Wang Yangming, *A Record for Practice*, §5, cited in Tiwald and Van Norden, *Readings in Later Chinese Philosophy*, 268.

114. Eric Schwitzgebel, "The Moral Behavior of Ethicists and the Role of the Philosopher," in *Experimental Ethics*, ed. H. Rusch, M. Uhl, and C. Luetge (New York: Palgrave, 2014); Schwitzgebel, "Do Ethicists Steal More Books?" *Philosophical Psychology* 22 (2009): 711–25; Schwitzgebel, "Are Ethicists Any More Likely to Pay Their Registration Fees at Professional Meetings?" *Economics and Philosophy* 29 (2013): 371–80; Eric Schwitzgebel and Joshua Rust, "The Moral Behavior of Ethics Professors: Relationships Among Self-Reported Behavior, Expressed Normative Attitude, and Directly Observed Behavior," *Philosophical Psychology* 27 (2014): 293–327; Schwitzgebel and Rust, "Do Ethicists and Political Philosophers Vote More Often Than Other Professors?" *Review of Philosophy and Psychology* 1 (2010): 189–99; Schwitzgebel and Rust, "The Self-Reported Moral Behavior of Ethics Professors," *Philosophical Psychology* 27 (2014): 293–327; Schwitzgebel and Rust, "Ethicists' and Non-Ethicists' Responsiveness to Student Emails: Relationships Among Expressed Normative Attitude, Self-Described Behavior, and

Experimentally Observed Behavior," *Metaphilosophy* 44 (2013): 350–71; Eric Schwitzgebel, Joshua Rust, Linus Huang, Alan Moore, and Justin Coates, "Ethicists' Courtesy at Philosophy Conferences," *Philosophical Psychology* 35 (2012): 331–40.

115. *Analects* 2.15, cited in Ivanhoe and Van Norden, *Readings in Classical Chinese Philosophy*, 6.

116. Ivanhoe, *Confucian Moral Self Cultivation*.

117. Zhu Xi, *Zhuzi yulei*, 190, cited in Tiwald and Van Norden, *Readings in Later Chinese Philosophy*, 184.

118. James Maffie, *Aztec Philosophy: Understanding a World in Motion* (Boulder: University Press of Colorado, 2014).

119. Thomas M. Norton-Smith, *The Dance of Person and Place: One Interpretation of American Indian Philosophy* (Albany: State University of New York Press, 2010).

120. Dale Turner, *This Is Not a Peace Pipe: Toward a Critical Indigenous Philosophy* (Toronto: University of Toronto Press, 2006).

121. Anne Waters, ed., *American Indian Thought* (Hoboken, NJ: Wiley-Blackwell, 2003).

122. Kwame Gyekye, *An Essay on African Philosophical Thought: The Akan Conceptual Scheme*, rev. ed. (Cambridge: Cambridge University Press, 1995).

123. Kwazi Wiredu, *Philosophy and an African Culture* (New York: Cambridge University Press, 1980).

3. TRUMP'S PHILOSOPHERS

The epigraphs to chapter 3 are from Donald J. Trump, Announcement of Presidential Candidacy, June 16, 2015, New York, NY; Mao Zedong, "Mount Liupan," translation mine but see Willis Barnstone, ed., *The Poems of Mao Zedong* (Los Angeles: University of California Press, 1972), 68–69 for the Chinese text and an alternative translation; Richard Nixon, "Exchange with Reporters at the Great Wall of China," February 24, 1972. (In context, Nixon's comment is not as silly as it sounds.)

1. 近平, "青年要自觉践行社会主义核心价值观" (speech delivered May 4, 2014, uploaded July 20, 2015), http://cpc.people.com.cn/xuexi/n/2015/0720/c397563-27331773.html. Translation mine.

2. Days after the election, Trump acknowledged that it could be "part wall, part fence" (interview with Lesley Stahl, "The 45th President," *60 Minutes*, aired November 13, 2016). A few weeks after that, he admitted that parts of the border do not need a wall "because you have, you know, you have mountains, you have other things" (interview with Sean Hannity, *Fox News*, December 1, 2016, http://insider.foxnews.com/2016/12/01/donald -trump-hannity-his-election-victory-message-protesters). This version of Trump's plan would involve no change from current policy, since the border already has a combination of walls, fences, and natural barriers.

3. Trump, Announcement of Presidential Candidacy.

4. Ana Gonzalez-Barrera, "Migration Flows Between the US and Mexico Have Slowed—and Turned Toward Mexico," *Pew Research Center*, November 19, 2015, www.pewhispanic.org/2015/11/19/chapter-1-migration -flows-between-the-u-s-and-mexico-have-slowed-and-turned-toward -mexico/#number-of-unauthorized-mexican-immigrants-declines.

5. Richard Pérez-Peña, "Contrary to Trump's Claims, Immigrants Are Less Likely to Commit Crimes," *New York Times*, January 26, 2017, www .nytimes.com/2017/01/26/us/trump-illegal-immigrants-crime.html.

6. The prevalence of the us vs. them mindset is illustrated by a comment from Representative Robert Pittenger (R, NC). When asked what motivated those who protested a police shooting in Charlotte, he asserted: "The grievance in their minds is—the animus, the anger—they hate white people because white people are successful and they're not." "NC Congressman: 'Protestors Hate White People Because They're Successful,'" *New York Post*, September 22, 2016, http://nypost.com/2016 /09/22/nc-congressman-protesters-hate-white-people-because-theyre -successful/. (Videos and photographs show what is clearly a multiracial group of protestors.)

7. Since the election, some conservatives have crowed that Trump's victory shows how out of touch the intellectual elite is with mainstream America. See Charles C. Camosy, "Trump Won Because College-Educated Americans Are out of Touch," *Washington Post*, November 9, 2016, www.washingtonpost.com/posteverything/wp/2016/11/09/trump-won -because-college-educated-americans-are-out-of-touch/. However, the reality is that 53 percent of those who voted opposed Donald Trump, Clinton won the plurality of the popular vote, and she won "big league"

among both Americans under thirty and people of color (who constitute the fastest-growing share of the US population). The future does not look bright for those who supported Trump.

8. Bob Herbert, "Righting Reagan's Wrongs?" *New York Times*, November 13, 2007, www.nytimes.com/2007/11/13/opinion/13herbert.html.

9. Alexander P. Lamis, ed., *Southern Politics in the 1990s* (Baton Rouge: Louisiana State University Press, 1999), 8. The Atwater interview was not noticed by the mainstream media until it was cited in an editorial by Bob Herbert, "Impossible, Ridiculous, Repugnant," *New York Times*, October 6, 2005, www.nytimes.com/2005/10/06/opinion/impossible-ridiculous-repugnant.html. The audio recording of the interview is archived at Rick Perlstein, "Exclusive: Lee Atwater's Infamous 1981 Interview on the Southern Strategy," *Nation*, November 13, 2012, www.thenation.com/article/exclusive-lee-atwaters-infamous-1981-interview-southern-strategy/.

10. Andrew Jacobs, "Confucius Statue Vanishes Near Tiananmen Square," *New York Times*, April 22, 2011, www.nytimes.com/2011/04/23/world/asia/23confucius.html.

11. I have visited Mao's mausoleum on several occasions. On each visit, I have been told that the body is not available for viewing because it is being "cleaned." I am beginning to think that he just doesn't want to see me.

12. Chris Buckley, "Mocking Mao Backfires for Chinese TV Host," *Sinosphere*, blog, *New York Times*, April 9, 2015, http://sinosphere.blogs.nytimes.com/2015/04/09/joking-about-mao-lands-tv-host-in-hot-water/.

13. Nonetheless, the amount of support for Mao, at least as a symbol, is often surprising to first-time visitors to China. A nontrivial number of young people, who have no firsthand knowledge of the Cultural Revolution, actually seem nostalgic about it. See Kiki Zhao, "Graduates' Red Guard Photos Cast Doubts on What They Learned," *Sinosphere*, blog, *New York Times*, June 26, 2014, http://sinosphere.blogs.nytimes.com/2014/06/26/graduates-red-guard-photos-cast-doubt-on-what-they-learned/. I have even met intellectuals who were "rusticated" during the Cultural Revolution (sent to do hard labor in the countryside) who feel that China under Mao had a positive moral spirit that is lacking in China today.

14. Paul Gewirtz, "Xi, Mao, and China's Search for a Usable Past," *China File*, January 14, 2014, www.chinafile.com/reporting-opinion/viewpoint /xi-mao-and-chinas-search-usable-past.

15. See, for example, Charles Taylor, *The Ethics of Authenticity* (Cambridge: Harvard University Press, 1992).

16. Fu Danni, "Life Is Meaningless, Say China's Top Students," *Sixth Tone*, November 23, 2016, www.sixthtone.com/news/life-meaningless-say -china's-top-students.

17. This is very similar to the view developed in *Mengzi* 6A15, cited in Philip J. Ivanhoe and Bryan W. Van Norden, eds., *Readings in Classical Chinese Philosophy*, 2nd ed. (Indianapolis: Hackett, 2005), 151.

18. Milan Kundera, *The Book of Laughter and Forgetting*, trans. Aaron Asher (New York: Harper Perennial, 1996), 4.

19. I originally developed the ideas in the preceding paragraph in "Zhuangzi's Ironic Detachment and Political Commitment," *Dao* 15, no. 1 (March 2016): 1–17.

20. I was the only philosopher at the conference who was not Chinese. When I showed my son the official group photograph of the conference, he quipped, "Where's Waldo?"

21. Chris Buckley and Didi Tatlow, "Cultural Revolution Steeled a Schoolboy, Now China's Leader," *New York Times*, September 25, 2015, www.nytimes .com/2015/09/25/world/asia/xi-jinping-china-cultural-revolution.html. After the Cultural Revolution, Xi studied chemical engineering and later earned an LLD from Tsinghua University (the MIT of China).

22. 我觉得我们当时那一代青年成长履历就是红卫兵时代跟着激动，那是一种情绪，那是一种氛围；到了文化革命理想破灭，最后变得甚至是一种虚无的。(央视《东方时空》省委书记系列专访:习近平) November 16, 2003, http://news.sina.com.cn/c/2003-11-16/11182145564.shtml. My thanks to Professor Wu Wanwei for locating the Chinese original of this quotation. English translation from Jonathan Watts, "Choice of 'Princeling' as the Country's Next President Came as a Shock to Many," *Guardian*, October 26, 2007, www.theguardian.com/world/2007 /oct/26/china.uknews4.

23. Max Fisher, "Trump, Taiwan and China: The Controversy, Explained," *New York Times*, December 3, 2016, www.nytimes.com/2016/12/03/ world/asia/trump-taiwan-and-china-the-controversy-explained.html.

24. See Chris Buckley, "Xi Touts Communist Party as Defender of Confucius's Virtues," *Sinosphere*, blog, *New York Times*, February 13, 2014, http://sinosphere.blogs.nytimes.com/2014/02/13/xi-touts-communist-party-as-defender-of-confuciuss-virtues/.

25. Xi Jinping, *How to Read Confucius and Other Chinese Classical Thinkers*, ed. Fenzhi Zhang (Jericho, NY: CN Times Books, 2015), 55. (This book consists of brief excerpts from Xi's speeches where he mentions classical Chinese texts, along with the editor's comments.) Xi is quoting *Analects* 2:1; translation from Ivanhoe and Van Norden, *Readings in Classical Chinese Philosophy*, 5. On the Confucian emphasis on rule by moral suasion rather than brute force, see chapter 2.

26. Xi, *How to Read Confucius*, 101–2. Xi was quoting the *Great Learning*, commentary 3, which states that the sage-king Tang had the following phrase inscribed on his bathtub: "Genuinely renew yourself daily. Day by day renew yourself, and continue to do so each day." As Zhu Xi (1130–1200) explains, the sage meant that "people cleanse their minds to remove evil just like they bathe their bodies to remove dirt." See Zhu Xi, *Daxue jizhu* (translation mine).

27. Xi, *How to Read Confucius*, 264–65. Xi is quoting *Analects* 2.4; translation from Ivanhoe and Van Norden, *Readings in Classical Chinese Philosophy*, 5. He does exactly the same thing with the phrase "at fifty, I understood Heaven's mandate" (also from *Analects* 2.4) in commemorating the fiftieth anniversary of the establishment of diplomatic relations between China and France (Xi, *How to Read Confucius*, 168–69).

28. Xi, *How to Read Confucius*, 185–86. Xi is quoting *Analects* 13.20; translation from Ivanhoe and Van Norden, *Readings in Classical Chinese Philosophy*, 40.

29. *Mengzi* 4B11, cited in Ivanhoe and Van Norden, *Readings in Classical Chinese Philosophy*, 139.

30. Kant, "On a Supposed Right to Lie Because of Philanthropic Concern," in *Grounding for the Metaphysics of Morals*, trans. James W. Ellington, 3rd ed. (Indianapolis: Hackett, 1993).

31. 习近平, "青年要自觉践行社会主义核心价值观." Translation mine. These quotations are largely drawn from the *Analects* of Confucius, and the *Mengzi*, but some are from other classics, including the *Classic of Changes* and *Record of Rites*.

32. Ahmed Ali, trans., *Al-Qur'an: A Contemporary Translation* (Princeton: Princeton University Press, 2001).

33. Jessica Taylor, "Citing 'Two Corinthians' Trump Struggles to Make the Sale to Evangelicals," *NPR*, January 18, 2016, www.npr.org/2016/01/18 /463528847/citing-two-corinthians-trump-struggles-to-make-the-sale -to-evangelicals.

34. Jenna Johnson, "Donald Trump Likes That Proverbs Verse That Might Not Exist," *Washington Post*, September 16, 2015, www.washingtonpost .com/news/post-politics/wp/2015/09/16/donald-trump-likes-that -proverbs-verse-that-might-not-exist/.

35. Jaroslav Pelikan, *The Vindication of Tradition* (New Haven: Yale University Press, 1986), 54–57.

36. Matt K. Lewis, *Too Dumb to Fail: How the GOP Betrayed the Reagan Revolution to Win Elections (and How It Can Reclaim Its Conservative Roots)* (New York: Hachette, 2016), xii.

37. Ibid., 26.

38. Ibid. (italics mine). Lewis's book is the best presentation of a moderate conservative position that I have read. However, not all those on the right are so well intentioned. In response to a suggestion that the GOP needs to extend its demographic base beyond older white voters, Representative Steve King (R, IA) replied, "This 'old white people' business does get a little tired. . . . I'd ask you to go back through history and figure out, where are these contributions that have been made by these other categories of people that you're talking about, where did any other subgroup of people contribute more to civilization?" Reporter Chris Hayes asked, "Than white people?" "Than Western civilization itself," King replied. "It's rooted in Western Europe, Eastern Europe and the United States of America and every place where the footprint of Christianity settled the world. That's all of Western civilization." (Interview with Chris Hayes at the Republican National Convention, MSNBC, cited in Philip Bump, "Rep. Steve King Wonders What 'Sub Groups' Besides Whites Made Contributions to Civilization," *Washington Post*, July 18 2016, www.washingtonpost.com/news/the-fix/wp /2016/07/18/rep-steve-king-wonders-what-sub-groups-besides-whites -made-contributions-to-civilization/.)

39. Lewis, *Too Dumb to Fail*, 98.

40. Ibid., 99.
41. See ibid., 4; Nussbaum, "Non-Relative Virtues: An Aristotelian Approach," in *The Quality of Life*, ed. Martha C. Nussbaum and Amartya Sen (New York: Oxford University Press, 1993), 242–70.
42. Alasdair MacIntyre, *After Virtue*, 2nd ed. (Notre Dame: University of Notre Dame Press, 1984), 221–22.
43. William F. Buckley, *God and Man at Yale: The Superstitions of "Academic Freedom,"* rev. ed. (Washington: Regnery Gateway, 1986). At a GOP fundraiser during the 1960s, my parents (both lifelong Republicans) met Buckley. My mother gushed, "I love you! I love you! I love you!" Buckley flashed his famous smile and said, "Can't you make up your mind?"
44. Allan Bloom, *The Closing of the American Mind: How Higher Education Has Failed Democracy and Impoverished the Souls of Today's Students* (New York: Simon and Schuster, 1987).
45. Richard Bernstein, "In Dispute on Bias, Stanford Is Likely to Alter Western Culture Program," *New York Times*, January 19, 1988, www.nytimes.com/1988/01/19/us/in-dispute-on-bias-stanford-is-likely-to-alter-western-culture-program.htm.
46. Bloom, *Closing of the American Mind*, 35–36.
47. Ibid., 37.
48. Ibid., 36. Bloom studied under Leo Strauss, who made similar claims about the need for myths in his seminal *The City and Man* (Chicago: University of Chicago Press, 1978).
49. Bloom, *Closing of the American Mind*, 60.
50. Ibid., 94.
51. Sam Levin, "After Brock Turner: Did the Stanford Sexual Assault Case Change Anything?" *Guardian*, September 1, 2016, www.theguardian.com/us-news/2016/sep/01/brock-turner-stanford-assault-case-did-anything-change.
52. Belinda-Rose Young, Sarah L. Desmarais, Julie A. Baldwin, and Rasheeta Chandler, "Sexual Coercion Practices Among Undergraduate Male Recreational Athletes, Intercollegiate Athletes, and Non-Athletes," *Violence Against Women*, May 30, 2016.
53. See Jean Edward Smith, *Bush* (New York: Simon and Schuster, 2016), 13–14; and Gwenda Blair, *The Trumps: Three Generations of Builders and a*

Presidential Candidate (New York: Simon and Schuster, 2015), 241. Bush the Younger and Trump are not isolated incidents. See Daniel Golden, *The Price of Admission* (New York: Broadway, 2007) for an exposé of how the wealthy routinely buy admission into elite colleges for their children.

54. Award-winning author Jennine Capó Crucet, the first person in her family to attend college, explains how absolutely incomprehensible and terrifying *everything* about college was to her and her family, including things so obvious to most students that they are never explained. "Taking My Parents to College," *New York Times*, August 22, 2015, http://nyti.ms/1Lr81YG.

55. Hendrik Hertzberg, "Buckley, Vidal, and the 'Queer' Question," *New Yorker*, July 31, 2015, www.newyorker.com/news/daily-comment/buckley-vidal-and-the-queer-question.

56. White House Press Briefing by Deputy Press Secretary Larry Speakes, October 15, 1982. See the brief documentary film with the audio of the exchange by Scott Calonic, "When AIDS Was Funny," December 1, 2015, http://video.vanityfair.com/watch/the-reagan-administration-s-chilling-response-to-the-aids-crisis.

57. The statement was in a direct mailing sent out over the signature of Gregory T. Angelo, president of the Log Cabin Republicans (a pro-LGBT conservative group), cited in Steve Rothaus, "Log Cabin Republicans: Party Passes 'Most Anti-LBGT Platform' in GOP History," *Miami Herald*, July 12, 2016, www.miamiherald.com/news/local/community/gay-south-florida/article89235362.html.

58. Will Drabold, "Here's What Mike Pence Said on LGBT Issues Over the Years," *Time*, July 15, 2016, http://time.com/4406337/mike-pence-gay-rights-lgbt-religious-freedom/.

59. See Saul Bellow, *Ravelstein* (New York: Penguin, 2001). Bellow, who wrote the foreword to *The Closing of the American Mind*, explicitly stated in interviews that Bloom is the model for the title character of this roman à clef.

60. D. T. Max, "With Friends Like Saul Bellow," *New York Times*, April 16, 2000, www.nytimes.com/2000/04/16/magazine/with-friends-like-saul-bellow.html. This review is an informative and insightful discussion of the general issue of the relationship between Bloom and Bellow's *Ravelstein*.

4. WELDERS AND PHILOSOPHERS

The quotation from Johst that is one of the epigraphs to chapter 4 is literally "Whenever I hear culture . . . I unlock my Browning" ("Wenn ich Kultur höre . . . entsichere ich meinen Browning"). The line is from a play written by Johst, and the ellipsis is in the original, indicating a pause, not text left out. A Browning is a kind of semiautomatic pistol, and to "unlock" it is to take the safety off. See *Quote/Counterquote*, July 7, 2014, www.quotecounterquote.com/2011/02/whenever-i-hear-word -culture.html. See below for the epigraph quotation of Marco Rubio.

1. "Republican Candidates' Debate in Milwaukee Wisconsin," *American Presidency Project*, November 10, 2015, www.presidency.ucsb.edu/ws/index.php?pid=110908.

2. For an interactive chart that will allow you to compare the lifetime earnings of specific majors, see www.payscale.com/college-salary-report/ degrees-and-majors-lifetime-earnings.

3. Bourree Lam, "The Earning Power of Philosophy Majors," *Atlantic*, September 3, 2015, www.theatlantic.com/notes/2015/09/philosophy-majors -out-earn-other-humanities/403555/.

4. "Value of Philosophy: Charts and Graphs," *DailyNous*, http://dailynous .com/value-of-philosophy/charts-and-graphs/.

5. Ibid.

6. See Paul Jung, MD, "Major Anxiety," www.amsa.org/wp-content/uploads/2015/05/Major-Anxiety.doc; "Philosophy for Pre-Law and Pre-Med," Philosophy Department, UC Davis, http://philosophy.ucdavis .edu/undergraduate-program/philosophy-for-pre-law-and-pre-med -students; and "Philosophy a Practical Choice," Department of Philosophy, Belmont University, www.belmont.edu/philosophy/general_information/. See also "Kaveh Kamooneh's Student Resource Pages," www2 .gsu.edu/~phlkkk/foryou.html#MCAT.

7. Emily P. Walker, "New MCAT: Hard Science No Longer Sole Aim," *MedPage Today*, n.d., www.medpagetoday.com/PublicHealthPolicy/ GeneralProfessionalIssues/31219.

8. David Silbersweig, "A Harvard Medical School Professor Makes the Case for Liberal Arts and Philosophy," *Washington Post*, December 24, 2015, www.washingtonpost.com/news/grade-point/wp/2015/12/24

/a-harvard-medical-school-professor-makes-the-case-for-the-liberal
-arts-and-philosophy/.

9. In chapter 5, I shall discuss the distinctive contribution that philosophy makes to the humanities and social sciences.

10. Examples include Yuanpei College of Peking University, College of Arts and Sciences of the University of Tokyo, Ashoka University, Delhi, College of Liberal Studies of Seoul National University, S. H. Ho College of the Chinese University of Hong Kong, and Yale-NUS College in Singapore. See Sergei Klebnikov, "The Rise of Liberal Arts Colleges in Asia," *Forbes*, June 3, 2015, www.forbes.com/sites/sergeiklebnikov /2015/06/03/the-rise-of-liberal-arts-colleges-in-asia/. A representative view is expressed by Po Chung, cofounder of the multinational corporation DHL, who explained that the liberal arts education he received at Whittier College in the United States paid off in his career in ways that he never expected. Consequently, he is now an ardent supporter of the growing liberal arts programs in Hong Kong ("How General Education Can Sharpen Hong Kong's Edge," *South China Morning Post*, October 23, 2012).

11. "Transcript: Marco Rubio: 'I Ask the American People, Do Not Give in to Fear,'" *Los Angeles Times*, March 15, 2016, www.latimes.com/politics /la-pol-prez-marco-rubio-speech-transcript-20160315-story.html.

12. Donovan Slack, "Whoops! Carly Fiorina Falls off Stage," *USA Today*, May 2, 2016, www.usatoday.com/story/news/politics/onpolitics/2016/05 /02/whoops-carly-fiorina-falls-ted-cruz/83831470/.

13. Phil Mattingly, "Ben Carson's Longshot Presidential Bid Suddenly Looks a Lot More Realistic," *Bloomberg Politics*, October 15, 2014, www.bloomberg.com/politics/articles/2014–10–15/carsons-longshot -presidential-bid-suddenly-looks-a-lot-more-realistic.

14. For discussions, see R. Bett, ed., *The Cambridge Companion to Ancient Skepticism* (New York: Cambridge University Press, 2010); John Cooper, "Arcesilaus: Socratic and Sceptic," in *Knowledge, Nature, and the Good: Essays on Ancient Philosophy* (Princeton: Princeton University Press, 2004); and Katja Vogt, "Ancient Skepticism," *Stanford Encyclopedia of Philosophy*, Fall 2015 ed., ed. Edward N. Zalta, http://plato.stanford.edu /archives/fall2015/entries/skepticism-ancient/.

15. For discussions of the various Western philosophical schools in this era,

see Gisela Striker, *Essays on Hellenistic Epistemology and Ethics* (New York: Cambridge University Press, 1996); Martha Nussbaum, *The Therapy of Desire: Theory and Practice in Hellenistic Ethics* (Princeton: Princeton University Press, 2009); and John M. Cooper, *Pursuits of Wisdom: Six Ways of Life in Ancient Philosophy* (Princeton: Princeton University Press, 2012).

16. Edward Gibbon, *The Decline and Fall of the Roman Empire*, chap. 38. See Gibbon, *The Decline and Fall of the Roman Empire*, abridged by Frank C. Bourne (Garden City, NY: Nelson Doubleday, 1963), 579.

17. Ibid., 239–40.

18. Ibid., 580.

19. For a more up-to-date account, see Peter Brown, *Through the Eye of a Needle: Wealth, the Fall of Rome, and the Making of Christianity in the West* (Princeton: Princeton University Press, 2014).

20. Gibbon, *Decline and Fall*, 579.

21. Richard Hofstadter, *Anti-Intellectualism in American Life* (New York: Vintage, 1966).

22. Jean Edward Smith, *Bush* (New York: Simon and Schuster, 2016), 14.

23. Matt K. Lewis, *Too Dumb to Fail* (New York: Hachette, 2016), 105.

24. The earliest political use of "Palinize" may be due to Sebastian Mallaby of the *Washington Post* in "McCain's Convenient Untruth," September 7, 2008, www.washingtonpost.com/wp-dyn/content/article/2008/09/07/AR2008090701950.html.

25. "Sarah Palin: Mama Grizzlies," *YouTube*, July 8, 2010, https://youtu.be/oF-OsHTLfxM?t=33s.

26. Schiff continues: "An actual grizzly mom is a single mom. . . . What Mama Grizzly wouldn't believe in school lunches, health insurance and quality childcare? Who's going to look after the kids while she's off hunting?" Gail Collins and Stacy Schiff, "Of Mama Grizzly Born?" *New York Times*, August 18, 2010, http://opinionator.blogs.nytimes.com/2010/08/18/of-mama-grizzly-born/. Palin is eminently easy to mock, but she is also a tragic figure, as her former supporter and editor, Matt K. Lewis, reminds us. Lewis, "You Betcha I Was Wrong About Sarah Palin," *Daily Beast*, January 28, 2015, www.thedailybeast.com/articles/2015/01/28/you-betcha-i-was-wrong-about-sarah-palin.html.

27. Michael Kazin, *A Godly Hero: The Life of William Jennings Bryan* (New York: Anchor, 2007), 114.

28. On Lincoln's fondness for Euclid, see David Herbert Donald, *Lincoln* (New York: Simon and Schuster, 1996), 142–43; and Henry Ketcham, *The Life of Abraham Lincoln* (New York: A. L. Burt, 1901), 64–65. For the influence of Pericles on Lincoln, see Garry Wills, *Lincoln at Gettysburg* (New York: Simon and Schuster, 1992).

29. See Patricia Zengerle, "Huntsman Wouldn't Be the Only U.S. President to Speak Chinese," *Reuters*, January 9, 2012, http://blogs.reuters.com/talesfromthetrail/2012/01/09/huntsman-wouldnt-be-the-only-u-s-president-to-speak-chinese/, and Georgius Agricola, *De Re Metalica*, trans. Herbert Hoover and Lou Henry Hoover (New York: Dover, 1950).

30. President Ronald Reagan, Televised Speech from the Oval Office, March 4, 1987. Reagan also believed that the Chernobyl nuclear accident fulfilled a prophecy in the Bible. Lou Cannon, *President Reagan: The Role of a Lifetime*, rev. ed. (New York: Public Affairs, 2000), 679. Haines Johnson probably gives the best overall assessment of Reagan: "He was much more than he seemed to his detractors, who continually disparaged him, and much less than his partisan followers believed him to be." Johnson, *Sleepwalking Through History: America in the Reagan Years*, rev. ed. (New York: Anchor, 1992), 41.

31. George W. Bush, Campaign Speech at Bentonville, Arkansas, November 6, 2000.

32. Donald J. Trump, Campaign Rally in Hilton Head Island, SC, November 25, 2016, video archived at http://dailycaller.com/2015/12/30/trump-i-know-words-i-have-the-best-words-obama-is-stupid-video/. As if to prove my point that the Democratic and Republican parties have traded identities, Trump has hung a portrait of Andrew Jackson in the Oval Office, and laid a wreath on Jackson's grave. Jamelle Bouie, "Donald Trump Sees Himself in Andrew Jackson," *Slate*, March 15, 2017, http://www.slate.com/articles/news_and_politics/politics/2017/03/donald_trump_sees_himself_in_andrew_jackson_they_deserve_one_another.html.

33. Francis Perraudin, "Scott Walker Dodges Question About Evolution Beliefs During Trade Visit to UK," *Guardian*, February 11, 2015, www.theguardian.com/politics/2015/feb/11/scott-walker-special-relationship-trade-cheese-republican-chris-christie.

34. Brian Tashman, "Rafael Cruz: Evolution Is a Communist Lie," *Right*

Wing Watch, November 4, 2013, www.rightwingwatch.org/content/
rafael-cruz-evolution-communist-lie-gay-rights-endanger-children.

35. Michael Hainey, "All Eyez on Him," *GQ*, November 19, 2012, www.gq
.com/story/marco-rubio-interview-gq-december-2012.

36. Augustine, *Confessions*, trans. R. S. Pine-Coffin (New York: Penguin,
1961), 113–16.

37. Ibid., bks. 11–13.

38. Francis Bacon, "Of Atheism," in *Essays*, ed. John Pitcher (New York:
Penguin, 1986), 107.

39. Including Marilyn McCord Adams, Karl Barth, Dietrich Bonhoffer,
Rudolf Bultmann, Hermann Cohen, Gustavo Gutierrez, Stanley Hau-
erwas, Bernard Lonergan, Jürgen Moltmann, Reinhold Neibuhr, Karl
Rahner, Rashid Rida, Franz Rosenzweig, Elizabeth Stuart, Shaykh
Abdal Hakim Murad, and Paul Tillich.

40. Including Elizabeth Anscombe, Martin Buber, Michael Dummett, Bas
van Fraassen, Emmanuel Levinas, Alasdair MacIntyre, Nicholas Re-
scher, Paul Ricoeur, Eleonore Stump, and Charles Taylor.

41. Cannon, *President Reagan*, 30. The transcript of the relevant press conference is archived as Alex C. Kaempfer, "Press Conference of Governor Ronald Reagan," February 28, 1967, http://chronicle.com/items/biz
/pdf/Reagan_press_conference_02–28–1967.pdf.

42. Cited in Dan Berrett, "The Day the Purpose of College Changed,"
Chronicle of Higher Education, January 26, 2015, http://chronicle.com/
article/The-Day-the-Purpose-of-College/151359/.

43. Ron Suskind, "Faith, Certainty and the Presidency of George W. Bush,"
New York Times Magazine, October 17, 2004, www.nytimes.com/2004
/10/17/magazine/faith-certainty-and-the-presidency-of-george-w
-bush.html. Suskind does not name the speaker, but he has been identified as Rove. See Mark Danner, "Words in a Time of War: On Rhetoric, Truth, and Power," in *What Orwell Didn't Know: Propaganda and
the New Face of American Politics*, ed. András Szántó (New York: Public
Affairs, 2007), 23.

44. The exception is Rand Paul, whose educational background is bizarre.
He was studying biology and English when he dropped out of college
and somehow got admitted to medical school. He is now an ophthal-
mologist who founded his own accreditation agency so that he would

not have to be accredited by the state. The original board members of this agency were Paul himself (as president), his wife Kelley (as vice president), and his father-in-law (as secretary). "Rand Paul's Doctor Credentials Questioned for Lacking Top Board's Certification," *Associated Press*, June 14, 2010, www.foxnews.com/politics/2010/06/14/rand -pauls-doctor-credentials-questioned-lacking-boards-certification .html.

45. John Dewey, *Democracy and Education* (New York: Macmillan, 1916), 373.

46. Ibid., 372.

47. Stuart Hampshire, *Innocence and Experience* (Cambridge: Harvard University Press, 1991), 70. On his experience interrogating leading Nazis, see ibid., 7–8.

48. Ibid., 71.

49. See Berrett, "The Day the Purpose of College Changed."

50. Martha C. Nussbaum, *Not for Profit: Why Democracy Needs the Humanities* (Princeton: Princeton University Press, 2012), 17–18.

51. Thomas Jefferson, preamble to "A Bill for the More General Diffusion of Knowledge," in *The Papers of Thomas Jefferson*, ed. Julian P. Boyd, Charles T. Cullen, John Catanzariti, Barbara B. Oberg, et al. (Princeton: Princeton University Press, 1950), 2:526–27.

52. Galileo, *The Assayer*, in *Discoveries and Opinions of Galileo*, trans. Stillman Drake (New York: Anchor, 1957), 237–38.

53. A seminal work on this point is Alexandre Koyré, "Galileo and Plato," *Journal of the History of Ideas* 4, no. 4 (October 1943): 400–28.

54. R. J. Hankinson, "Science," in *The Cambridge Companion to Aristotle*, ed. Jonathan Barnes (Cambridge: Cambridge University Press, 1995), 162–63.

55. Aristotle himself was influenced by Plato's method of dichotomous division. For an introduction to the issues, see Montgomery Furth, "Aristotle's Biological Universe: An Overview," in *Philosophical Issues in Aristotle's Biology*, ed. Allan Gotthelf and James G. Lennox (Cambridge: Cambridge University Press, 2009), 21–52. For more on Aristotle's contribution to biology, see Max Delbrück, "Aristotle-totle-totle," in *Of Microbes and Life*, ed. Jacques Monod and Ernest Borek (New York: Columbia University Press, 1971), 50–55.

56. Drake, *Discoveries and Opinions of Galileo*, 252–256. Galileo couches his point in hypothetical terms, but this is presumably because he was wary of making unqualified assertions that would get him in trouble with the Inquisition.

57. "Rapport fait a l'Académie Royale des Sciences, par MM. Fougerous, Cadet & Lavoisier, d'une observation, communiquée par M. l'abbé Bachela, sur une Pierre qu'on pretend être tombée du ciel pendant un orage," *Observations sur la Physique* (June 1772): 63–76, cited in Matt Salusbury, "Meteor Man," *Fortean Times* 265 (August 2010), http://mattsalusbury.blogspot.com/2010/08/meteor-man-from-fortean-times-265.html.

58. Arthur Fine, *The Shaky Game: Einstein, Realism, and the Quantum Theory*, 2nd ed. (Chicago: University of Chicago Press, 1996).

59. Nietzsche, *Beyond Good and Evil*, trans. Walter Kaufman (New York: Vintage, 1989), §18, 24.

60. Thomas Kuhn, *The Copernican Revolution* (Cambridge: Harvard University Press, 1957), 117. For more on medieval Scholastic criticisms and refinements of Aristotle's view, see ibid., 115–23.

61. Jaroslav Pelikan, *The Vindication of Tradition* (New Haven: Yale University Press, 1984), 16.

62. Bertrand Russell, *The Problems of Philosophy* (Indianapolis: Hackett, 1990), 155.

63. Matt Warman, "Stephen Hawking Tells Google 'Philosophy Is Dead,'" *Telegraph*, May 17, 2011, www.telegraph.co.uk/technology/google/8520033/Stephen-Hawking-tells-Google-philosophy-is-dead.html. I have a philosophical colleague who was at a public lecture that Hawking gave on the problem of free will and determinism. He said he was honored to have been invited, but wanted to slink out in embarrassment after hearing the talk. He explained: "If Hawking's talk were turned in as an essay in a freshman philosophy course, it would have earned a B+ at best." Sounds like Stephen should keep his day job.

64. This distinction comes from Thomas Kuhn, *The Structure of Scientific Revolutions*, 3rd ed. (Chicago: University of Chicago Press, 1996).

65. Albert Einstein, Letter to Thornton, December 7, 1944, Einstein Archive, 61–574.

66. Erwin Schrödinger, *Nature and the Greeks* (New York: Cambridge University Press, 1996), 95.

67. It goes without saying that I just used the rhetorical device of apophasis.
68. John Cleese, "Ideas Transform," public service announcements by John Cleese in honor of the hundredth anniversary of the American Philosophical Association, 2000, www.publicphilosophy.org/media/100 YearsofPhilosophyInAmerica/18-IdeasTransform.mp3.

5. THE WAY OF CONFUCIUS AND SOCRATES

The epigraphs at the beginning of chapter 5 are from Plato, *Republic*, bk. 1, 352d (translation mine), and *Analects* 7.6, cited in Philip J. Ivanhoe and Bryan W. Van Norden, eds., *Readings in Classical Chinese Philosophy*, 2nd ed. (Indianapolis: Hackett, 2005), 21.

1. As I have noted in other publications, we can further divide relativism according to whether claims are taken to be relative to individuals or cultures. This gives us four possibilities: subjective ethical relativism, cultural ethical relativism, subjective cognitive relativism, cultural cognitive relativism. See Bryan W. Van Norden, "Competing Interpretations of the Inner Chapters of the *Zhuangzi*," *Philosophy East and West* 46, no. 2 (April 1996): 248; and Van Norden, review of Scott Cook, ed., *Hiding the World in the World*, *China Review International* 12, no. 1 (Spring 2005): 1–2.
2. Plato, *Theatetus* 170e; *Mozi*, "Canon" B79, translation in Angus C. Graham, *Disputers of the Tao: Philosophical Argument in Ancient China* (La Salle, IL: Open Court, 1989), 185.
3. This point is made very convincingly by Justin E. H. Smith in *The Philosopher: A History in Six Types* (Princeton: Princeton University Press, 2016).
4. I am influenced here by Richard Rorty's notion that hermeneutics is "abnormal discourse": "Normal discourse (a generalization of Kuhn's notion of 'normal science') is any discourse (scientific, political, theological, or whatever) which embodies agreed-upon criteria for reaching agreement; abnormal discourse is any which lacks such criteria." Rorty, *Philosophy and the Mirror of Nature* (Princeton: Princeton University Press, 1979), 11.
5. I am indebted to an anonymous referee and to Wendy Lochner for encouraging me to address the issues raised in this paragraph and the next.
6. Alasdair MacIntyre, "Incommensurability, Truth, and the Conversation

Between Confucians and Aristotelians About the Virtues," in *Culture and Modernity*, ed. Eliot Deutsch (Honolulu: University of Hawaii Press, 1991), 113.

7. Aristotle's *Organon* and Descartes's *Discourse on Method* are just two classic examples of philosophical works whose authors think they have solved the problem of correct methodology. And neither Confucius nor the Buddha thinks there is any fundamental methodological problem that they have yet to solve. See also Smith, *The Philosopher*, on the variety of conceptions of philosophy.

8. Wang Chong, *Balanced Inquiries*, chap. 24, "Dao xu." (Translation mine, but compare Alfred Forke, trans., *Lun-hêng*, part 1, *Philosophical Essays of Wang Ch'ung* [1907].)

9. The conclusion of George Lucas's film *THX 1138* invokes the Platonic allegory of the cave.

10. Plato, *Republic* (Stephanus 514a–517b), trans. G. M. A. Grube and C. D. C. Reeve (Indianapolis: Hackett, 1992), 186–89.

11. Aristotle, *Nicomachean Ethics*, bk. 10, chap. 4. (My translation, but compare Aristotle, *Nicomachean Ethics*, trans. Terence Irwin [Indianapolis: Hackett, 1985], 276.)

12. Ryle, *The Concept of Mind* (Chicago: University of Chicago Press, 2000), chap. 2.

13. Lee H. Yearley, *Mencius and Aquinas: Theories of Virtue and Conceptions of Courage* (Albany: State University of New York Press, 1990), 144–68; and Bryan W. Van Norden, "Mencius on Courage," *Midwest Studies in Philosophy* 21, no. 1 (September 1997), ed. Peter French, Theodore Uehling, and Howard Wettstein, 237–56.

14. *Analects* 1.2, cited in Ivanhoe and Van Norden, *Readings in Classical Chinese Philosophy*, 3. See also the discussion of the passage in Zhu Xi's commentary, cited in Tiwald and Van Norden, *Readings in Later Chinese Philosophy* (Indianapolis: Hackett, 2014), 195–96.

15. I am not denying that they also engage in the other forms of philosophical dialogue I have identified, but it would be presumptuous of me to assert that they do based on my current level of knowledge.

16. Jean-François Lyotard, *The Postmodern Condition*, trans. Geoff Bennington and Brian Massumi (Minneapolis: University of Minnesota Press, 1984), 63–64.

17. Bernard Williams, *Ethics and the Limits of Philosophy* (Cambridge: Harvard University Press, 1985), 1.

18. Hillary Putnam, *Reason, Truth, and History* (Cambridge: Cambridge University Press: 1981), 1–21.

19. Derek Parfit, *Reasons and Persons* (New York: Oxford University Press, 1986), 199–201.

20. Philippa Foot, "The Problem of Abortion and the Doctrine of the Double Effect," in *Virtues and Vices* (New York: Clarendon, 1993), 19–32.

21. David Lewis, *On the Plurality of Worlds* (Oxford: Oxford University Press, 1986).

22. Nelson Goodman, *Fact, Fiction, and Forecast*, 4th ed. (Cambridge: Harvard University Press, 1983), chap. 3, "The New Riddle of Induction."

23. Martha Nussbaum, *Love's Knowledge: Essays on Philosophy and Literature* (New York: Oxford University Press, 1990), 171.

24. Bryan W. Van Norden, "Unweaving the 'One Thread' of *Analects* 4.15," in *Confucius and the "Analects": New Essays* (New York: Oxford University Press, 2002), 216–36.

25. Bertrand Russell, *The Problems of Philosophy* (Indianapolis: Hackett, 1990), 161.

26. Bertrand Russell, *The Autobiography of Bertrand Russell* (London: Unwin, 1975), 149. Russell also discussed how important the poetry of Shelley (35) and Blake (55) had been to him.

27. That such a horrible experience of a friend's suffering could have a positive effect on one's character illustrates Iris Murdoch's insight that "the kind of suffering which brings wisdom cannot be named and cannot without blasphemy be prayed for." Murdoch, *The Nice and the Good* (New York: Penguin, 1978), 56.

28. Plato, *Seventh Letter*, in Paul Friedländer, *Plato: An Introduction* (Princeton: Princeton University Press, 1973), 5. Some question whether the *Seventh Letter* is authentic; see, for example, Myles Burnyeat and Michael Frede, *The Pseudo-Platonic Seventh Letter*, ed. Dominic Scott (Oxford: Oxford University Press, 2015). However, I am inclined to agree with my old teacher, Charles Kahn, that the arguments against its authenticity are unpersuasive. See Kahn, review of Buryneat and Frede, *The Pseudo-Platonic Seventh Letter*, *Notre Dame Philosophical Reviews*, November 9, 2015, http://ndpr.nd.edu/news/62135-the-pseudo-platonic-seventh-letter/.

29. Iain King, "Thinkers at War: John Rawls," *Military History Monthly*, June 13, 2014, www.military-history.org/articles/thinkers-at-war-john-rawls.htm.

30. John Rawls, "Fifty Years After Hiroshima," *Dissent* (Summer 1995), www.dissentmagazine.org/article/50-years-after-hiroshima-2.

31. Ved Mehta, *The Fly and the Fly-Bottle: Encounters with British Intellectuals* (New York: Columbia University Press, 1983), 50.

32. James Stockdale, "The World of Epictetus," in *Vice and Virtue in Everyday Life*, 3rd ed., ed. Christina Sommers and Fred Sommers (New York: Harcourt, Brace, Jovanovich, 1993), 658–74.

33. See chapter 4.

34. See chapter 3.

35. Stockdale, "World of Epictetus," 670–71.

36. King, *A Testament of Hope: The Essential Writings and Speeches of Martin Luther King, Jr.*, ed. James M. Washington (New York: HarperCollins, 1986), 372.

37. Ibid., 291.

38. Ibid., 46–48.

39. Plato, *Apology*, 38a (translation mine).

INDEX

abortion, 23, 49; Buddhist
perspectives on, 174n28
Adluri, Vishwa, 163n9, 170n73
affirmative action, 105–6
African Americans, 87, 101, 120,
124; in philosophy, 1, 7. *See also*
Africana philosophy; King,
Rev. Martin Luther, Jr.;
Obama, Barack Hussein II
Africana philosophy, 3, 9, 22, 32,
34, 82, 84, 149, 199n15; examples
of, 83, 157–58; exclusion from the
Anglo-European canon, xviii,
xix–xx, 21–22; and origin of
Greek philosophy, 19, 168n56;
where taught, 163n8. *See also*
King, Rev. Martin Luther, Jr.
Aggregates. *See* Five Aggregates
Akbar the Great, 98
akrasia. *See* weakness of will
Albertus Magnus, 18
Ambrose (saint), 122
Analects, xvi, 153, 168n61, 171n88,
175n46, 180n95, 180–81n97,

187n27, 187n31, 199n14; difficulty
of appreciating philosophically,
28–29, 171n86; first translated
into a European language, 19.
See also Confucius (Kongzi),
quoted; Youzi; Zigong
analytic philosophy, 32–33, 80, 83,
151–52; and ethnocentrism, 13, 15,
26, 108, 166n28; and openness to
multicultural philosophy, 8, 24,
29. *See also* Hare, R. M.; Moore,
G. E.; Rawls, John; Russell,
Bertrand; Strawson, Peter
anātman. *See* self, nonexistence of
Anaxagoras, 130
Angle, Stephen, 164n15
Anglo-European philosophy, 2,
9–10, 38, 66, 92, 150, 159;
historical divisions of, 32;
individualism in, 39; not
identical with all of philosophy,
16–28, 82–84, 108; strategies to
broaden, 31–36. *See also*
philosophy

Anscombe, Elizabeth, 178*n*72, 195*n*40

Anselm (saint), 124

Aquinas, Thomas. *See* Thomas Aquinas

Aristotle, 1, 86, 124, 159, 180*n*93, 199*n*7; on contradictions, 6; on ethics, 62–67, 135, 147, 178*n*72; not always a part of the European canon, 18; on substance, 40, 41, 172*n*7; as scientist, 63–64, 131–33, 134, 177*n*67, 196*n*55, 197*n*60; use by conservatives, 99–101, 104. *See also* prime matter; substance

Asian philosophy. *See* Chinese philosophy; Indian (South Asian) philosophy

Atwater, Lee, 88, 185*n*9

Augustine, 104, 124, 172*n*95; on metaphorical reading of the Bible, 122

Aung San Suu Kyi, 113

Averroes, 18, 124

Avicenna, 10, 124

Bachelard, Gaston, 13

Bacon, Francis, 123–24

Bagchee, Joydeep, 170*n*73

Barnhart, Michael G., 174*n*28

Beauvoir, Simone de, 33

Bell, Daniel, 163*n*12

Bellow, Saul, 107, 190*nn*59–60

Benedict XVI, 113

benevolence. *See* virtue, benevolence as a

Bennett, William, 113

Berkeley, George, 124

Bhagavad Gita, 10, 105

Bible, 63, 96–97, 104–5, 108–9, 117–18, 121–23, 157, 181*n*100, 194*n*30

Blake, William, 200*n*26

Bliss, Ricki, 172*n*4

Bloom, Allan, 102–107, 179*n*83, 189*n*48, 190*nn*59–60

Bommarito, Nic, 163*n*6

Bradbury, Ray. *See* butterfly effect

Breyer, Stephen, 112

Bryan, William Jennings, 120

Buber, Martin, 195*n*40

Buchanan, Patrick, 113

Buck, Pearl, 113

Buckley, William F., 102, 104, 107, 157, 189*n*43

Buddha, 45, 48, 84, 155, 159, 173*n*18, 199*n*7

Buddhist philosophy, 4, 8, 13, 17, 23, 29, 30, 39–40, 52, 81–83 (passim), 101, 149, 159, 176*nn*57–58, 180*n*93, 199*n*7; compared with Hume, 172*n*4; examples of, 6, 14, 31, 43–51, 57–59, 69–71, 173*n*18, 174*n*28, 174*n*31, 174*n*34; influence on Bertrand Russell, 155; Madhyamaka distinguished from Yogacara, 174*n*29; Mahāyāna distinguished from Theravāda, 49. *See also* Candrakīrti; Dharmakīrti

building and rafter example. *See* rafter dialogue

Burke, Edmund, 99–102

Burnyeat, Myles, 179*n*82, 200*n*28
Bush, George H. W., 88, 121, 126
Bush, George W., 106, 119–21
    (passim), 125, 190*n*53
Bush, Jeb, 126
Bussanich, John, 163*n*6
butterfly effect, 50–51
Byrne, Patrick, 112

Cambridge University, 137
Camosy, Charles C., 184*n*7
Camus, Albert, 113
Candrakīrti, xv, xvii–xviii, 10
Carman, Taylor, 170*n*78
Carmichael, Stokely, 113
Carneades, 117
Carson, Ben, 116–17, 126, 156
Cato the Elder, 117
celibacy, 58
Chakrabarti, Arindam, 163*n*6
Chan, Joseph, 163–64*n*12
Chan, Wing-tsit, 180*n*96
Changes, 19, 187*n*31; difficulty of
    reading philosophically, 28–29,
    171*n*86
chariot, simile of the, 47–48
Chase, Alston Hurd, 24
Cheng Hao, 58, 59
Cheng Yi, 75–76
Cherry, Myisha, 7–8
child at the well thought
    experiment, 55–56, 68, 74
Chinese Communist Party, 89–91,
    94
Chinese philosophy, xvi, 9, 17,
    30–31, 32, 34; contemporary

disciplinary divisions in, 92;
    examples of, 5–7, 14, 26, 53–62,
    66–82, 94–96, 144–45, 148, 149;
    exclusion from Anglo-
    European canon, xviii, xix–xx,
    22–24, 26–28; influence on
    laissez-faire economics, 20–21;
    where taught, 8, 162*nn*4–5.
    See also Buddhist philosophy;
    Confucianism; Daoism
Christianity, 19, 97, 100, 102, 157,
    169*n*72, 188*n*38; and philosophy,
    3, 6, 18, 20, 117–18, 121–24,
    195*nn*39–40. *See also* Bible
Chung, Po Yang, 192*n*10
Cicero, 12, 24
City College of New York, 154
Cleese, John, 137
Cline, Erin, xxiv, 162*n*4, 164*n*16
Clinton, Bill (William), 126
Clinton, Hillary, 100, 184–85*n*7
Coen, Ethan, 113
Cohen, Hermann, 195*n*39
Columbia University, 112, 121,
    163*n*8
Confucianism, 4–6, 13, 17, 22, 23,
    26, 30, 39–40, 52, 54, 62, 67, 101,
    149; rites (or rituals) in, 175*n*46.
    See also Confucius (Kongzi);
    Mengzi; New Confucianism;
    Neo-Confucianism; Xunzi;
    Wang Yangming; Zhu Xi
Confucius (Kongzi), 10, 19, 28, 83,
    149, 153, 167*n*35, 171*n*86, 179*n*79,
    180*n*94, 199*n*7; Chinese
    attitudes toward 4, 85, 88–89,

Confucius (*cont.*)
90, 107–8; compared with
Socrates, 158–59; dismissed as a
philosopher, xiii, xv–xvii,
12–13, 22–24; praised as a
philosopher, 19–20, 24; quoted,
54, 57, 73, 81, 94–96 (passim),
138, 187*n*27. See also *Analects;*
Confucianism
Continental philosophy, 3, 32, 83;
ethnocentrism in, 108, 152. *See
also* Derrida, Jacques; Hegel,
G. W. F.; Heidegger, Martin;
Nietzsche, Friedrich
Cook, Francis C., 174*n*34
courage. *See* virtue, courage as a
Crucet, Jennine Capó, 190*n*54
Cruz, Rafael Bienvenido, 122
Cruz, Ted (Rafael Edward), 116,
121–22, 126
Csikszentmihalyi, Mark, 168*n*61
Cullen, Christopher, 168*n*53
Cultural Revolution, 90, 93, 102,
185*n*13
CUNY Graduate Center, 162*n*4,
162–63*n*6, 163*n*8

Dai Zhen, 14
Dalton, John, 130, 134
Daodejing, 20–21, 26, 170*n*78,
171*n*88; difficulty of
appreciating philosophically,
28–29, 171*n*86
Daoism, 4, 6, 13, 17, 30, 149. *See also*
Daodejing; Zhuangzi
Darrow, Clarence, 120

Darwin, Charles, 57, 134. *See also*
evolutionary theory
Dasgupta, Surama, 15
Davidson, Donald, 13, 182*n*107
Daxue. See Great Learning
Defoort, Carine, 162*n*5, 170*n*79
Democratic party, 126, 184–85*n*7,
194*n*32; anti-intellectualism
and racism in, 87, 120; and
Aristotelian values, 99–100;
and Confucian values, 60–61.
See also Bryan, William
Jennings; Clinton, Bill
(William); Clinton, Hillary;
Gore, Al (Albert); Jackson,
Andrew
Democritus, 130, 134
Deng Xiaoping, 90
Derrida, Jacques, 152;
ethnocentrism of, 25, 27,
170*n*80
Descartes, René, 31, 44, 82, 104,
124, 147, 172–73*n*10, 199*n*7; on
individual substances, 39–43,
46, 48, 49, 52, 57–58, 60, 172*n*5;
on potentiality, 63
development model of ethical
cultivation. *See* virtue, models
of cultivation of
Dewey, John, 83, 127
dharma, 59, 176*n*57
Dharmakīrti, 31
Diogenes, vii
discovery model of ethical
cultivation. *See* virtue, models
of cultivation of

Dole, Bob (Robert), 126
Drabinski, John, 166*n*28
Du Bois, W. E. B., 1
Duhem, Pierre, 13, 134
Durkheim, Emile, 91
Dussel, Enrique, 33–34

egoism, 52, 55, 61, 68, 174–75*n*36
Einstein, Albert, 132, 133; on value
    of philosophy, 2, 134, 137
Eisenhower, Dwight D., 121
Epictetus, 31, 126, 156
Epicurus, 117
ethics, 5–6, 19–20, 26, 32, 39, 80–81,
    83, 115, 135, 137, 144, 149, 153, 154,
    179*n*82, 181*n*100; meta-, 14, 26,
    58, 70–72, 78, 180*n*93; utilitarian,
    135–36, 155–56. *See also* virtue;
    weakness of will
ethnocentrism: examples of, xiii,
    xiv, 11–16 (passim), 21–27, 34,
    103–4, 188*n*38. *See also* racism
Euclid, 17, 120
evolutionary theory, 120, 121–22; on
    origin of altruistic motivations,
    56–57, 176*n*52.
existentialism, 64, 135. *See also*
    Beauvoir, Simone de; Camus,
    Albert; Sartre, Jean-Paul

Fanon, Frantz, 10
Fazang, 14, 49–50, 58–59, 174*n*29
feminist philosophy, 3, 14, 25, 27, 33,
    41, 82, 117, 119–20, 149, 154,
    193*n*26. *See also* sexism
Feyerabend, Paul, 13

filial piety, xvi, 6, 58, 60, 77–78,
    149
Fingarette, Herbert, 24, 175*n*46
Fiorina, Carly, 2, 116, 126
Five Aggregates, 44–49, 176*n*57;
    defined, 43
Flanagan, Owen, 164*n*20
Foot, Philippa, 178*n*72; runaway
    train example of, 151–52, 153
Ford, Harrison. *See Regarding
    Henry*
fortune cookies, xiii, 12, 147
Foucault, Michel, 13, 136
Freud, Sigmund, 136
Frost, Robert, 138
Fung, Yu-lan, 180*n*96

Gadamer, Hans-Georg, 149–50
Galileo Galilei, 130–31, 132, 134,
    197*n*56
Gandhi, Mahatma, 33, 98
Garfield, Jay, xi–xxi, xxiii–xxv
    (passim), 8–10, 16, 35, 36, 44,
    165*n*22, 174*n*29
Geertz, Clifford, 113
Gervais, Ricky, 113
Gewirtz, Paul, 91
Gibbon, Edward, 118
Gleick, James, 174*n*32
God. *See* theism
Goodman, Charles, xxiv, 163*n*6
Goodman, Nelson, 83; "grue"
    paradox of, 152
Gore, Al (Albert), 119
Graham, Angus C., 165*n*23, 177*n*64,
    198*n*2

Great Learning, 72–78, 180*n*94, 180*n*97, 181*n*98; quoted, 72, 94, 187*n*26

Great Proletarian Cultural Revolution. *See* Cultural Revolution

Great Wall (of China), 85–86

Gyekye, Kwame, 83

Habermas, Jürgen, 149–50

Hampshire, Stuart, 128, 196*n*47

Hanfeizi, 14, 29, 61–62, 171*n*88

Han Yu, 176*n*58

Harbsmeier, Christoph, 165*n*23

Hardwick, Chris, 113, 162*n*1

Hare, R. M., 156, 178*n*71

Harris, Eirik, 171*n*88, 177*n*65

Harvard University, 113, 121, 163*n*6, 163*n*8

Havel, Vaclav, 113

Hawking, Stephen, 133, 134, 137, 197*n*63

Hayes, Chris, 188*n*38

Hegel, G. W. F., 39; role in excluding non-Western philosophy from the Anglo-European canon, 23–24, 25, 27, 170*n*73

Heidegger, Martin, 104; ethnocentrism of, 25, 27, 149–50, 170*n*78

Hellenistic philosophy, 32, 117–18, 192–93*n*15

Heraclitus, xiii, 29, 45

Herbert, Bob, 185*nn*8–9

hermeneutics, 91, 139–40, 142, 149–50, 198*n*4

Hispanic. *See* Latino/a and Hispanic Americans

Hobbes, Thomas, 6, 82, 104; on metaphysical individualism, 39, 52; political philosophy of, 52–55, 57–58, 64, 70, 174–75*n*36, 175*n*41; on potentiality, 63–64, 177*n*67; similarities and differences with Mohists, 61, 177*n*64

Hoffman, Martin L., 176*n*50

Hofstadter, Richard, 193*n*21

Hong Kong, 93, 192*n*10

Hoover, Herbert, 121

Huiyuan, 176*n*58

Hume, David, xv, 10, 70, 82, 135, 172*n*4, 180*n*93; racism of, 169*n*66

Hursthouse, Rosalind, 178*n*72

Hutton, Eric, 162*n*5

Icahn, Carl, 112

icons and idols. *See* traditions, icons distinguished from idols in

Indian (South Asian) philosophy, xiv, xvi, xvii, 2, 9, 15, 30, 32–33, 34, 82, 149; exclusion from the Anglo-European canon, xviii, xix–xx, 21–22, 27–28, 170*n*73; and origin of Greek philosophy, 19, 168*n*56; where taught, 162–63*n*6. See also *Bhagavad Gita*; Buddhist philosophy; Candrakīrti; Dharmakīrti; Orientalism

Indigenous Americans, 120; in philosophy, 7. *See also* Whyte, Kyle Powys

Indigenous philosophy, xiii, 2–3, 83, 149, 199*n*15; examples of, 83; exclusion from Anglo-European canon, xviii, xix–xx, 22; where taught, 163*n*7. *See also* Indigenous Americans

infanticide, 23, 169*n*70, 169*n*72

integrity. *See* virtue, righteousness (or integrity) as a

intellectual imperialism objection, xvii–xviii, 29–31, 143–44. *See also* noble savages

intuitionism. *See* ethics, meta-

Islam, 11, 93, 96–97; and philosophy, xiv, 3, 9, 18, 28, 34, 82, 149. *See also* Averroes; Avicenna; Murad, Shaykh Abdal Hakim (Timothy Winter); Rida, Rashid

Ivanhoe, Philip J., 81, 178*n*78

Jackson, Andrew, 120, 194*n*32

Jackson, Frank, "Mary" thought experiment, 78–79

Jefferson, Thomas, 129–30

Jesus, 96, 123, 181*n*100

Jiang Qing, 164*n*12

John Paul II, 113

Johnson, Haines, 194*n*30

Joseph, George, 166*n*31

Judaism, 97, 128, 149; and philosophy, 3, 18, 82. *See also* Buber, Martin; Cohen, Hermann; Levinas, Immanuel; Maimonides; Rosenzweig, Franz

justice, 6, 8, 98, 116, 128, 144, 154–56 (passim); as a virtue, 5, 65

Kahn, Charles, 200*n*28

Kang Youwei, 98

Kant, Immanuel, xv, xx, 5, 10, 14, 30, 113, 148; on normative ethics, 95, 136; role in excluding non-Western philosophy from the Anglo-European canon, 1, 21–23, 27, 169*nn*65–66, 169*n*68

Kasich, John, 116, 126

Kennedy, Anthony, 12, 167*n*35

Keown, Damien, 174*n*28

Keynes, John Maynard, 15

Kierkegaard, Søren, 124, 136

King, Rev. Martin Luther, Jr., 1, 33, 98; inspired by Plato, 157–58

King, Steve, 188*n*38

King Milinda. *See* Milinda (king)

Kongzi. *See* Confucius (Kongzi)

Koyré, Alexander, 196*n*53

Krishnamurthy, Meena, 166*n*28

Kuhn, Thomas S., 13, 132, 133–34, 197*n*64, 198*n*4

Kundera, Milan, 92

Kupperman, Joel, 28

LaFleur, William R., 174*n*28

Lame Deer, 10

Laozi. *See Daodejing*

Latin American philosophy, 3, 33–34, 82

Latino/a and Hispanic Americans, 7, 85, 86–87, 101, 149
Lavoisier, Antoine, 132
LCTP. *See* less commonly taught philosophies (LCTP)
Legalism. *See* Hanfeizi; Shen Dao
Leibniz, Gottfried Wilhelm, 19–20, 124, 133
Leiter, Brian, 166n28, 172n94
Lenin (Vladimir Ilyich Ulyanov), 157
less commonly taught philosophies (LCTP), 2–3, 8, 32–34, 38, 82, 108, 149; origin of term, 163n6
Leucippus, 130
Levinas, Immanuel, 195n40
Levi-Strauss, Claude, 113
Lewis, David, multiple world metaphysics of, 152
Lewis, Matt K., 98–102, 104, 119, 121, 188n38, 193n26
LGBTQ: issues, 12, 101, 107, 167n35, 181n98; philosophy, 3, 82–83, 149
Liberty University, 97
Li Dazhao, 14
Lincoln, Abraham, 88, 120
Linnaeus, Carl, 131
Liu Shaoqi, 14
Li Zhi, 14
Lochner, Wendy, xxiii, xxiv, 198n5
Locke, Alain, 1
Locke, John, 104, 136, 175n40
Lorenz, Edward, 51
Louden, Robert, 168n59
Lucas, George. See *THX 1138*

Lugones, Maria, 10
Lu Xiangshan, 176n58; quoted, 69
Lynne, Richard John, 171n86
Lyotard, Jean-François, 13, 150

Macaulay, Thomas Babington, xiv, xvii
Machiavelli, Niccolò, 172n1
MacIntyre, Alasdair, 195n40; on comparative philosophy, 6, 143; on tradition, 100–1; on virtue ethics, 62–65, 177n66, 178n72
Mackie, J. L., 136
Mad Max: Fury Road, 52
Maffie, James, xxiv, xxv, 83
Maimonides, 124
male gaze. *See* Mulvey, Laura
Manicheanism, 159
Mao Zedong, 85, 89–90, 92, 94, 100, 185n11, 185n13
MAP. *See* Minorities and Philosophy
Marx, Karl, 136, 157
Marxism, 14, 83, 92, 122, 157. *See also* Chinese Communist Party
mathematics, 6, 9–10, 11–12, 16–17, 19, 32, 120, 131, 133, 143, 144, 147, 153
Mattice, Sarah, 167n49
Max, D. T., 107, 190n60
May Fourth Movement, 4
McCain, John, 126
McDowell, John, 178n72
McGuire, Patricia, 11
McLeod, Alexus, 162n4
Mencius. *See* Mengzi

Mengzi, 5, 6, 20, 29, 31, 81, 83, 105,
171*n*88, 187*n*31; on human nature
and political philosophy, 14,
54–57, 176*n*49; on ethical
cultivation, 66, 67–69; on
normative ethics, 95, 148
meta-ethics. *See* ethics, meta-
metaphysics, 17, 25, 31, 32, 40–52,
58–60, 80, 83, 144, 151, 172*n*7;
defined, 39. *See also* mind-body
problem; personal identity
problem; prime matter; soul;
substance
Milinda (king), 44, 46–48
mind-body problem, 14, 46–47, 124,
173*n*18
Minorities and Philosophy, xi, xxv,
8, 34
Mohism, 7, 14, 29, 69, 141;
contrasted with Hobbes, 61,
177*n*64
Molière (Jean-Baptiste Poquelin),
63, 177*n*67
Mommsen, Theodor, 24
Moore, G. E., 15
Mou Zongsan, 14
Mozi. *See* Mohism
multicultural philosophy, xxiii,
xxiv, 10–11, 35–37 (passim), 84;
objections to: xii; Anglo-
European philosophy matters
too objection, 102–3, 159; area
studies objection, 5, 9, 27;
comprehensiveness objection,
32–33, 38, 143; essentialist
objection, xiv–xv, 16–19, 25, 108;

language competence objection,
33–34; nonexistence objection,
xiii, xviii–xix, 5–7, 14, 29,
143–44, 149; quality objection,
xiv, 5–7, 12–16, 108, 147–48. *See
also* intellectual imperialism
objection; less commonly taught
philosophies (LCTP); noble
savages; pipeline problem
Mulvey, Laura, 181*n*98
Mungello, David E., xxiv, 23
Murad, Shaykh Abdal Hakim
(Timothy Winter), 195*n*39
Murdoch, Iris, 178*n*72, 200*n*27
Murray, Bill, 101–2

Nāgasena, 44, 46–49
Native American. *See* Indigenous
Americans; Indigenous
philosophy
naturalism. *See* ethics, meta-
Neo-Confucianism, 14, 29, 39–40;
on personal identity, 58–61;
on ethical cultivation, 69–72.
See also Wang Yangming;
Zhu Xi
New Confucianism, 4, 29. *See also*
Mou Zongsan
Newton, Isaac, 133, 134
New York University, 112, 163*n*8
Nietzsche, Friedrich, 25, 29, 104,
125, 132, 136, 152
Nivison, David S., 80, 179*nn*87–88,
181*n*104, 182*n*107
Nixon, Richard M., 85, 121, 183
(epigraph sources)

noble savages, xv–xvi, 25, 86. *See also* intellectual imperialism objection

nonaction. *See wúwéi* (non-interference)

Norton-Smith, Thomas M., 83

Nussbaum, Martha, 178n72, 193n15; on Aristotelianism 100–1; on comparative philosophy, 6; on Derrida, 152; on education, 129, 179n83

Obama, Barack Hussein, II, 48, 152; election of 2008, 126; quoted, 60–61

objections to multicultural philosophy. *See* multicultural philosophy, objections to

Olberding, Amy, 162n5, 166n28

Orientalism, xiv, 21, 170n80; defined, 27–28

Oxford University, 119

Ozbey, Sonya, 162n4

Paley, William, 15

Palin, Sarah, 119–120, 193n24, 193n26

Parfit, Derek, teleporter thought experiment of, 151, 153

Park, Eugene, 26–27, 150

Park, Peter K. J., 19, 21, 168n56, 169n65

Parmenides, 3, 16, 29, 39, 163n9

Pascal, Blaise, 104, 136

Patil, Parimil, 163n6

Pattern, 59–60, 69

Paul (saint), 117, 118, 122, 123

Paul, Rand, 195–96n44

Peking University, 91, 94–95, 192n10

Pelikan, Jaroslav, 97–98, 132

Pence, Mike (Michael), 107

Peone, D. Kyle, 16

Pericles, 120

Perkins, Franklin, 162n5, 168n58

Perry, John, 173n13

personal identity problem, 10, 41–51, 57–60, 173n13. *See also* self; soul; substance

Phillips, Stephen, 163n6

Phillips, Stone, 113

philosophy: of language, 3, 6–7, 155; political, 4, 5, 14, 19–20, 32, 33, 39, 52–62, 64, 80, 83, 92, 101, 104, 135, 144, 155–56, 166n28, 172n1, 174–75n36, 175n40; problem of defining, 13, 16–19, 25, 29–31, 108, 142–49, 151; renaming departments of, xii, xxiii, 9–10, 11, 35; subfields in, 32, 135. *See also* analytic philosophy; Anglo-European philosophy; Continental philosophy; ethics; less commonly taught philosophies (LCTP); metaphysics; multicultural philosophy; weakness of will

Pigliucci, Masimo, 13–14, 27

pipeline problem, 33–34

Pittenger, Robert, 184n6

Plato, xxvi, 1, 14, 30, 86, 116, 124, 148, 159, 200n28; on Heraclitus,

45; influence on other thinkers, 18, 27, 101, 131, 134, 157–58, 196*n*55, 199*n*9; quoted, xvi–xvii, 145–47, 155; refutation of relativism, 140–41; *Republic,* xiv–xv, 10, 16, 104, 157. *See also* Socrates

Poincaré, Henri, 51

political correctness, xiii, 12, 116–17

political philosophy. *See* philosophy, political

Popper, Karl, 148–49

Powell, Colin, 125

Pratt, Scott L., 163*n*7

Prichard, H. A., 70–71

Priest, Graham, 162–63*n*6, 165*n*22

prime matter, 44, 60, 178*n*70; defined, 41

psychology: philosophical, 52, 55–56, 68–69, 75, 135, 174–75*n*36, 181*n*100; scientific, 6, 56–57, 80, 107, 126

Putnam, Hilary, brain-in-a-vat thought experiment of, 10, 151

Pythagoras, 16–17

Quesnay, François, 20

Quine, W. V. O., 13

racism, xii–xiii, 21–22, 87–88, 94, 101, 105–6, 107–8, 139, 158, 169*nn*65–66, 184*n*6; structural, xix–xx, 7–8, 26–28, 108. *See also* Orientalism

rafter dialogue, 14, 49–50, 59–60, 174*n*31

Ramsey, F. P., 83

Rawls, John, 136, 155–56, 164*n*16

Reagan, Ronald, 119, 121, 126, 194*n*30; anti-intellectualism of, 124, 125, 128; press secretary joked about AIDS, 107; quoted *Daodejing,* 20–21; on states' rights, 85, 87–88

Red Guards. *See* Cultural Revolution

re-formation model of ethical cultivation. *See* virtue, models of cultivation of

Regarding Henry, 42, 48–49

relativism, 18, 139, 140–42, 198*n*1

Republican party, 2, 110, 177*n*62, 184–85*n*7, 189*n*43, 194*n*32; anti-intellectualism in, 116–21, 124–27, 130; denial of evolutionary theory in, 121–22; opposition to LGBTQ rights in, 107, 190*n*57; racism and ethnocentrism in, 87–88, 184*n*6, 188*n*38. *See also* Bush, George W.; Carson, Ben; Paul, Rand; Rubio, Marco; Trump, Donald J.

Ricoeur, Paul, 148–49, 195*n*40

Rida, Rashid, 195*n*39

rights, human, 53, 61, 87, 101, 107, 113, 124, 129, 136, 156. *See also* states' rights

Robinson Crusoe, 61, 177*n*63

Rome, 23; fall of, 116–19, 193*n*19. *See also* Hellenistic philosophy

Roosevelt, Teddy (Theodore), 120, 121
Rorty, Richard, 13, 149–50, 198*n*4
Rosenthal, Andrew, 177*n*62
Rosenzweig, Franz, 195*n*39
Rousseau, Jean-Jacques, 6, 68, 104
Rove, Karl, 125, 195*n*43
Rubio, Marco, 1–2, 110–11, 114, 115–16, 122, 126–27
Russell, Bertrand, 30, 82, 113, 148; moral vision of, 153–55, 200*n*26; philosophical views of, 3, 6, 133, 136, 153
Ryle, Gilbert, 148

Said, Edward. *See* Orientalism
Sarkissian, Hagop, 162*n*4
Sartre, Jean-Paul, 82, 83, 113, 178*n*71
Scalia, Antonin, 12–13, 14, 24, 27, 167*n*35
Schiff, Stacy, 120, 193*n*26
Schofer, Jonathan, 178*n*78
Scholl, Sophie, 113
Schrödinger, Erwin, 134; on limitations of science, 136–37
Schweitzer, Albert, 113
Schwitzgebel, Eric, 7–8, 28–29, 80, 162*n*4, 164*n*18, 179*n*82
science, natural, 11, 22, 51, 63–64, 78, 112, 122, 123, 195*n*44; and philosophy, 1–2, 9–10, 13, 32, 130–37, 143, 144, 148–49, 198*n*4. *See also* evolutionary theory; mathematics
self: nonexistence of, 43–49, 172*n*4, 173*n*18, 174*n*28; transpersonal,

49–51, 58–59, 74–75; unity and conflict as ideals of, 181*n*100. *See also* personal identity problem
Sellars, Wilfred, xvii, 13
Seneca, 172*n*95
sexism, 23, 101, 105–6, 139, 181*n*98; reflected in use of effeminacy as symptom of decay, 99, 118; structural, 7–8
Shelley, Percy Bysshe, 200*n*26
Shen Dao, 29, 61–62, 171*n*88
Shun (king). *See wúwéi* (non-interference)
Shun, Kwong-loi, 162*n*4, 175*n*46
Sidgwick, Henry, 180*n*93
Siger of Brabant, 18
Sim, May, 164*n*15
skepticism, 14, 116–117, 192*n*14
Skinner, B. F., 66
Slingerland, Edward, 162*n*4, 171*n*86, 179–180*n*89
Slote, Michael, 178*n*72
Smith, Justin E. H., 30, 166*n*28, 198*n*3, 199*n*7
Socrates, 1, 83, 126, 138, 145–47, 151, 152, 157–59
Solzhenitsyn, Alexander, 113
Soros, George, 112
soul, 39, 40, 41–43, 46–47, 49, 147, 154, 172*n*5
Souter, David, 112
Speakes, Larry, 107
Spinoza, Baruch, 39, 104, 124, 126
Spivak, Gayatri, 25
sprout metaphor, 68
Stalnaker, Aaron, 162*n*4, 164*n*19

Stanford University, 102–3, 105–6, 112, 156

Star Trek, 103

state of nature argument, 14, 52–53, 57, 61, 175nn40–41

states' rights, 85, 87–88

Stockdale, James, 156–57

Stoicism, 36, 102, 117–18. *See also* Cicero; Epictetus; Seneca

Strauss, Leo, 189n48

Strawson, Peter, 3

Stump, Eleanore, 195n40

substance, 40–44, 48, 60, 172n5, 172n7; Aristotelian definition of, 40; Chinese concepts related to, 58, 59, 95, 176n56

Suppes, Patrick, 178n70

Suskind, Ron, 125, 195n43

Swanton, Christine, 178n72

Taber, John, 163n6

Taiwan (Republic of China), 93–94

Tampio, Nicholas, xiv–xviii, 16

Taoism. *See* Daoism

Taylor, Charles, 186n15, 195n40

Terence, 38

Teresa (saint), 48

Terkel, Studs, 113

theism, 20, 97, 102, 104, 117–18, 122–24, 130, 136, 172n5, 177n63. *See also* Christianity; Islam; Judaism

Thiel, Peter, 112

Thomas Aquinas, 5, 18, 124, 136

THX 1138, 199n9

Tibet, 93

Tillich, Paul, 195n39

traditions, philosophical, 5, 8–11, 13, 27, 43, 82–84, 85–86, 91, 92, 99, 101–5, 108, 148, 149–51, 158–59; icons distinguished from idols in, 97–98; not hermetic or static, 17–18, 29–30, 38–39, 65, 101. *See also* Burke, Edmund

Trebek, Alex, 113

Trinity Washington University, 11

Trivers, Robert L., 176n52

Truman, Harry S., 87

Trump, Donald J., 85, 86–87, 93–94, 97, 106, 107, 116, 121, 126, 127, 184n2, 184–85n7, 190n53, 194n32

Turner, Dale, 83

Twilight Zone, 175n41

Tyson, Neil deGrasse, 1–2, 130, 134, 137

unity of knowing and acting. *See* Wang Yangming; weakness of will

University of Michigan, 112, 162n4

University of Paris, 18

University of Pennsylvania, xi, xxv, 8; Wharton School of, 106

utilitarianism. *See* ethics, utilitarian

Vedanta, 15, 149

Vidal, Gore, 107

virtue, 4, 14, 23, 24, 26, 54, 73, 94–96 (passim), 117, 118, 129, 148, 149, 157, 180n97; benevolence as a, 5, 54–58, 66, 74–75, 81, 149, 174–75n36, 175n41, 176n49;

virtue (*cont.*)
  courage as a, 5, 65, 148, 157;
    ethics, 5, 29, 62–66, 164*n*15,
    165*n*21, 177*n*66, 178*n*72, 181*n*98;
    models of cultivation of, 66–72;
    righteousness (or integrity) as a,
    54, 66, 67, 81, 94, 95, 148, 156,
    175*n*41; wisdom as a, 5, 24, 99,
    130, 146, 200*n*27. *See also* justice
virtus dormitiva. See Molière
  (Jean-Baptiste Poquelin)

Walker, Scott, 121
Walking Dead, The, 52, 175*n*41
Wang, Robin R., 167*n*48, 171*n*92
Wang Bi, 171*n*86
Wang Chong, 144–45
Wang Yangming, vii, 14, 74, 77–81
Washington, Booker T., 120
Waters, Anne, 83
wax example, 40–41
weakness of will, 14, 76–80,
  181*n*104, 182*n*107; defined, 72
Whitman, Walt, 181*n*100
Whittier College, 121, 192*n*10
Whyte, Kyle Powys, xxiv, 163*n*7,
  165*n*25
Williams, Bernard, 151
Wills, Garry, 194*n*28
Wiredu, Kwasi, 10, 83
Wittgenstein, Ludwig, 29

Wolff, Christian, 20
Wong, David, 68–69, 162*n*4,
  164*n*20
Wordsworth, William, xxvi
Wu Wanwei, xxiv, 186*n*22
wúwéi (non-interference), 20–21,
  168*n*61

xiào. See filial piety
Xi Jinping, 4, 85, 93–96, 107–8,
  187*nn*25–28
Xunzi, 6, 29, 67, 81, 171*n*88

Yale University, 91, 102, 106, 119,
  121, 157
Yale-NUS College, 192*n*10
Yang Zhu, 55
Yearley, Lee H., 5, 178*n*78,
  199*n*13
Yijing. See Changes
Youzi, 149
Yu, Jiyuan, 164*n*15

Zengzi, 180*n*94
Zhuangzi, 14, 29, 164*n*18, 171*n*88,
  186*n*19, 198*n*1
Zhu Xi, 31, 59–60, 76–77, 80–82
  (passim), 159, 180*n*97, 187*n*26,
  199*n*14
Zigong, 38
Zongmi, 14

CPSIA information can be obtained
at www.ICGtesting.com
Printed in the USA
LVOW11s0838291217
561194LV00001B/6/P